MASTERING
THE
BUSINESS
OF
WRITING

Richard Curtis

Allworth Press • New York

Published by Allworth Press
an imprint of Allworth Communications, Inc.
10 East 23rd Street, New York, NY 10010

Cover design: Douglas Design Associates, New York, NY

Book design: Sharp Des!gns, Holt, MI

ISBN: 1-880559-55-2

Library of Congress Catalog Card Number: 96-84618

Printed in Canada

Some of the material in this volume was previously published in the book *Beyond the Bestseller*. The original work has been substantially revised and updated, and new text has been added.

This book is lovingly dedicated to Leslie,
my wife and best friend

Contents

Preface *11*

Acknowledgments *15*

SECTION ONE: AGENTS DEMYSTIFIED

1. **Clout**   *What do we mean when we say a literary agent has clout? And is it all it's cracked up to be? In truth, agents are only as powerful as their clients* *18*

2. **All Agencies Great and Small**   *Compares the benefits and short-comings of gigantic, medium, and sole practitioner agencies* *23*

3. **Rivals**   *Are literary agents really in competition with each other? Or are they friendly and cooperative?* *29*

4. **What I Have Done for You Lately**   *Some unusual tasks that agents are required to do for their clients beyond selling books and collecting money* *32*

5. **Building Careers**   *The agent's ultimate goal is to guide an author's career from category writing to mainstream, and then to stardom* *38*

SECTION TWO: BREAKING IN

6. **Sometimes a Great Notion** *How do professional authors generate ideas, and how do agents convert them into hard cash? The one thing professionals do not need is more ideas* 44

7. **Outlines** *There are two kinds of outlines: the kind authors follow when they are writing their books, and the kind they use when they are selling them. How authors can write more effective outlines* 48

8. **Hardcover vs. Softcover vs. Hard-Soft** *Addresses the confusion over which books should be published in which format. Sometimes even publishers don't know* 54

9. **A Modest Wager** *Prolific authors need a strategy to find outlets for their output. Many can write books faster than publishers can cut checks* 60

10. **Movies into Books** *Novelizing movie and television screenplays is a lot harder than it looks. Some tips for would-be novelizers* 65

11. **Work-for-Hire** *Are book packagers a blessing or a menace?* 69

12. **Audio** *Audiocassette rights have become a valuable commodity. What you need to know about the market and the kinds of deals being made* 74

13. **Multibook Deals** *The advantages and disadvantages of contracts tying up more than one book at a time. When to sign them and when to sell one book at a time* 80

14. **Payout Schedules** *How advances are divided into installments, and how authors can negotiate more favorable payouts* 86

15. **Escalators** *Understanding best-seller, movie, and other bonuses in book contracts* 92

16. **Acceptability** *Examines the acceptability clause of contracts. Takes the position that advances should be considered investments rather than refundable loans to authors* 97

SECTION THREE: BREAKING OUT

17. Are Editors Necessary?   *Deals with assertions that editing has declined in modern times. Today's editors must be far more versatile than their forebears* 104

18. Sales Conference   *What happens when editors present your book to the sales people, and why sales conferences are critically important to the fates of books* 110

19. "P & L"   *Profit-and-loss statements. How publishers analyze the profitability, or lack thereof, of books they are considering acquiring* 116

20. Pub Date   *How significant is the season, month, or date of publication of your book* 121

21. Great Expectations: Advertising and Publicity   *Advertising, publicity, and promotion of books and authors, and how publishing is becoming more like show business* 125

22. Brand Names   *Questions the wisdom of prohibiting ads in published books. The revenue from "sponsors" might balance some shaky ledgers for publishers and put a few extra dollars in authors' pockets* 129

23. Book Clubs   *Are they necessary? Are they in competition with paperback publishers? And how do they work, anyway?* 134

24. Bookstore Buyers: The Book Stops Here   *What buyers for bookstore chains do, and why they are among the most important people in your book's journey to success or failure. The growth of chains and their tremendous influence* 140

25. Audits   *What happens when an accountant examines the ledgers of your publisher? When should you think about conducting an audit?* 146

26. Never the Twain   *How West Coast movie agents have transformed into movie producers and packagers. It's getting harder to find an agent to perform the simple task of selling your book to a movie company* 151

27. Books into Movies *Adaptation of books by the film industry. How it is now versus how it used to be. The big buyer of books for adaptation today is television* 156

28. Take This Job and Shove It *When to leave your job to become a full-time writer, and are you suited financially and emotionally to make the move?* 162

29. Breakout Books *What is a breakout book, and how and when do authors move into that stratosphere?* 168

SECTION FOUR: SINS OF COMMISSION

30. Publishing Spoken Here *How agents diplomatically translate the strong emotions of editors and authors to keep their relations smooth* 174

31. Timing *How agents use timing effectively* 179

32. Is Life Too Short? *Why patience in an agent is a virtue. And so is restraint* 185

33. To Fee? Or Not to Fee? *Should agents charge reading fees to review the work of unpublished authors? Have agents become the slush pile readers for the publishing industry?* 189

34. Extraordinary Expenses *The major categories of out-of-pocket expenses that many agents charge off to clients, and why it is vital for agents to recover these from authors* 194

35. Bad News about Your Agent's Death *What authors can do to protect themselves against having their money tied up when their agents die* 200

SECTION FIVE: MANNERS AND MORALS

36. Courtesy *Manners and protocol in the publishing industry, and the ten commandments that authors should obey when dealing with agents and publishers* 208

37. Pet Peeves *An agent's humorous account of the strange and annoying things that authors do* *214*

38. This Sporting Life *How agents, publishers, and authors take gambles when they make vital decisions* *220*

39. Back to Basics *Writing well is still the best strategy for writers* ... *226*

40. Lawyers (Groan!) *Why lawyers who don't understand the uniqueness of publishing law may be more obstructive than helpful* *231*

41. "Let's Run It Past Legal" *The role of the house counsel in determining a publisher's legal policies, and how legal readings affect your manuscript* *236*

42. Moral Rights *American publishing lawyers are re-examining a European legal principle that gives authors greater control over their work* *242*

43. Earn Big Bucks From Old Copyrights in Your Spare Time! *Some obscure and subtle aspects of copyright law may make it easier for authors or their heirs to control or recapture their literary properties* *247*

44. Sacred Honor *The old-fashioned concept of honor still counts, or at least should, in the dealings among authors, agents, and publishers* *253*

45. Scruples *Ambulance chasing among agents and publishers. There is still a place for taste and restraint in the publishing business* *258*

Index *265*

Preface

THIS BOOK WAS born out of my frustration with the fact that nobody seemed to be making sense out of the terrible upheavals taking place in the publishing industry over the last few decades, or expressing alarm over the threat they posed to everyone associated with books. In the early 1980s, as I began to grasp the immensity and the implications of these changes, I proposed to write a monthly column for *Locus,* the leading trade publication catering to science fiction writers, publishers, and fans. Science fiction writers have always been among the most concerned members of the writing profession, and among the most aggressive in the protection of authors' interests. I suspected that a series of articles written by an active literary agent examining and evaluating publishing practices would find a responsive audience. This turned out to be true.

The column, "Agent's Corner," first saw the light of day early in 1981, and out of the first two dozen or so pieces I developed my book, *How to Be Your Own Literary Agent.* Although the book contained a number of critical observations about the way things are done in the book trade, its purpose was largely instructional. I had realized that most authors were appallingly uninformed about the business side of writing. Despite many unhappy experiences they'd had in their dealings with publishers, they did not seem to realize that knowledge is the best armor, and my book set out to enlighten them about contracts, rights, royalty statements, and other fundamentals.

After publication of that book in 1983, I continued to produce my column but ventured to explore in it some provocative issues revolving around business ethics, authors' rights, and the future of the publishing and writing professions. How does the acquisition of one publisher by another ruin authors, paralyze editorial processes, and orphan books? Why is the publishing industry collapsing under the weight of an archaic merchandising system? Is unionization of authors a realistic possibility? Should publishers turn down books on moral grounds? Are editors necessary any longer?

However, not all of the matters I wrote about were of such profound moment. I've continued to instruct and, on the principle that a drop of honey makes the medicine taste better, tried where appropriate to entertain. So you will also discover in this book my thoughts about such topics as: How should writers behave when they deal with editors? What are some of the things authors do that annoy their agents? Are there better and worse publication dates for your book? And—one of my favorites—should agents lend money to their clients? Though these questions are pretty basic, I am constantly amazed to discover that most writers I meet have seldom been given any guidance on them by their agents, editors, or writer friends.

The response to these articles has been inspiring. They seem to have had an impact not only on novice writers but on successful professionals, as well as on my fellow literary agents, on publishing people at every level, and on members of other professions such as accountants and lawyers. Apparently, a great many people connected with this business are worried and disillusioned, and not a few are angry. I was particularly impressed by the supportive reactions of editors, who have begun to realize that they are becoming as alienated from the system as authors.

Having pinpointed some of the most pressing problems, I have not been content to lament the decline of our industry and let it go at that. I have instead attempted to prescribe specific and positive solutions. Some are simple and practical. Others are visionary, even revolutionary. If they stimulate a dialogue and produce some healthy changes, I shall be quite content. Some of the criticisms I leveled in my previous book, *How to Be Your Own Literary Agent,* about the way publishers report royalties to authors, raised the consciousness of a whole generation of writers about these procedures and led to improvement at a number of houses in the rendering of statements. So, change for the good is possible once everybody has enough information to work with.

The most important discovery I made as I assembled this manuscript was how strongly I feel that publishers and literary agents, in whom tremendous power is vested, have a social responsibility. The publishing and writing professions find themselves in, perhaps, the most precarious state of all time. Stupendous economic and technological forces have radically transformed both in recent times, and the emerging inter-relationships among editors, authors, and agents are almost unrecognizable from what they were even a few short years ago. Authors, editors, and even whole publishing companies are being swept out of the business, and the stability of an industry that nurtured the development of America's greatest literary figures has been shattered.

If anything stands out for me as I prepare this book for publication, it is the realization that we are in equal jeopardy from the volcanic changes that the publishing industry is undergoing. If we do not find a way to confront the perils courageously, we may all one day find ourselves victims of a tragedy that will leave everyone connected with literature—author, agent, publisher, and even you the reader—irreversibly impoverished.

RICHARD CURTIS
New York City

Acknowledgments

VIRTUALLY ALL OF the material in this book originally appeared in *Locus*, the trade publication of the science fiction world. Its publisher, Charles Brown, offered me carte blanche in the selection and treatment of my subjects, a rare commitment for which I am immeasurably grateful. Without the forum provided by Charlie, there would be no book here.

I wish to thank my publisher, Tad Crawford of Allworth Press, for his astute reorganization of my material.

Above all, I thank my wife, Leslie, who among her countless other virtues is an inspiring editor and shrewd critic. Her influence is palpable on every page of this work.

And now for a word about sex.

Though I've tried wherever possible to refer to persons of both sexes as "he and she," the English language has yet to create a graceful solution to this frustrating problem. It is particularly galling for people in the publishing business, an industry as sensitive to feminist sensibilities as any in the world and one whose work and executive forces are at least 50 percent female. The best I can do is to rely, as I did in my previous book, on the publishing tradition in which, on most contracts, the masculine pronoun signifies writers of either sex. But I don't like it, and I apologize to any reader who may take offense.

Section One

AGENTS DEMYSTIFIED

CHAPTER 1

Clout

WHENEVER AUTHORS GATHER to discuss the merits of their agents (it may legitimately be wondered whether they ever discuss anything else), the word "clout" inevitably enters the conversation. Clout is the measure of an agent's influence over publishers, and though it is by no means the sole criterion by which agents are judged, it is certainly the ultimate one. What is clout? How do agents wield it? And is it everything we crack it up to be?

The definition of clout has two important components. The first is access: the enclouted agent is intimate with the most powerful men and women in the publishing industry. "They put me through to the head of the company whenever I call," an agent might boast. Or, "I can have your manuscript on the editor-in-chief's desk tomorrow morning." The second component is power, the capability to effect, yea to coerce, positive decisions. The agent with clout does not merely have access to the honchos (and honchas) of certain publishing companies, he has the ability to make them say yes, and to say yes when they would have said no to some other agent.

Unquestionably, clout exists in our business as it does in any other, and there are indeed agents who can make publishers jump every time they call them on the phone, or render a positive verdict when they were originally inclined to render a negative one. At the same time, there are many erroneous impressions about clout stemming from the widely held belief that power in publishing is concentrated in the hands of an elite circle of men and women, a belief promoted by the press, which tends to quote the same people every time it does a story on industry trends. Let's look a little closer at these impressions.

1. *Agents with clout know the top people in the business.* It is not that hard to meet and know, or at least claim to know, the top people in publishing. For one thing, ours is an extremely small industry consisting, according to my short list of key contacts, of no more than two hundred men and women with acquisition authority in the trade book field—a number sufficiently small so that in the course of a season of publishing parties, lunch and drink dates, and office visits, any agent could meet 75 percent of them.

Of course, it is one thing to be acquainted with these folks and quite another to truly know them as one knows friends or family. Among that two hundred I mentioned, I doubt if I know more than half a dozen in a way that goes beyond the superficial. More pertinent is whether an agent *should* be too tight with the people he does business with. If my own experience is indicative, I would say there are few true friendships between agents and publishers for the simple reason that business all too often gets in the way of consistently close friendship. A time inevitably comes when one or the other must get hard-nosed about something, and few friendships survive the test of a knock-down drag-out negotiation, for it's impossible to dig in and take a hard stand when you're afraid of hurting the other guy's feelings. Bear in mind also that as genuinely warmly as agent and publisher may feel toward each other, the former is responsible to his clients, the latter to his company, and the pressures exerted on them are immensely daunting to friendship. The most one can hope for, I think, is solid mutual respect.

As for an agent's boasts of his ability to get an author's manuscript promptly on a publisher's desk, it's hard not to laugh, for if you could see some publishers' desks you would wonder why anyone would want to add to the mountainous chaos to be found there. I know of one editor whose office is so cluttered with unread manuscripts that his staff calls it the Bermuda Triangle. A story is told that one day an agent received a manuscript that this editor had finally gotten around to reading and rejecting. The agent dropped him a line thanking him for at last returning the manuscript, but pointed out that the book had been sold to another publisher, published, gone on and off the best-seller list, and been remaindered.

The truth is that most heads of publishing companies have too much administrative work to read manuscripts or even, for that matter, read all the books their firms publish. I would guess that more than half the time, when an agent submits a manuscript to the head of the company, that person is going to turn it over to an editor or reader and ask for a report. Unless the report is a rave, this executive will take the reader's word about the merits of the work. And again one has to ask, is going to the head of the company necessarily the wise thing to do? This tactic can backfire for an agent, for if the publisher thinks the manuscript is a stinker, he may be less inclined the next time to spend a valuable evening reading that agent's submission. An agent's credibility is his stock in trade, and once lost it's extremely hard to retrieve. Best to go through channels 99 percent of the time, and to be damned sure about the one time in a hundred you attack at the top.

One more myth about accessibility. It's commonly believed that clout among agents is the power not to return phone calls. Although executives in all industries have their phone calls screened by subordinates, I know of few agents who are not available to the lowliest of editors or to any professional author desirous of speaking to them.

2. *Agents with clout can make publishers buy things they wouldn't ordinarily buy.* The judicious use of a close association with a publisher can make a difference in certain cases, particularly when a close decision teeters on the fulcrum of the key man's or woman's opinion. On such an occasion the agent may call in a favor, or beg one, or utilize any of his countless wiles, ranging from bluster to blarney, in order to elicit a yes decision. But because of the democratic process by which most decisions are reached by publishing companies today, few chief executives are going to make it a practice to overrule their editorial boards. The agent who tries to force positive decisions too often will eventually antagonize even his closest buddies in the business.

But I'm not sure that making the head of a company buy books is the best use for such personages, for, as I say, they are not as influential editorially as they are in other areas of the publishing process. The higher in a company an editor rises the less he is involved in editorial matters and the more in administrative ones. The editor-in-chief, publisher, and other titled executives are the principal transmitters of corporate policy. Such matters as advertising and promotional budgets, payout schedules, royalty scales, and reserves against returns are controlled by those persons, and if there is any flexibility on policies in such areas, it's to be found in their offices. And it's there that the agent is best advised to use his clout, except that clout is a terribly brutish word for a process that calls for the utmost finesse and diplomatic skill.

Because publishing in the last four decades has become highly conglomeratized and bureaucratized, decisions that used to be made by just one person who was accountable to nobody are now made by committee. Consensus is achieved by the input not merely of editors but of financial, legal, production, marketing, advertising, design, art, promotional, publicity, and advertising specialists. These individuals form a dismaying picket of decision-makers, each a potential naysayer. The agent's task thus becomes far more challenging than it used to be: it is no longer a matter of bullying, coaxing, or charming one person but of manipulating an entire system. Naturally, an agent can't approach the art director, head of subsidiary rights, in-house counsel, marketing director, vice-president in charge of publicity, and the half dozen editors who sit at a publisher's weekly convocations, whenever he tries to sell the company a book. But he might speak to one or two key board members whose reluctance to vote yes might be jeopardizing a deal or other important decision. The full measure of the agent's tact must be used here, for if he blunders the reaction may be likened to what happens when one inserts one's arm into a hornet's nest. Only at the utmost risk do you play office politics with somebody else's office.

One of the advantages a literary agent has over the unagented author is that the agent is usually familiar with the dynamics of each publishing house, and is able to adapt his methods to the style and structure and personality of each company. He knows all about their organizational structure and power hierarchy, their policies, their negotiating strategies, knows all about the friendships and rivalries that form the corporate profile. To know how a company reaches its decisions is to know how to influence those decisions.

There are other techniques for influencing decisions from without, ranging from relatively harmless ones such as cultivating and flattering secretaries (of either sex, I hasten to add) to the extremely dangerous one of going over the head of the person you're dealing with. For the agent who does not understand the company dynamic, who misjudges it, or who overplays the game, serious and possibly permanent damage may be rendered to his relations with that publisher. Some firms are so rigidly structured that any attempt to tamper with the system will create terrible turmoil.

3. *Agents with clout get higher prices.* There is a good deal of truth to this, but not necessarily for the reasons you think. High prices are a function of boldness; you get big money only if you ask for big money. Agents with reputations for landing huge deals earn their celebrity by seeking prices that other agents would hesitate to demand, and by risking everything by refusing to back down. But it takes two to make a deal, and if publishers accept an agent's demands, it's because the profit-and-loss statements they've drawn up before negotiations commence indicate that they can make a profit even if they meet the agent's outrageous terms. If a publisher takes a bath, the fault rests with the executives who wanted the book so badly they were willing to delude themselves about its prospects in order to acquire it. Of course, one thing that agents with clout do best is foster such delusions by reassuring publishers that they will earn back all that money. But seldom can an agent charm a publisher into overpaying again and again, for at a certain point along the chain of failures, people start getting fired.

One last myth about clout that deserves to be punctured: it is seldom exercised by means of a raised voice. The image of a cigar-chomping agent-bully browbeating an editor into submission is not one with which I'm familiar except in movies. Almost all of the agents I know speak to editors in conversational tones, even when the going gets rough. One of the most clout-laden ones I know seldom raises his voice above a whisper, but heaven help the publisher who does not detect the apocalyptic undertones in his voice when he murmurs, "Are you sure that's your final offer?"

There are hundreds of literary agents plying their trade in New York, California, and many locations between coasts, and I'd guess that you've never heard of most of them. They don't get their names and faces in the trade papers every week like some agents we all know. Yet almost all of them make a living, and some make very good livings, simply because they know that a good book is the master key to most editorial doors. So perhaps you should ask not what your agent can do for you, but what— by way of a good book—you can do for your agent.

⤙⤚

CHAPTER 2

All Agencies Great and Small

I'M NOT SURE that authors understand the structures of literary agencies much better than they understand those of publishing companies. For those of you who are shopping for an agent or thinking of switching agencies, or who are simply interested in organizational dynamics, it might be interesting to compare agencies of different sizes and structures and to discuss the advantages and disadvantages of each type.

First, but not least, is the one-man or one-woman agency. And when I say one man or woman I don't mean one man or woman plus a secretary, for, as we shall soon see, the presence of a second person can radically alter an agent's style, service, and clout. Most such agents start out either as editors of publishing companies or as staff members of large agencies; a few join our profession from the legal and other related fields. To agenting they bring their special knowledge and experience, and those are always big plusses for prospective clients. They can also be handicaps, however. The lawyer who becomes a literary agent will soon discover that publishing law is so vastly different in theory and practice from any other kind of law as to render his training and experience virtually useless. Agents who leave big agencies to set up their own don't always make good agents, as they may be unused to operating outside the context of a supporting organization. Editors who become agents may know a great deal about publishing procedures, but that knowledge doesn't necessarily make them good deal-makers.

The sole practitioner must do everything by and for himself, and from an author's viewpoint there are many desirable aspects of such a setup. Chief among them is accessibility. Phone answering machines or services notwithstanding, you know that when you call your agent, you will get him or her. That means you can maximize your input, communications, and control, which is great unless your input, communications, and control happen to be lousy. Remember that you hired an agent in the first place because you need someone who understands the publishing business better than you, someone who is more experienced and skillful in negotiations, is more objective, and remains calm when push comes to shove. If you take advantage of your agent's accessibility, then all you are doing is manipulating him like a puppet, programming into him the very same emotional shortcomings that you most desperately need to be defended from.

For the sole practitioner, the credit for success belongs exclusively to him or her, and deservedly so. But so, deservedly, does the blame for mistakes. Because there is no insulation between author and agent, both positive and negative emotions tend to run stronger than they might if the author were not so intimate with everything having to do with the handling of his business. Indeed, the author represented by a sole practitioner is all too often quite intimate with the business of his agent's other clients, too, and among the emotions that run strongly in these cases, therefore, is jealousy.

In short, you cannot ask for more personalized service than you get when you engage a one-man or one-woman agency, and if the relationship is solid and harmonious it can be like owning a custom-made automobile. But custom-made automobiles tend to react oversensitively to every bump in the road. And their owners tend to tinker with them.

From the viewpoint of one who has been a sole practitioner, the biggest disadvantage is that the one-person company cannot utilize what businesspeople refer to as a "devil," someone to blame.

It is essential for the new agent to cultivate and ingratiate himself with the influential editors in the business. Needless to say, this agent will be loath to alienate those editors by being overly tough and demanding in negotiations. If an agent starting out in business gets a reputation for being unreasonable, he may lose business. He can of course blame his intransigence on his clients, but in most cases the editors will know it's not the author who's the troublemaker, but his agent. Besides, one of the things authors hire agents for is to take the fire for hard decisions in order to allow their clients to maintain pleasant working relationships with editors. If only there were someone working for your agent with whom he could play Good Guy–Bad Guy, he could have some leeway when it comes to playing hardball. His associate might sometimes serve as the devil, taking tough positions in negotiations. Then, just when it looked as if a deal were going to fall through, his boss would intervene and offer a compromise that mitigated his employee's inflexibility. In other cases the assistant could be the good guy who wishes he could be more lenient but, well, his boss is a tough bird who simply will not yield.

This may be the commonest game played by businessmen and women, but it requires two to each side, and the sole practitioner is one shy of that minimum. Exposed as he or she is, the one-man or one-woman agent must, almost by definition, be a courageous individual.

With the introduction of a second person into the agency—even a secretary with no discretionary power—the dynamics of the firm usually alter sharply. The agent can if he chooses make himself less accessible, a state that is often tactically desirable. He at last has somebody to blame, perhaps not for negotiating and other serious mistakes, but at least for some of the clerical screwups that bedevil all business enterprises. On the other hand, the operation of the business should become more efficient, a fair tradeoff for the agent's withdrawal from the firing line. If the employee is anything more than a warm body occupying a desk, he or she can create some important opportunities for strategic games, can serve as a reader, rendering a second viewpoint on the salability of manuscripts, or as a sounding board for marketing, negotiating, and other decisions. And if that person is interested in and good at certain specialized tasks— handling movie, television, magazine, or foreign rights, for example—or has a good grasp of certain markets that the boss has no interest in or feel for, or if he or she is good at handling certain clients, then you have the makings of a potent team and the foundation for a successful agency.

From that point on it becomes a matter of adding new staff members and deploying them according to the organization that best suits the agent's style—a style that may transmute as the agent gains experience.

As a rule, the smaller the agency the less specialized are the tasks performed by its staff: in other words, everybody handles everything. As the firm grows, a structure usually emerges along lines of staff specialization. One structure might be described as vertical, with the agent at the pinnacle handling the clients, supported by a staff that services the clients' properties but does not necessarily have contact with the clients themselves. One staff member might handle foreign rights, another movie, another serial, another bookkeeping, another filing, and so on.

The advantage of a vertical system, generally, is excellent service, for every aspect of the client's needs; every facet of the property, will be taken care of by a specialist. The disadvantage is that the client list must be kept relatively small—no larger than the capacity of the head of the company to handle his clients' work and needs comfortably. Another disadvantage is the vulnerability of the agency in the event of the death or disability of its owner, for there will be no one with deep experience at handling clients to take his or her place. If the agent should go out of town for an extended trip or vacation, the agency may be reduced to a maintenance capacity and not be capable of dealing forcefully with the sorts of emergencies that always seem to attack writers the moment their agents board an airplane.

As an agent becomes successful he will be solicited by many authors seeking representation. Many are excellent writers with good track records who need the guidance and assistance of a good agency. A combination of profit motive and compassion will compel the agent to offer representation to them. But how can he fit them into his stable without curtailing the time, attention, and service he is now able to lavish on the rest of his clients?

Some agents resist this temptation, harden their hearts, and shut their doors to newcomers. Others resort to hiring employees to handle the overflow of clients. An agency engaging a roster of agents might be described as horizontal, and obviously there is no limit to the number of clients such a firm can take on, for, as soon as it reaches capacity, it can always add a new agent to take on the excess. The boss will still be the boss, and there will still be a staff of specialists to handle subsidiary rights and clerical and administrative functions. But on the middle level will be those other agents, replicating what their boss does. They may be generalists, handling the gamut of literature from genre to mainstream, or they may deal in such specialties as juveniles, nonfiction, or science fiction. I would say that most middle-sized and large agencies fit this horizontal pattern; in fact, it's hard to imagine how an agency can become large unless it does expand horizontally.

From the writer's viewpoint, an agency of this type is attractive for several reasons. First, it enables him to locate within the organization the individual agent best suited to his work and style. Second, if the organization is well run, he will enjoy the benefit of a team approach under the supervision of the principal agent. And third, if one's agent is out of town or on vacation, or is so thoughtless as to die, there is a good likelihood that he will find a replacement in the ranks of the other agents at the same firm. In other words, the bumpy ups and downs you often experience with a one-person agency will be absorbed by a larger organization, and that is a secure feeling. But there's also a catch.

Most clients of middle-sized and large agencies are content to be represented by an agent who is not the head man or woman, as long as there is a sense that the chief is at least overseeing the work of the subordinate agents and making sure that all of the agency's authors are being properly serviced. Inherent in the very nature of large organizations, however, is a degree of insulation between the head of the company and the activities of those clients he or she does not directly represent. If an author begins to feel that the agent handling his work is not doing an adequate job, he may conclude that the head of the company has more important concerns than the scribblings of a fifteen-thousand-dollar-a-year midlist writer. Thus is created what might be described as the "A List–B List Syndrome," meaning that the agency has two client lists: the Grade A clients handled by the boss, and the Grade B ones handled by the secondary agents. When that sort of suspicion begins to gnaw at a client, he may eventually decide he must either move up or move out and seek an agency where he will receive more personal attention from the top agent.

It is therefore incumbent on the heads of agencies to make sure that the subordinate agents keep in very close touch with him and with each other. At many agencies, that is precisely what happens. In others, the boss has administrative and client demands that make supervision of the other agents' activities difficult. Now, it can certainly be assumed that some of those agents are ambitious, and so an atmosphere is created in which a subordinate agent, operating with little supervision, begins to wonder just what he needs a boss for anyway. He may be making a good salary and even collecting commissions, but as so much of the revenue he generates must go to paying overhead and a profit to the firm he works for, as surely as the sun will rise tomorrow the idea will occur to him that he could do better on his own. For many of his clients, the notion of joining this agent when he starts his own agency is extremely appealing, for in a stroke those clients will be transformed from B Listers to A Listers. Things don't always turn out to be as satisfying as that fantasy, though, for the agent may discover that he does not, on his own, enjoy the same success he did when he was a member of a large and influential organization. It is extremely hard and perhaps impossible for the client of a larger agency to sort out just what is the true source of his agent's power and success. Does the person handling you consult with the head of the company or is he handling your account strictly on his own? Is his effectiveness due in good measure to the influence, reputation, and support of his organization, or are these incidental to his performance? Some authors discover the answers to these questions by leaving; others, by staying on.

At the summit are the giant agencies, representing many illustrious authors, extremely well-connected in the movie and television area, and moving tremendous amounts of properties, rights, and money. These firms are often broken down into departments, and you the author will be handled by someone in the literary department. These departments usually have senior and junior staff members and operate as potent fiefdoms in a great bicoastal kingdom. Because the overhead of these firms is stupendous, the clients they take on must be pretty heavy hitters and often are authors whose work is highly adaptable to film and television. The disadvantage is the intimidating vastness of such organizations.

Somewhere in all this is a place for you, and in few businesses is it more true that what's great for one person may be awful for another. I doubt if many authors retain one agent for the span of their entire career. Indeed, for the sake of an author's personal growth, having the same agent from cradle to grave may be a very poor idea.

At least, that's what I tell myself whenever I lose a client.

CHAPTER 3

Rivals

RE LITERARY AGENTS friendly with each other? Are they mutually suspicious or hostile? Do they steal authors from each other at every opportunity? Do they cooperate with one another? Do they have a code of behavior? Are they too competitive to act collectively?

To the extent that the book publishing business is a pie to be sliced into just so many pieces, and the number of profitable authors is a finite one, I suppose it can be argued that agents are rivals. Yet I don't think most agents feel that way. Unlike some other businesses we can think of, where the survival of one firm is achieved only at the expense of another, there appears to be enough business in the publishing field to enable all literary agents who stay in the game long enough and run their businesses prudently to earn a living and to be gracious toward each other while doing so. Though we have seen bad times in our industry, they have never been so bad that no publisher was buying books. Nor has the pool of potential clients ever shrunk to the degree that a resourceful agent could not find authors to make money with. In short, I don't believe agents lose too much sleep worrying that the supply of or the demand for their products and services is going to dry up.

What agents do worry about is maximizing the earning power of their clients, helping their authors realize the full measure of their talents, and exploiting every bit of financial potential in their work: to put it plainly, making them rich and famous. Obviously, the agent whose clients become rich and famous will become rich and famous too. And, just as obviously, a dissatisfied author will eventually seek new representation.

And it is here that agents sometimes start throwing elbows.

Antagonism between agents flares up over the interpretation of just how loudly, sweetly, and aggressively an agent sings his firm's praises to an author represented by another agent. You might think of it as the Smoking Gun theory of client-stealing: if the author walks in the door of another agency in a state of uncertainty but walks out clutching a signed agreement with his new agent, it can be inferred that something considerably more than a soft-sell occurred behind that door. At least, most of the time such an inference is justified. But not always. Many an author not comfortable with his agent has visited another agency and, with little persuasion, realized from a brief chat and a look around and a sniff of the atmosphere that he has actually been quite miserable with his old agent, but could not admit it until that moment.

However that may be so, the author's old agent is going to strongly suspect that the other agent gave a snow job to his former client. Because I treasure the friendships of (most of) my colleagues, I call them when I become the beneficiary of a former client of theirs to reassure them that I did not actively solicit that client, and to pave the way for cooperation on old business concerning that author. And I have always appreciated it when my colleagues did the same for me. In some cases, when the parting is friendly and by mutual consent, agents will refer authors to other agents.

Most agents have had the experience of having their colleagues refer clients to them. In point of fact, agents work with each other to a much greater degree than they work against each other. I know of a few suspicious, curmudgeonly types who jealously guard their flocks as if their colleagues were wolves poised to pounce on helpless clients and carry them off to their lairs. On the whole, though, agents enjoy each other's company, help each other, are anxious to remain on one another's good side, and to a degree act collectively on matters that affect their community of interest.

Agents call each other frequently seeking advice on all manner of problems: Who do you know at Random House? How do you phrase your option clause? Who's buying westerns? How did you conduct that auction? How did you get that terrific price? What should I do about this problem client?

On occasion, agents cooperate on deals. For instance, if an author leaving Agent A wishes Agent B to handle subsidiary rights to his old books—a situation fraught with the potential for mean-spirited behavior—the two agents might work things out so that they split a commission. Agent A will be satisfied because he doesn't have to do all that much work to earn his share of the commission, and Agent B will be satisfied because he didn't have to sell the books originally.

In other cases, such as collaborations, there may be two agents for two authors and the agents work out the division of labor and commissions. I may have a client with a fantastic story to tell who can't write, but I don't represent quite the right author to team up with him. And my buddy Agent X may have just the right author. After exploring the questions of our clients' compatibility and the division of work and money, Agent X and I discuss just how we're going to cooperate. Am I going to be the principal agent in making a deal with the publisher? If so, am I to take my commission off the top—off the total advance, that is—or do I take my commission only on that portion of the advance allocated to my client? Who is going to handle the subsidiary rights, Agent X or my agency? You can see that unless there is a solid friendship and abundant goodwill between agents, there is going to be friction, and in potentially fatal doses. Many a lucrative deal has gone down the tubes because two agents couldn't reach agreement on such matters.

CHAPTER 4

What I Have Done for You Lately

ONE DAY, I got a phone call from an agitated editor. His voice was trembling and he could scarcely contain his emotion. The emotion was fear.

It seems that a hotheaded client of mine had gotten so upset over some editorial work done on his book that he'd threatened in a loud voice, during a visit to the editor's office, to pulp his face. Some of his colleagues had interceded and ushered the distraught author out of the building. Of course, beating up your editor is a time-honored writer's fantasy, but my client had taken it further than most authors do. Pulping an editor's face is a serious breach of etiquette. "What can I do to help?" I offered.

"Restrain him," the editor said.

"You mean, physically?"

"Yes, if need be."

I could not suppress an ill-timed laugh.

"What the hell is so funny?" he demanded.

"Well," I said, "I've done everything else, I might as well be a bodyguard for an editor, too."

After settling the dispute by eliciting promises of good behavior from my client and assurances of more thoughtful blue-pencilling from the editor, I reflected on some of the unusual things that agents are called upon to do in the course of their careers. I am often asked to speak to groups of aspiring writers and to explain just what literary agents do. I wonder how the audience would react if I told them that among other things, literary agents babysit for their clients' kids, paint their clients' houses, and bail their clients out of jail. They even fall in love with their clients and marry them. In fact, I have done all these things and more.

Years ago, before it merged with another agents' organization to form the Association of Authors' Representatives, the Society of Authors' Representatives issued a brochure describing some functions that authors should not expect their agents to perform. Most of my colleagues would lose half their clients overnight if they took these guidelines seriously, however. For instance, the brochure advised that you shouldn't expect your agent to edit your book. But most agents I know would consider themselves remiss if they did not do some light, and sometimes heavy, editing to improve a book's chances of acceptance, help the author modify a manuscript for magazine serialization, or simply make it the best book it can be.

Here are some other things the brochure mentioned:

- *The agent cannot solve authors' personal problems.* As a writer myself, and a friend or agent of many writers, I can testify to how tightly interconnected the personal, financial, and creative elements of an author's life are. Trouble in one area almost invariably indicates trouble in the others. The agent who turns his back on an author's personal problems may well be diminishing that author's earning power. So for reasons of self-interest if not compassion, an agent may find himself playing psychiatrist to a client, sticking his nose into an author's marital disputes, or taking a depressed author to a baseball game.

- *The agent cannot lend authors money.* Ha! In this age of glacial cash flow, agents are being asked more and more frequently to play banker. I'm not sure authors always appreciate that the agent who advances them money lends it interest-free, or that the agent's total advances to clients at any given time may come to tens of thousands of dollars. But I don't know too many agents who can gaze unflinchingly into the eyes of a desperate client and say, "If you need a loan, go to a bank."

- *The agent cannot be available outside office hours except by appointment.* Many business and personal crises arise for authors at times that, inconveniently, do not correspond to regular business hours. Book negotiations can carry over into the evening, and global time differentials put Hollywood three hours behind New York, New York at least five hours behind Europe, and Japan half a day away. An agent's day is not the same as a civil servant's.

  Many of my clients have my home phone number. I only ask them to use it sparingly.

- *The agent cannot be a press agent, social secretary, or travel agent.* A lot of agents I know take on these functions to supplement the author's or publisher's efforts. Literary agenting is a service business, and anything within reason that an agent can do to free a client from care should be given thoughtful consideration. Rare is the agent who has not driven clients to the airport or booked them into hotels, arranged business or social appointments, or helped them secure tickets to a hot Broadway show.

Like my colleagues I have a large quiver full of sales techniques ranging from sweet talk to harangues. But I wonder how many agents have donned costumes and performed burlesque routines to sell books? It happened. Some clients of mine had written a satire of the best-selling book *The One Minute Manager.* Theirs was called *The One Minute Relationship,* demonstrating how you could meet, fall in love, marry, and divorce within sixty seconds of the first heartthrob. It was to be published by Pinnacle, but about a week before Pinnacle's sales conference, the editor-in-chief called me. "I'm thinking of something different for presenting this book to the sales staff. Could your clients cook up a cute skit?"

I promised to see what I could do, and called my clients. They came to my home and we brainstormed a skit over take-out Chinese food. The shtick we came up with featured an Indian swami who has developed the One Minute Technique. He has to wear a white robe and a turban with a jewel in it. The "jewel" in this case was a thick slice of kosher salami, and we called it the Star of Deli. My clients and I fell on the floor laughing. Then they suggested that since I had the robe, the turban, and the salami, and did a passing fair imitation of a Hindu fakir, I should perform the starring role in front of the Pinnacle salespeople. It took several bottles of Chinese beer to make me agree, but at length I went along, reasoning that these days, whatever it takes to sell books is okay by me. The skit went over well, climaxed of course by my gleefully stuffing the Star of Deli into my mouth. Pinnacle loved it so much they took our show on the road, videotaping our performance and featuring it at the American Booksellers Association convention.

Agents are not the tight-lipped stiffs that some have made us out to be. Like Shylock, we bleed if you prick us and laugh if you tickle us. I have cried with and for my authors when misfortune strikes, and rejoiced with them at their weddings and the births of their children.

I have also had some great laughs, not a few at the expense of clients and colleagues, for I am an inveterate practical joker. A client and good friend bought himself a telephone answering machine, and was so anxious about missing important calls that whenever he was away for any length of time he called home every fifteen minutes to get his messages by means of a remote control signal. He worried that machine to death. If he returned to find no messages, he would examine the phone and the answering machine for malfunctions.

One day, I decided to indulge his worst paranoid fantasy, and left the following message on his answering machine: ". . . Studios. If you don't return my call by five P.M. we will assume you're not interested and we will withdraw our offer." The poor fellow spent an hour phoning movie studio executives on both coasts explaining that his phone machine had malfunctioned in the middle of a message, and asking if they happened to be the people who left an offer on his machine that day.

Most people do not think of literary agents as leading adventurous lives, and that is largely true. Most of the time our conduct is as tightly circumscribed as that of businesspeople in any other profession. Our greatest thrill is grappling in close combat with an editor during a six-figure negotiation, or stalking a check through the treacherous thickets of a publisher's bookkeeping system. Accounts of such adventures make for exciting listening only if you happen to be another literary agent, but somehow they don't carry the same weight as the tales of mountainous seas and mutinous tribes, challenging mountains and charging rhinos, that you can routinely hear at any meeting of the Explorers Club.

Nevertheless, because our profession brings us into contact with unusual characters, we do occasionally find ourselves carried far from the stereotypical role of submitting manuscripts in the morning, collecting checks in the afternoon, and going to lunch for three hours in between.

In 1966 I was in London setting up the English office of Scott Meredith's literary agency. Novelist Evan Hunter and his wife were passing through London on their way to the Cotswolds, and we spent a delightful afternoon dining al fresco at my boss's expense. I bade them good-bye and wished them a pleasant journey, and figured that was that. About a week later, however, I got a call from Evan in Southampton. They were about to embark on a ship for America when his wife realized she had left her jewelry in a safe in the Ligon Arms Hotel in the Cotswold town of Broadway. "I'm going to ask an important favor of you," Evan said. "I want you to take a train out there and get the jewels back. Bring them to London and we'll arrange for them to be shipped home."

At that time I was in my twenties and, beyond getting stuck in an elevator for two hours and having my tonsils taken out, I had never been at hazard in many "real life situations." This sounded like an opportunity to experience the kind of peril that confronted the Burtons, Spekes, and Hilarys through whom I'd lived vicariously.

"They're not just going to hand the jewels over to me," I protested.

"Of course not," said Evan. "There'll be a password."

"A password?"

"When you get to the hotel, go to the desk and tell the lady you're there to recover our jewelry. Then say the password."

A password! This was a scheme worthy of Evan Hunter, who under the pen name of Ed McBain had created my favorite police procedural series, "The 87th Precinct."

"And what is the password?" I asked.

There was a long pause and I sensed that Evan was looking furtively around for eavesdroppers. He uttered a phrase in a voce so sotto I had to ask him to say it again. "'Phoenix Rising'," he said. "Repeat it."

"'Phoenix Rising'," I said. "Heavy!"

That afternoon I caught a British Railways train to Evesham, the station closest to Broadway. The taxi driver I hired to take me to Broadway looked like Central Casting's notion of a Dickensian cutpurse, including addressing me as "Guv'nor." When he asked me, just being friendly, my business in Broadway, I told him, "Just touring." He arched an eyebrow. I wore a three-piece English-cut suit and a tense smile and didn't look remotely like a tourist. I looked like a man trying not to look like a man who was soon to bear tens of thousands of dollars' worth of jewelry on his person.

The Ligon Arms Hotel had been built in an era when Englishmen were four feet tall, as I quickly discovered when I grazed my skull on a lintel. I wobbled to the desk and found a diminutive woman peering at me who looked as if she would crumble into powder if I spoke too loudly. I cleared my throat and murmured, "Phoenix Rising." She gazed owlishly at me and my heart sank. Something had gone wrong. Evan had not told her the password. He had told her the wrong password. She had not heard it correctly. She had stolen the jewels.

"Phoenix Rising. Phoenix Rising," she muttered, searching at least ninety years of memory for an association with this mysterious phrase. Then the light of recognition kindled in her eyes. Her hand leaped to her mouth. "Phoenix Rising! You're Phoenix Rising! EVERYONE, IT'S PHOENIX RISING! HE'S HERE, HE'S HERE!" Whereupon bellhops, maids, cooks, and guests poured into the lobby to see The Bearer of the Password. I doubt if anything quite like this had happened here since the Norman Invasion.

We crowded around the safe as the jewels, rolled in a pocketed length of embroidered velvet, were set before me. Delicately, my friend untied a drawstring, making certain not to touch the jewelry itself. I stared at a handsome collection of baubles. There was a hurried conference when we realized I had no inventory of what was supposed to be there, and I was required to sign a receipt itemizing each piece. The staff gathered at the entrance to bid adieu to Alias Phoenix Rising. "Quick tour, Guv'nor," my driver observed as I stepped back into the taxi. "Saw what I came to see," I replied tersely, clutching the pouch in a death grip.

Obviously, these days authors don't merely ask their agents what they've done for them lately, but rather, what else they've done for them lately, and I guess just about anything goes.

∽

CHAPTER 5

Building Careers

A S YOU CAN see, a literary agent's life involves far more than reading, lunching, and deal-making. His or her services embrace the literary, legal, financial, social, political, psychological, and even the spiritual; and the jobs we are obliged to tackle run the gamut from computer troubleshooting to espionage. But because our business is a day-to-day, book-to-book affair, we tend to lose perspective. With our preoccupation with advances and royalties, payout schedules and discounts, with movie rights and foreign rights and serial rights and merchandise rights, with option clauses and agency clauses and acceptability clauses and termination clauses, it is all too easy for us to forget that our primary goal is to build careers, to take writers of raw talents, modest accomplishments, and unimpressive incomes and render them prosperous, successful, and emotionally fulfilled.

This endeavor demands the application of all the skill and experience we command, plus something else: vision. Vision in this context may be defined as an agent's ideal of the best work an author is capable of achieving, matched to the best job his publishers can perform. An agent's vision should illuminate the author's path, oftentimes far into his future, if not for his entire career.

In order for our vision to be fulfilled, three conditions must be met. First, we have to learn and understand what the author's own vision is. Second, we have to align his vision with our perception of his talent: do we believe he has what it takes to realize his dream? And finally, we have to help the author fashion his work to suit the demands and expectations of the marketplace.

I cannot overstate how much easier said than done the process of building an author's career is. Human nature being what it is, the forces militating against success are heartbreakingly formidable. The agent's vision and the author's vision may be at serious odds with one another, or at odds with the publisher's. The author's talent or stamina or financial resources may simply not be up to the task he has cut out for himself. His publisher may not like or understand his work. His audience may reject it. Every imaginable contingency may beset an author along life's path: death and disability, divorce and disaster—the same ones that beset everybody else, plus a few that are indigenous to creative people. The attrition rate for authors and their dreams is extremely high, and the odds against talent flourishing under perfect conditions are prohibitive. With so much at stake, it should come as no surprise that agents approach the building of their clients' careers with the utmost solemnity.

When a writer becomes my client I sit down with him or her to explore immediate and long-term goals. I ask writers how much it costs to live comfortably, how much they earn per book, and how long it takes them to write. It should then be a matter of simple arithmetic to determine what I must do to keep their careers on a steady keel: simply divide their yearly nut by the number of books they are capable of producing annually. This gives me the amount of money they must earn (after commission, I hasten to remind them) per book to make a living.

Unfortunately, life is not a matter of simple arithmetic. Even in the unlikely event that the author lives within his means and nothing un-toward befalls him and his family, there is no room in the above equation for profit, and visions of greatness require an author to earn a profit.

Now, books that earn a profit for authors are not easily come by (not, at any rate, as easily come by as books that earn a profit for publishers). Good luck and good agenting may sometimes make one happen, but it is unwise for an author to depend on either. This means the author has to make it happen on his own by writing a breakout book. But how can he do that if he can't buy the time?

Even if you are blessed with an unexpected windfall, there is no guarantee that you will achieve your dream, thanks to Fehrenbach's Law. T. R. Fehrenbach, the brilliant Texas historian, once wrote to me that,

"Expenses rise to meet the cost of every sellout." In other words, the profit that authors make does not necessarily go into the fund marked, "This Time I'm *Really* Going to Write That Book." More likely, it will go toward something that is easier to grasp, like a new Buick Regal, a twenty-one-inch Sony Trinitron, or a two-week vacation on Lake George.

The truth is that writers are no better equipped to fulfill their dreams than are other middle-class people, because compromise is an easy habit to get into when it is rewarded with comforts and luxuries. Austerity, integrity, sacrifice, relentless determination, and other virtues associated with uncompromising artistic endeavor are seldom a match for a brand-new living room suite or wall-to-wall carpeting for the master bedroom. So an author's dream gets postponed a bit longer, and a bit longer after that, until perhaps that terrible day comes when the dream deferred pops, in Langston Hughes's phrase, "like a raisin in the sun." Death and disability, divorce and disaster are not the only terrible things that can befall an author, or even the worst things. Giving up his dream is the worst thing, and that is truly tragic. I believe it is an agent's sacred duty to keep this from happening, to keep the flame of hope burning in the author's breast, to encourage him in every way possible to seize the moment when an opportunity to reach for greatness presents itself.

Just as importantly, the agent must make a judgment as to whether the author's talents are up to his ambitious projects. They are not always, by any means. Authors are no more objective about their strengths and weaknesses than anyone else, and when their self-perceptions are deficient, it is vital for their agents to shed light on those blind spots.

Another way that agents help authors build their careers is to match their "product"—an unpleasant but useful word—to the demands of the marketplace. In other words, to make it commercial. It is not enough for a writer to fulfill his dream if his dream happens to be to write perfect imitations of Virgil, parodies of Thackeray, or metaphysical poetry. The agent must therefore be as intimate with publishing and reading trends as he is with the soul of his author, and to make sure the author's work plays into those trends.

The problem doesn't always lie with the author. Some publishers are simply better at publishing certain types of books than others, and an author's development may eventually reach the point where his publisher simply can no longer accommodate it. Then it may be time to move the author to a house that understands his needs and his work and offers an environment in which these can be nurtured properly. It is not always greed that motivates agents to switch authors to new publishers. Most of the time, yes, but not always.

If all goes well—and we have seen how seldom it does—you will gradually, or perhaps suddenly, move on to a new and lofty plateau, maybe even onto the very summit itself. Hand clasped in your agent's, you will breathe the heady, rarefied atmosphere of success. You will have fulfilled your dream, your talent will now be a splendidly fashioned tool, and you will be published by a publisher that knows how to realize every dollar of commercial value from your masterpieces for your mutual enrichment. Only one thing remains to be done to place the capstone on your sublime triumph.

Why, fire your agent, of course.

↬

Section Two

BREAKING IN

CHAPTER 6

Sometimes a Great Notion

M OST PUBLISHING PEOPLE can relate to the following scenario: You are attending a party and are introduced to another guest. "So, what line of business are you in?" the guest asks, a respected opening social gambit.

"I'm in the publishing business," you reply. "I work with authors."

"Hey, that's great. You must lead a really interesting life." He then goes on to explain that he is a postal clerk, a fabric salesman, a dishwasher repairman, a sanitation worker. Your companion suddenly brightens. "Hey, you may be just the guy I've been looking for!" He then takes you by the arm and furtively escorts you to an isolated corner of the room. Your stomach begins to sink, because you know what's coming.

His eyes dart suspiciously from guest to guest as he takes you by the lapels and puts his mouth close to your ear. "You got any writers looking for a *great* idea? *Because I've got one!* I would write it myself, but I don't have the time or the talent. But if you got somebody, I'll go in with him, fifty-fifty."

You look past him, seeking your host to rescue you, but it is hopeless.

The fellow has an iron grip on your lapels. "Okay, I'll tell you the idea if you swear not to tell another soul."

"Stack of Bibles," you say, raising your palm to the sky.

He leans even closer. "Okay. What it is, is . . ."

What it is, is usually awful. But even if it isn't, the truth is that I cannot help him. For how can I explain to him that the last thing that professional writers need is ideas, that most of the writers I know have enough ideas to last a lifetime? They may need time, yes. They may need money. They may need peace and quiet. They certainly need love. But the one thing they have more than enough of is ideas.

Most people who have never seriously attempted to write books subscribe to what might be termed the Big Bang theory of inspiration. They perceive artistic ideas to be stupendous epiphanies that are visited once in a lifetime on a chosen few, like Moses receiving the Ten Commandments from God.

There is no denying that many sublime works of art, music, and literature are born that way. Most of us take ideas for granted, and why shouldn't we? We have dozens of them every day, and seldom do they seem to be of such moment that we pause in wonder to contemplate their splendor. Only when we examine books, pictures, and other artistic endeavors closely do we think about the intellectual processes that gave birth to them, and if these works are truly great, we may well be reminded that the generation of ideas is a phenomenon worthy of genuine reverence. By what mysterious mechanism they originate is surely as unknowable as how life itself was first created. Indeed, as the word "inspiration" literally means the entering of spirit into that which was hitherto lifeless, it could well be said that at no time are humans closer to divine than when they are inspired with noble ideas.

But ask a professional writer about his ideas and he may well respond as inarticulately as my friend at the party. In all likelihood, he'll ask, "Which ideas?" because he's got a million of them, and his biggest problem is choosing one. His next biggest problem is finding the time and money to develop it. For this kind of writer, the real inspiration comes when he is writing. It magically flows from a remote region of his unconscious into his fingertips and seems almost unfailingly to illuminate every character description, every plot twist, every metaphor, perhaps every sentence. Big Bang? No, the image of a water tap is probably more apposite. Turn it on for an hour or two and out comes a daily ration of good, maybe great work. I hesitate to say "inspired" because most professional writers are too modest and self-critical to call it that. But the creative process by which literature—even popular literature—is produced may legitimately be described as miraculous.

At first glance, most people would say that literary agents operate far from this ethereal realm of ideas. After all, we make our livings appraising the value of the commodities known as books, and helping the producers of those commodities turn them into hard cash. But look again. Unlike rug dealers, car salesmen, or bond brokers, the merchandise we traffic in is intellectual. Our stock in trade is ideas, ideas that have been smelted and fashioned by authors into the precious metal called literature. A manuscript may be no more than a pound or two of paper, but when an agent pitches that book to an editor, it isn't the value of the paper he's describing. It's the value of the idea.

As I talk with an author about ideas, I ask myself some very pragmatic questions. How do those ideas fit in with the author's career goals and financial circumstances? He may have a magnificent vision that takes my breath away, but where is he going to find the forty thousand dollars he needs to write that book under the tranquil conditions he requires, particularly since he is currently getting five thousand dollars a book!

Another thing I look and listen for is energy. An author may well have dozens of ideas for books, but he does not hold them all equally dear. When writers relate their ideas to me, do their eyes kindle with fire and their voices resonate with passion? Do they gesture frenetically with their hands or seem to lapse into a sort of trance? Do they speak in a singsong tone, as if it's all the same to them which book they write and which one they abandon?

The agent who encourages an author to develop the wrong idea, or who doesn't help him realize an idea fully, or who doesn't take into account that idea's appropriateness for its intended market, or doesn't consider an idea in the context of an author's talent and skill, or doesn't calculate the time and money that the author will require to fulfill his idea—that agent may inflict serious harm on his client's career. It's a very big responsibility, and my fellow agents and I worry about it a lot.

Once we are satisfied that we have the right idea, and that we have it where we want it, we must help the author develop it into an outline form that is useful both as a scenario for the writer to follow and as a sales instrument we can pitch to publishers. As you'll see in the next chapter, the two functions can differ vastly. The key difference is that in the latter, the idea is presented with as much intensity as author and agent can possibly endow it with. We try to boil a book's complexity down to its very essence, and to articulate that essence with words that stimulate associations in editors' minds with such abstractions as beauty, as well as with less abstract values like profit. We strive (and sometimes slave) to make every word of description pique an editor's imagination.

Obviously, many and perhaps most books are more complex than any one-line summary can possibly convey. And many of them are not half as good. One agent friend of mine is fond of saying that his idea of a book is usually a lot better than the book itself. "I don't sell the book, I sell my idea of the book," he says.

The process doesn't stop with the agent's pitch to the editor. It continues down the line as the editor tries to conceptualize the book for his or her colleagues. The publisher's sales force must in turn transmit the idea to the bookstore buyer, and the store's sales staff must get the message across to its customers. And because no one in this chain of people has a great deal of time (including the customer), the idea must be expressed in the pithiest possible way, otherwise attention may wander and the sale will be lost. So we all practice refining our descriptions of books into concepts that are so concentrated and potent they are practically radioactive. And we use a wide variety of audio and visual aids to get the idea across: good titles and subtitles, eye-catching covers, arresting dust jacket blurbs, intriguing advertising copy, plugs by celebrities.

What concerns me is that the publishing business is becoming entirely too idea-driven. In our frenzy to encapsulate concepts so that we can sell them to each other effectively, we may well be forgetting that it is not the idea that excites us when we read a book, not the idea that makes us laugh or cry or stay up to the small hours turning pages raptly while our hearts thunder with the thrill and suspense and tragedy and comedy of it. It's the way the author realizes that idea and evokes it in our own imaginations. To put it succinctly, it's good writing. But there is a tendency today to presell great ideas—we call them "high concepts" in the trade—then develop them in predictably formulaic plots and package them for an audience that has been conditioned for formulas by television.

The next time you're struck by a great idea for a book, don't forget to ask yourself if you know what to do with it.

CHAPTER 7

Outlines

MANY EXCELLENT WORKS are available about how to write, but there is one category of writing that even topflight professionals struggle with, and that's outlines. I have seldom seen outlines covered adequately in the how-to literature I've read, probably because most writers who write about writing have never seriously examined why we need outlines. If you think we need them only to help us write books, you're probably doing something wrong.

Too many writers dismiss outlines as unworthy of serious attention, or not essential to the practice of their trade. "I'm a good writer, but a lousy outliner," I frequently hear, and the statement often sounds like a boast. "What does it matter?" goes another typical remark. "My finished books don't resemble my outlines anyway, so why bother?" Still others say, "The outline is in my head, and as long as my books turn out well, why should I have to outline them on paper?"

These scoffers have failed to understand the critical truth about outline writing: publishers are less interested in what's going into your book than they are in what's going onto your cover.

From what I know about publishing history, the use of outlines to sell books to publishers is a relatively recent phenomenon. Before World War II, it was de rigueur for authors to submit completed manuscripts to their publishers. Even established authors wrote their books before seeking contracts with their regular publishers. They might consult with them in the formative stages, but it was pretty much taken for granted that the author knew what he was doing and where he was going with his book, and that editors served to help shape or tidy up the finished product. The purpose of outlines was, as you might expect, to help authors conceptualize and develop their books. It didn't matter if the outlines were long or short, well written or scribbled, highly compressed or elaborate (Henry James composed forty thousand word summaries of his later novels): an outline was a working sketch for the sole use of the author. It was not designed for display, particularly to publishers.

After World War II, the nature of publishing changed dramatically, affecting not only what kinds of books were written but how they got sold. Not the least of the transformations was that of the outline from writing tool to selling tool.

With the emergence of publishing as big business, with the acquisition of publishing companies by conglomerates or their absorption into immense entertainment complexes, a schism was created between the editorial and the business functions. Tremendous tensions were created as publishers demanded better justification for the purchasing of books. Profit-and-loss statements and market projections had to be drawn up before submissions were accepted. Editorial and publishing committees replaced the judgments of individual editors whose rationales for acquisition were often no more than intuition, enthusiasm, or personal pleasure.

In order to crack this increasingly formidable system, authors were required to produce detailed and polished presentations that answered not merely the question "What is it about?" but such questions as "How does it differ from similar books?" "What is the target market and how large is it?" and "Can a publisher make a profit on it?" It no longer mattered if an individual editor was wild about a book or a proposed book, because he was no longer the only person making the decision. Indeed, many of the people now making the decision might not have read the work at all, and not a few of them weren't particularly interested in books except in terms of their bottom line value as merchandise: how to "package" them, how to position advertising and promotion for them, how to price them, how to "move" them. Some writers realized that in order to satisfy this growing cadre of specialists, they'd have to learn a kind of writing very far from the sort of thing they'd been doing until then—not synopses but sales pitches cunningly contrived to subdue the anxieties of publishing personnel ranging from art director to head of sales to subsidiary rights director to publicity chief to vice-president in charge of marketing to editor.

If you piled all the outlines I have read in my lifetime on top of each other, they would reach the summit of Kanchenjunga. So I can say with some authority that few writers have grasped this crucial distinction between outlines designed to guide oneself through the complex terrain of plot and character and those written to turn on the staff of a publishing company. All too often I see chapter-by-chapter outlines of fifty or a hundred pages describing every twist of story and every nuance of character development, outlines that are 95 percent longer than most editors have the time or inclination to read, and that are deficient in many elements that are tempting to potential buyers. Such outlines should go back where they belong: beside the author's typewriter, helping him construct his book. But they don't belong on an editor's desk.

Let's look at the components of a solid outline. Naturally, we have to divide proposals into two categories: those for nonfiction books and those for novels.

Nonfiction books are both easier to outline and easier to sell from an outline. A nonfiction work lends itself to easy encapsulation because its subject is finite and usually defines itself. A war, a biography, a history of a period, a murder case, seventeenth-century Dutch art, Greek cooking, traveling through Japan—all are limited by the factual information available, at which point it becomes a matter of selection and arrangement of that information. It is relatively easy to convey in an outline an author's familiarity with his subject, his enthusiasm for it, his authority, the uniqueness of the proposed work, its organization, and so forth. It is even possible to convey in an outline how good a writer the author is. A good nonfiction outline is a pleasure from the viewpoint of publishers. It takes five minutes to read, requires little imagination to grasp, and enables an editor (or anyone else at a publishing company) to make his mind up quickly and decisively. It is hard for most writers to visualize the joy it gives an editor to be able to reach a clean, fast decision, and this factor may have contributed in no small measure to the increased predilection for nonfiction at most trade publishing companies over the last few years.

A solid nonfiction outline should follow these basic precepts:

- *Establish your authority.* At the very outset you must show the publisher your credentials. It has become extremely difficult to sell proposals by writers who do not have a Ph.D. or M.D. after their names or cannot otherwise demonstrate long and vast experience in the field in which they are writing. As you might do with any other resume, if you have great bona fides, pile them on; if you don't, then stress the next best thing, to wit: "Although I am not an M.D. I have written about medical subjects for leading national magazines for the last twenty years." And if you cannot even boast that much, I strongly advise you to write a large piece of the book so that your authority and familiarity with your subject shine through by virtue of the writing itself.

- *Present your thesis dramatically.* The best outlines read like the best short stories, and like great stories should have a beginning, a middle, and an end. In enunciating the subject, you should present a disturbing problem that cries out for resolution: "The teenage suicide rate has tripled in the last ten years." "As the First Continental Congress convened, the American colonies seemed very far indeed from the unification we take for granted today." "Although there are many books available on Jewish cooking, to date there is no comprehensive work on cheese blintzes."

You now have the editor worried: how did the teenage suicide rate get to be so bad, what is the profile of a potential teen suicide, what can parents do about it? Here is where you display your intimacy with your subject, for as these questions occur to the editor considering your presentation, one by one your outline answers them satisfyingly and, if possible, entertainingly.

Like a good short story, your outline should rise to a satisfying climax, and here is where your writing skills must be displayed in all their splendor, for editors know that an author's interest and energy tend to flag in the final stages of a book and they want to see whether you can sustain the same level of intensity in the finale as you did in the opening stages of the work. You should therefore describe in vivid detail the culmination of your book. Whatever it was that originally inspired you to write it must be communicated here, and whether you're writing a biography, history, medical self-help book, or even a blintz cookbook, you must demonstrate in these final passages of your synopsis your intense absorption in your material. Depict in full dress that final battle, that cure, that turning point in the life of your biographical subject. Let your editor know you're in love with this idea and will live in a constant state of torment until you have gotten it out of your system.

- *Furnish a table of contents.* Each chapter of your proposed book should be summarized in a short paragraph. Although a table of contents would appear to go over the same ground as your synopsis, it actually serves a different purpose. A synopsis is a narrative summarizing the topic and exhibiting the author's grasp of his material and writing skill. A table of contents demonstrates the author's organizational abilities and conveys the "feel" of the final book. It may seem redundant, but editors demand it. Don't leave home without one.

- *Anticipate a publishing committee's questions.* However masterfully you have synopsized your book, some important questions will probably linger in the editor's mind, and others will be raised by noneditorial staff members of the publishing committee. What competitive books exist or are in the works? What is the potential audience, and how can a publisher be sure that that audience will buy the book? Could a Big Name be induced to write an introduction or endorsement? Can you state with assurance that this organization or that society will approve the book, recommend it to members, purchase a minimum number of copies?

It is unfortunate that authors must do the sort of research that is the rightful province of publishers, but because publishing people have so little time and money to spare for market surveys, library searches, legal investigations, profit-and-loss evaluations, and the like, any author who does the publisher's homework for them will definitely raise his chances of landing a sale. So go the extra mile. You've always said you could do a better job than a publisher: here's your chance to prove it.

The outlining of fiction is an entirely different ball game. None of the criteria that enable editors to make quick and easy decisions about nonfiction book proposals applies to fiction outlines, for almost everything is subjective. Although it is even more important for a novel outline than it is for a nonfiction book outline to read like an enthralling short story, even wonderful novel outlines don't necessarily demonstrate convincingly that the writer is a good storyteller, has fine descriptive abilities, is capable of capturing subtleties of emotion, or knows how to build character and relationships. And, paradoxically, any attempt to portray such elements in an outline often results in a long and tedious one that is excruciatingly dull. Furthermore, nothing in an outline can demonstrate whether the author can go the distance or will falter or lose energy or inspiration during the writing of the novel. It is far more common for novelists to slump in the midst of a book than for nonfiction writers, whose inspiration derives from already existing material rather than from anything they have to create. And while editors who have the novelist's track record to go by can say, "See? He finished six novels, what makes you think he isn't going to finish his seventh?" a novel proposal must be judged by a lot of noneditorial people at a publishing company. Many of them are a little suspicious of, or even downright hostile to, the creative process, and therefore skeptical that a novelist will be able to stay the course. What is worse, they can relate many unfortunate experiences bearing their skepticism out. Resistance to fiction outlines runs extremely high at most publishers, and that's why one finds prodigious piles of them on so many editors' desks.

There are important exceptions, of course. The well-established novelist can land a contract on the basis of an outline, and often a brief one. And writers doing novels in a series or proposing books for a particular line, will of course have to do outlines. But authors who have no solid fiction track record are going to get nowhere in their quest to raise funds to complete their books. Or if they do, miraculously, get an offer, it will undoubtedly be a stingy one, because the publisher is being asked to invest his risk capital, and the costs of risk capital are extremely high.

I therefore advise anyone in that position to write a long, boring, detailed outline of his novel-to-be, take it to his word processor, and sit down and write the novel. Not a third; not a half; *all* of it. Shift the risk from the publisher to yourself—because it means shifting the rewards as well. Give an agent a finished novel that he likes and watch him do his thing: he can auction it, set a tight deadline for decisions, get a high price, break the author out.

What's that you say? You can't afford to write that novel on speculation? I'm afraid you'll have to do what the novelists of yore did: they begged, borrowed, stole, got day jobs, or married into money.

CHAPTER 8

Hardcover vs. Softcover vs. Hard-Soft

I'M AFRAID THAT the topic of this chapter is so complex and subtle that I wonder how much light I will be able to shed on it. And that's the question of what makes some novelists better suited to being published in hardcover and others to paperback.

I must confess at the outset that I'm far from certain I know the answer. My only consolation is that publishers often don't know it either. For every book they cite that must, incontrovertibly, be published in hardcover, I can name a similar one that enjoyed immense success as a paperback original. And for every piece of "trash" that, indisputably, was meant to be published originally in paperback, I can name an even trashier book that rode the crest of the best-seller list for twenty or thirty weeks.

The distinctions between what is appropriately hardcover and appropriately paperback have crumbled, and cross-pollination, as healthy in literature as it is in nature, is becoming commonplace. Literature that was once restricted to the paperback side of the street has crossed over to hardcover, is enjoyed by a more affluent and cultivated segment of our society, and appears with growing frequency on hardcover best-seller lists. It's even studied in college courses. Who would have imagined, a few decades ago, that science fiction, western, and romance novels would one day move hundreds of thousands and even millions of hardcover copies? Meanwhile, "serious" authors, literary writers who might have recoiled at the notion of initial publication in mass market or trade paperback, now appear in that format willingly and even happily, enriching both themselves and their readers in the process.

The prejudice against paperback originals still strongly persists, however, and by no means merely among elitist literati; it is extant in the minds of publishing and movie people, the reading public at large, and indeed, in the minds of many writers themselves. It is a formidable prejudice and, like most prejudices, is backed by enough truth to make me feel that it will not be dislodged for a long, long time to come.

In the dawn of the paperback revolution at the end of World War II, the distinctions between hardcover and paperback were pretty simple. Paperbacks fell roughly into three categories: the classics, reprints of hardcover best-sellers, and paperback originals aimed largely at male audiences: westerns, space operas, lusty thrillers, soft porn, and the like. But as publishing entered the 1960s, competition among paperback publishers for reprint rights to best-sellers intensified. These publishers, after spending and spending and overspending, realized they needed more money and clout to survive in this auction-dominated jungle. They therefore resorted to a number of strategies: they merged with, acquired, or were acquired by hardcover publishers to create hard-soft combines; they sold out to conglomerates and entertainment complexes in order to lay their hands on big capital for the acquisition of best-sellers; and they intensified the development of original paperback fiction, particularly the type aimed at the women's market—gothics, historicals, and contemporary romances.

Another trend in the mid-sixties was that original paperbacks became a powerful tool used by paperback companies to offset the spiraling costs of reprint acquisitions. Why, the reasoning went, should we invest half a million dollars or more to buy the reprint of a best-seller when we can hire an author for ten thousand dollars to write a book almost as good, spend fifty thousand dollars to promote and advertise it, and sell almost as many copies?

This philosophy took firmer and firmer grip in the paperback industry, and over a decade came to dominate it. The original eventually became the principal stock in trade of the paperback industry.

The yanking of the paperback rug from under the feet of the hardcover industry forced hardcover publishers to become extremely discriminating about what they acquired. The word was, if it can't make it on its own in hardcover, don't acquire it. A great many authors who'd been breezing along with midlist books now found themselves without hardcover publishers, or with hardcover publishers pressing them to accept cutbacks in terms. Not a few of these authors dropped out. Some of them tried harder and wrote blockbusters. A great many of them, however, lined up outside the doors of paperback houses and asked if there was any work for them. There was. Whatever else had happened to the paperback industry, it was still populated by folks who preferred good writing to bad. But, ironically, the entry into paperback originals of all those terrific writers depressed the prices paid for originals. The old hands, feeling themselves shouldered out of the business, accepted lower terms for their work just to hang on; the new hands, seeking reentry into publication at whatever price it took, accepted whatever price it took.

Among the many other benefits of this renaissance was the driving out of business of some schlocky paperback outfits, and the raising of quality among the survivors. Indeed, the quality, as well as the quantity, of genre books became so high that it attracted the attention of hardcover publishers, who reasoned that if five hundred thousand or a million people bought an author's paperback originals, surely a few tens of thousands of them at the very least would buy the same books in hardcover. This reasoning proved correct. Writers who were selling big in paperback were moved up into hardcover. A great many of them thrived. Today, the hardcover best-seller lists are chock-full of successful graduates of the paperback original school, with genre stuff like westerns, romances, science fiction and fantasy, and action-adventure making appearances there in unprecedented numbers.

For those of you who have not followed my drift, let me now draw you to it: The overall quality of popular literature is genuinely higher than it was twenty, ten, or even five years ago. After the Great Shakeout, the standards of acceptability among both hardcover and paperback publishers rose steeply, and because marginal publishers got driven out, the markets for marginal authors have all but disappeared. In the good old days of the sixties and seventies an agent could always find a quickie paperback assignment, a sex novel or a movie tie-in, to offer to a desperate client, or could sell something out of that author's trunk to some end-of-the-line paperback house. Those days are gone. The remaining paperback publishers are leaner, and if they also seem meaner, some of that may be attributed to authors, agents, and hardcover publishers having been spoiled by the extravagance of a decade ago, when even indifferent first novels were getting banged down for twenty or thirty thousand dollars on the reprint auction block. The rest is attributable to the fact that today's market belongs to the buyer. The message to today's professional writer is crystal clear: Be tough or be gone.

This raising of the stakes is reflected most vividly in hardcover. The principal reason is that most hardcover fiction is review-dependent. Hardcover books that get panned are, with one notable exception, going to lose money for their publishers, whereas paperback originals get scant review attention, and if that attention is negative the effect on sales is seldom fatal. We are seeing a little more attention paid by reviewers to paperback originals, and a few originals have experienced remarkable flights with the help of well-timed and well-placed favorable reviews. These, I am convinced, are only exceptions that prove the rule.

Here, then, we come to the crux: The single most important difference between hardcover and paperback publication is review coverage. But not, as most people think, because it satisfies author vanity or helps to sell books. As I see it, the true importance of reviews is that they *legitimize* books. A reviewed book, for most of us, is a "real" book, and that's why hardcover books are considered more "real" than paperbacks. Although we can all think of exceptions, in great measure a book brought out in hardcover is likelier to be seriously considered by magazine editors, foreign book publishers, and most particularly by movie people, than the same book published originally in paperback.

There is, as I indicated, one exception. When best-selling paperback writers advance into hardcover, their sales will usually not become much more dependent on reviews than they were when their books came out in paperback. That is because these authors bring with them a ready-made audience, one that has never been susceptible to reviews. Fans of paperback authors usually don't ask if the new book is any good, they just ask when does it go on sale, and this passionate loyalty follows the author into hardcover. If the hardcover happens to get good notices, that's great, for it will bring new fans into the fold. But that substantial hardcore audience will not be affected. Promotion, at this level, is far more effective than reviews in moving books.

If, in your efforts to figure out what's a hardcover and what's a paperback, you've also wondered what kind of book is more appropriate for hard-soft publication, it's the kind I have just described. Hard-soft combines were created to accommodate both the hardcover publisher's desire to have a guaranteed paperback reprint when it acquired a big book and the paperback publisher's desire to buy reprint rights to best-sellers for less than astronomical advances. But hard-soft deals also accommodate major authors. First, they give them the huge advances they demand, something few hardcover publishers can afford without paperback back-up. And second, by allowing them to retain 100 percent of both hardcover and paperback royalties, hard-soft neutralizes the resentment best-selling authors begin to feel when they see their hardcover publishers keeping 50 percent of the money collected from licensing reprint rights to outside paperback houses.

Assembling all these factors, the answer to our original question would seem to be that very little fiction is too good to be published originally in paperback. Rather than try to force your way into hardcover before it is timely to do so, I would recommend that you think paperback for just about everything you turn out, and let the hardcover market discover you in its own time.

If I were plotting the ideal career of a talented new author, I would establish him in paperback in whatever genre he produces best, for genre books offer the most opportunities for writers to break into the business. He will develop his craftsmanship and make a living, too—earn while he learns. I would advise him not to be ashamed to be a paperback writer. It has become a respectable profession populated by many fine writers and interesting people. Don't worry about reviews; there won't be that many and you will therefore be allowed to build up your confidence without being unduly influenced by public opinion.

Stay in paperback as long as possible, establishing an audience, winning the respect of editors at your own and other publishing companies, and making money not just for yourself but for your publisher. In due time, natural processes (and, I would hope, a smart agent) will lead you into hardcover publication. You may write that long-awaited breakout novel, or you may simply be recognized for a consistent and excellent body of work. Don't try to do anything differently once the question of hardcover is raised. Hardcover publication does not mean you now have to become a better writer; more likely it means that professionals in the publishing industry *think* that you are a better writer. In due time, thanks to review coverage and promotion, your books will sell to movies and television, to magazines, and to foreign publishers. Book club and reprint rights to your books will start to reach spectacular proportions. That will be the time for you to switch to a hard-soft publisher if you're not there already. Then your biggest problem will be income taxes.

CHAPTER 9

A Modest Wager

I HAVE A STANDING bet with many publishers, backed by one thousand dollars payable to the charity of their choice. The bet is that a professional author can write a book faster than a publisher can write a check. And I hereby reaffirm the bet publicly.

So far nobody has taken me up on this wager, and I doubt if anybody will. But if someone wants to, just make your check payable to the Special Olympics.

There is no gimmick here. At least a dozen professional writers on my client list are capable of turning out a novel in two to four weeks, even less if their publisher is desperate. But I know of scarcely any major publisher capable of routinely preparing contracts or, once contracts have been signed, cutting a check in that period of time. Unless it's an emergency, in which case it takes about three weeks longer.

I don't believe my clients are unique in this respect. Many agents handle or know of authors capable of turning out genre fiction, male adventure, westerns, romances, and the like, within weeks. In fact, many writers would go under if they were not capable of producing at least a book a month.

But are the books good? What is the relationship between the quality of a book and the time it takes to produce it? I'll be exploring these questions in a moment. But I'm not quite through with publishers.

The contracts and accounting departments of most publishing companies are extremely burdened with work and, under the best of circumstances, move with maddening bureaucratic casualness. Absent, it seems (to authors and agents), is the sense that the papers being shuffled have any bearing on the basic needs, the food and clothing and rent and car payments and college tuitions, of the human beings "hereinafter referred to as Authors." One agent, in a frothing fit of frustration, likened the process to the admitting office of a hospital emergency room, where the life fluids of victims trickle out of their bodies while the admitting clerk takes down their address, Social Security number, and mother's maiden name. I don't know if I would go that far, though I do remember a case of one crazed client who informed his editor he had just had his cat destroyed because an unconscionably late contract and check had made it impossible for him to pay for the poor creature's medical treatments. But I might, if I were of a cynical turn of mind, be tempted to suggest that the torpid pace of the contracts and accounting departments of some publishing companies is yet another example of how publishers cling to money as long as possible at the expense of authors. Luckily, I am not of a cynical turn of mind.

In fact, one's heart might almost go out to the gallant minions of the contracts and accounting departments. Anyone who has actually seen them in action, or inaction, must appreciate that the choreography of procedures for drafting a contract and drawing a check is highly complex in even the most efficiently run publishing houses. Once an editor has concluded negotiations with an agent or author, he or she draws up a contract request enumerating all of the deal points plus any variations in the boilerplate language that the author or agent may have requested. This contract request joins the many others awaiting action by the contracts department. The terms in the contract request are then transferred onto contract forms.

These forms must now be reviewed, sometimes by the original editor, sometimes by department heads, sometimes by the chief executive of the company, sometimes by all of them. The contracts are then submitted to author or agent, and if, heaven forbid, there should be but one or two minor items to be negotiated or renegotiated that the editor or contracts person does not have sole authority to decide, approval of those changes must be secured from someone at the company who *is* in authority. I have seen a contract held up for a month because I requested upping the number of free authors' copies from ten to twenty, or extending the delivery date by one month. Some contract department heads are fanatical about initialing alterations, requiring weeks of additional back-and-forthing. Some agents have become quite masterful at forging their clients' initials on contracts, and though this is a potentially dangerous practice, it seems like the only practical tactic to counter massive delay. One of my colleagues grinningly boasts, "If I spent a day in jail for every set of initials I've forged, you'd never see me again."

Once the contracts have been signed by the author, the machinery for procuring the check begins to grind. The contracts department issues a voucher instructing the accounting department to draw the check due on signing the contracts. Such vouchers must in the normal course of things be reviewed by the comptroller or some other executive in charge of financial affairs. Once the check is drawn, it will be examined by that executive and possibly by the publisher before it is signed by one or both of these officers. Needless to say, it is not as if these folks have nothing else to do.

If, therefore, you wonder why a publishing company can't just type up a contract the way you might scribble a thank-you note, and dash off a check the way you dash one off to pay your landlord, now you know, and perhaps you'll feel a bit more compassion for the clerical staffs of publishers.

I do. But my bet still stands.

Despite this lengthy digression and a muffled tone of querulousness, this chapter is not about how slow publishers are. It's about how fast writers are.

Outsiders—by which I mean people with little firsthand experience of the creative and technical aspects of writing—have difficulty making peace with the idea that any kind of book, let alone a good one, can be turned out in thirty days or less. But I know of several professional writers who have written full-length novels over a weekend, not because they wanted to, but because they had to in order to accommodate publishers in a jam. A tightly scheduled manuscript had not been delivered on time, covers were printed, rack space reserved, the printer's time booked. "Can do," these heroes quietly said, and on Monday morning, looking like The Thing From The Crypt, they dragged into their publisher's offices with a manuscript.

Ah, you murmur, but were they *good* manuscripts?

This annoying question arises again and again whenever prolific writers are mentioned. It's easy to understand how the public at large would classify such feats as belonging to that end of the spectrum of human accomplishment reserved for flagpole sitting and marathon dancing. It's harder to understand why many editors feel that way too. But a large number have the attitude that the quality of literature rises in direct proportion to the time required to produce it. Publishers, even those who publish lines of genre fiction that call for short and rigid deadlines, are quite suspicious of prolific authors. They can't believe a book written that fast can be that good.

I have always felt that in order to qualify to practice their profession, editors should be required to write a novel. They would then undoubtedly discover that many of the skills they now consider dismayingly hard are actually quite easy, while many they regard as a cinch are inordinately difficult. One thing they would appreciate, I'm certain, is that an experienced professional writer working an eight-hour day and typing at average speed can produce five thousand words daily in clean first draft without pushing. That's a finished book in twelve to fifteen working days.

But one draft? How can a writer produce a first draft that is also a polished draft?

One reason is that he has no choice. The author who writes a good book in one draft will earn twice as much money as one who writes the same book in two. And when the pay scale is twenty-five hundred to five thousand dollars per book, one simply cannot afford to write a second draft.

It is also a matter of training. Many professional writers reach a level of craftsmanship where whacking out clean copy is as natural as hitting balls is for a professional baseball player or dancing *en pointe* is for a ballerina. The amateur who writes fast usually writes sloppily; the professional who writes fast will most likely write masterfully.

And let us not forget inspiration. It is not uncommon for writers to talk about writing as if in a trance, or feeling like a channel through which a story is being poured from some mystical source. Some writers rehearse a scene or story so often in their heads that when they finally commit it to paper, it all comes in a rush, as if they're writing from memory rather than from a sense of original creation.

All this is helped by the development of computerized word processors, which enable their owners to write two drafts in the time it used to take writers working on conventional typewriters to write one. But now that the technology is at hand, will the prejudice against prolificness finally be overcome? I'm not too sure.

For, in the last analysis, it isn't the editors or public who cling most tightly to the myth that fast writing is poor writing. It's the writers themselves. Almost all the professional writers I know equate speedy writing with money and slow writing with love, to the point where their personalities actually bifurcate and the halves declare war on one another. Authors capable of knocking off a superb genre novel in one draft will agonize over every sentence of their "serious," "important," "literary" novel as if they were freshmen in a creative writing course. They seem to believe that anyone wishing to cross the line between popular entertainment and serious literature must cut his output and raise frustrating obstacles in his own path, and that legitimacy may be purchased only through writer's block. It is futile to point out that Dickens, Balzac, Dostoyevski, and Henry James wrote as if possessed, in many cases with scarcely a single emendation, yet turned out a body of sublime classics. And they did it in longhand, by the way.

CHAPTER 10

Movies into Books

NOVELIZATIONS OF MOVIES and television shows are among the most intriguing subspecies of commercial fiction. I say subspecies because they obviously cannot be spoken of in the same breath as *The Magic Mountain* or *Portrait of a Lady;* indeed, even commercial novelists look down their noses at novelizations as possessing not a shred of redeeming social value, as the literary equivalent of painting by numbers. On the spectrum of the written word, tie-ins are as close to merchandise as they are to literature.

Tie-ins are kin to souvenirs, and in some ways are not vastly different from the dolls, toys, games, calendars, clothes, and other paraphernalia generated by successful motion pictures and television shows. Those who write them usually dismiss them with embarrassment or contempt, or brag about how much money they made for so little work. Yet, when pressed they will speak with pride about the skill and craftsmanship that went into the books and assure you that the work is deceptively easy. And if you press them yet further, many will puff out their chests and boast that tie-in writers constitute a select inner circle of artisans capable of getting an extremely demanding job done promptly, reliably, and effectively, a kind of typewriter-armed S.W.A.T. team whose motto is, "My book is better than the movie."

How are tie-ins created? Their birthplace of course is the original screenplay. The Writers Guild of America Basic Agreement entitles the screenwriter to ownership of literary rights to his screenplay. When he sells his screenplay he may retain the novelization rights or include them, at terms to be negotiated, in the screenplay deal. Most of the time the screenwriter sells his novelization rights to the buyer—the film's producer or a studio. The new owner of these rights now tries to line up a publication deal for the tie-in. He contacts paperback publishers and pitches the forthcoming film.

If the film has a big budget, terrific story, bankable actors, unique special effects, or other highly promotable features that promise a hit, publishers will bid for the publication rights. (In the case of television tie-ins, the producers almost always wait till a series is a hit before arranging for tie-ins. And one-shot movies of the week seldom trigger novelizations because of the brief period—one evening—in which they are exposed to the public.) A deal is then struck, the publisher paying an advance against royalties to the producer or studio.

The publisher then engages a writer to adapt the screenplay. It should be readily apparent that if the movie is indeed shaping up to be a hit, or the television show is already a hit, the publisher will be forced to pay such a high advance and royalty to the producer or studio that little will be left for the writer. That's why novelizations are generally low-paying affairs, with modest advances and nominal royalties of 1 or 2 percent. Flat fees are by no means unheard of. And, because the competition among writers for novelizations is intense, few writers are in any position to bargain. But if the pay scale is so miserable, why do authors seek novelization assignments so ardently? Because they think it's easy money. Sometimes it is. But it's not like falling off a log, as we shall soon see.

Publishers are nowhere near as enamored of movie tie-ins as authors are, and they weigh the profit potential of such books as critically as they do that of the thousands of other manuscripts submitted to them annually. They know that most movies do not translate well into books. There are also technical and timing problems with tie-ins that are daunting to publishers. For instance, the screenplay may undergo alterations, some of them radical, right up to or even during the shooting of the film. By the time filming is complete there is insufficient time before the release of the movie for a writer to write the novel and the publisher to publish it.

Another problem for publishers is the greed that has set in at the studios. Originally, tie-ins were regarded as free publicity for movies, and publishers regarded them as little more than list-fillers. For a modest payment to the studio a publisher would get the screenplay, stills, cover photo, and promotional material, and everybody was happy. Then the studios began to smell profit, and arranging tie-ins became a little less complex than building a space shuttle.

Anyone who thinks that tie-in writing is a mere matter of adding he-saids and she-saids to the screenplay dialogue has certainly never attempted such an adaptation. For one thing, most screenplays are too short to convert page for page into book manuscripts. Therefore, even if you are following the script scene by scene, you are required to amplify on character, action, and location descriptions. Any good novelist can translate a terse screenplay direction ("EXTERIOR, OLD MACDONALD'S FARM, A STORMY NIGHT") into a few pages of descriptive prose ("A bitter, shrieking north wind lashed the trees and hurled sheet after sheet of icy rain against the clapboard siding of Old MacDonald's farmhouse . . ." etc.). The problem is that when you analyze screenplays you realize that most of them don't lend themselves comfortably to scene-for-scene conversion. In fact, many of them present nightmarish challenges.

The reason is that movies are seen with one lobe of the brain, and books read with another. If you'll take the trouble to compare a novel with its film adaptation, you'll immediately realize that whole chapters have been cut or reduced to takes that last a few seconds on the screen; or that, conversely, a sentence or paragraph has been dramatized into a full-dress scene that consumes five or ten minutes of movie time. This is because some material in books is distinctly more cinematic than other material. (It also explains why few novelists make good screenwriters, and most screenwriters are dreadful novelists.)

By the same token, owing to the demands of the book reader's imagination, elaborate scenes in a movie may seem far too long to merit the same expansive treatment in a novelization; fast transitional scenes, flashbacks, establishing shots, short takes, and the like may require a novelizer to build them into whole chapters.

Every tie-in writer talking shop will tell you how he or she overcame such challenges, challenges complicated by the insistence of the producer on approval of the novel or a run-in with some middle-management studio exec who demanded that whatever was in the movie must go into the book, and whatever wasn't in the movie must not go into the book. The fact that novelizations may take only a few weeks does not mean that many, many hours of thought and years of writing experience did not go into them. Novelizers earn every penny, and for all but the biggest books, pennies are what they make. Leonore Fleischer, one of the genre's top authors, earned a total of some $45,000 in royalties for a labor of less than a week on the film tie-in of *Annie,* but that is exceptional. Joan Vinge, who wrote *The Jedi Story Book,* a juvenile tie-in to *The Return of the Jedi,* did it for a modest flat fee for Random House. The movie was a phenomenal success, and so was the book, but Vinge was not entitled to a penny of royalty. Only by the goodness of Random House's heart, tinged perhaps with a dollop of guilt plus a healthy measure of pushing by her agent, was she awarded a $10,000 bonus.

The best advice I can give prospective tie-in writers is, if possible never write one for a flat fee, no matter how dumb the movie, no matter how quick and simple the job. Years ago, Ace hired me to write a tie-in for a perfectly dreadful and quite disgusting horror movie called *Squirm,* which portrayed in all its graphic revoltingness what happened when a small town was invaded by millions of bloodsucking earthworms. Ace offered me a flat fee of $2,500, and, seeing the prospect of earning $250 a day, I grabbed the deal. The movie came and, blessedly, went. But my book went through numerous editions for Ace, and was sold to English and other foreign publishers where it endured for years.

My book was better than the movie. Big deal! That and a good agent would have earned me a nice profit. Unfortunately, I don't have an agent. I don't trust them.

CHAPTER 11

Work-for-Hire

I F ONE WERE to compose a Bill of Rights for authors, ownership of copyright to their works would certainly be close to the top of the list. We hold self-evident the truth that if a person produces an original book-length work, he or she is entitled to proprietorship under the law, and to full benefit of its commercial exploitation.

Yet, it has not always been so. The piracy of literature by printers, publishers, and booksellers has been common practice throughout the world from the dawn of the printed word, and was prevalent in this country until well into the present century. Until the establishment of the first International Copyright Convention in 1891 and its refinement after World War II, respect for the sanctity of copyright was largely a matter of gentlemen's agreements based strictly on self-interest—don't steal from me and I won't steal from you. There are still vast areas of our globe where publishers think nothing of stealing and distributing works of literature from authors and publishers of law-abiding countries, and the emergence of electronic and online media have made it a big business. A recent *New York Times* article asserted that piracy of books, videotapes, music, and other intellectual property in China may be condoned if not sponsored and supported by the nation's government.

Lest you become too smug that such barbarities cannot happen here, I am compelled to report my observation that the appropriation of authors' copyrights by publishers and book packagers seems to be on the upswing. Nothing so gross as piracy, mind you. More, I would say, like extortion. But the effect is the same: the deprivation of authors' rights to enjoy the fruits of their labors. The fruits of an author's labors include such bounties as royalties on copies of books sold, participation in reprint income, and revenue deriving from the exploitation of serial, translation, dramatization, electronic, and other subsidiary rights. Not everyone shares the conviction that the enjoyment of these monies is a natural and God-given right, however. Indeed, not everybody behaves as if the enjoyment of these monies is protected by statutory law.

The engagement of writers for flat fees falls into a category of employment known as "work-for-hire." Work-for-hire is a doctrine defining the relationship between a copyright owner and a writer. Note that the owner may or may not be an author; he, she, they, or it may be a corporation (like a movie studio or television production company), a syndicate of investors, or an individual who is not a writer. These entities hire writers to perform a service in pretty much the same way a homeowner hires a cabinetmaker, a painter, or a gardener, except that in this case the task is writing a text for the "boss"—the creator or owner of the idea. The owner is then free to exploit the text in any way he desires with no further obligation to the author.

Some provisions of the 1976 Copyright Act attempt to define the work-for-hire concept, but they do not do so very clearly and have left the door open to unfair exploitation of authors.

I hasten to make clear that all work-for-hire is by no means exploitive. Authors sometimes voluntarily sell all rights to their copyrighted work. And there are numerous situations in which work-for-hire may be considered reasonable and acceptable by normal ethical standards. For instance, the engagement of writers to do articles for an encyclopedia. The copyright holder of the total work is the publisher, and because it would be impractical and uneconomical to pay a royalty to each contributor, the normal arrangement is a one-time fee. As long as the fee pays for the time and effort, the author is usually content, particularly if he or she gets byline credit, for a contribution to an encyclopedia bears great prestige that helps the author endure the low wages.

Another application of the work-for-hire concept that most of us accept unquestioningly is ghostwriting. Authorities or celebrities who cannot write well or are too busy to write their own books engage writers to draft books for them. Although the principal author may agree to share some of the proceeds of the book with his ghost, the principal is the sole signatory of the contract with the publisher, thus making him the copyright owner. He then signs a separate agreement with the ghost, removing that person from claim to copyright and direct participation in revenue generated by publication of the book. Occasionally, what may have seemed a fair fee at the time it was negotiated with the ghostwriter may not seem so if the work demanded of him turns out to be excessive, or if the book becomes a runaway best-seller. Under ordinary circumstances, however, the ghostwriter accepts his lot as a worker-for-hire, and may at least secure more work for himself by telling publishers, "That book was actually written by me."

If all this seems a bit remote to you, let me point out that many garden variety authors employ other writers on a work-for-hire basis. Take the creator of a popular fictional series who, growing bored with his characters or too busy with other projects to turn out new books in his series, farms them out to other authors. He signs contracts with his publisher, then negotiates separate agreements with ghostwriters to produce first drafts or even final ones for him, which he passes off as his own. In some instances the publisher is aware of the existence of these subcontractors, in others it is not. But seldom is the subcontractor a signatory to the publication contract, and though he may receive a piece of the action as part of his deal with the principal author, it is not strictly a royalty in the sense we usually understand it, and of course the ghost forfeits any claim to copyright ownership.

Although I'm not at liberty to detail the many instances I know of authors who farm their work out, fans of those authors might be shocked to learn that their favorite books are produced, as it were, in a shop. There is in particular one best-selling male action-adventure series whose creator, to my knowledge, no longer writes his own books at all. In conjunction with his publisher, he puts the production of his books on an assembly line basis. A series "bible" describing the characters and general story line of the series is issued to writers, who submit plots for the approval of the creator and/or the publisher. Upon approval, a contract is issued to the writers. At first glance it looks like a typical publishing contract, but closer scrutiny reveals that the copyright is owned by a corporate entity; the advance is not called an advance (it's simply called a "sum"); and the royalty is not called a royalty (it's called a "bonus payment") and is expressed in cents rather than as a percentage of the list price of the book, presumably to further remove the writer-for-hire's labor from any association with creation of the work. I estimate the payments to the writer-for-hire to be approximately one-fourth to one-third of the traditional royalty that might normally accrue to him if he were the original creator of the book. I assume that the balance of the royalty is shared between the originator and the publisher.

In the above example, the originator of the series is in effect a packager. Packagers, as I have stated elsewhere, are sui generis. They are not exactly authors even though they frequently create the ideas and story lines for books; they are not exactly agents even though they take a kind of commission for their roles as go-betweens among authors and publishers; and they are not exactly publishers even though they buy the services of authors.

I've never been comfortable with packagers either in theory or in practice. Packagers are both buyers and sellers at the same time (so that "broker" might be the most apposite synonym), and there is inherent in their function the potential for mischief, abuse, and downright dishonesty. Some book packagers are as honest, open in their business dealings, and caring about authors as is possible under the circumstances. But a number are little short of rapacious, hiring authors for the smallest fees they can get away with and paying them no royalty or participation in subsidiary rights revenue whatsoever, while selling their books to publishers for very large multiples of what they pay the writers for them.

Furthermore, while these packagers manage to sell publishers on the concepts of books or series, they often contribute little or nothing by way of editorial input or guidance. An author is given the most general ideas ("How about a *Dirty Dozen* set in Bosnia!"), then is required to create characters, situations, and plots—create, in short, the entire series. The packager's argument is that were it not for his initiative in creating an idea and selling it to a publisher, writers would have no work and no pay. As the level of pay is all too frequently subsistence, the cause for heartfelt gratitude frequently escapes the writer-for-hire.

Because many publishers don't particularly care where their product comes from as long as it is good, is delivered on time, and is not too expensive, they provide fertile ground in which packagers can flourish. That is one key reason for my concern that the packaging phenomenon, with all the implications of author exploitation that it represents, is on the rise. The other reason is that some publishers are taking their cues from packagers and doing the same thing. They cook up series ideas in their offices, produce a series bible, then hire writers to write books in the series under a house pseudonym. Because such publishers maintain that they created the series, they have been scaling back advances, royalties, and author participation in subsidiary rights for those books, and their contracts are, in fact if not in actual language, work-for-hire agreements. In many instances, the publishers offer flat fees to authors interested in writing books for publisher-originated series, take it or leave it.

Of more recent vintage, but a phenomenon that will grow to major proportions as time goes by, is the use of writers-for-hire for electronic and multimedia works, where text is but one element along with still and moving pictures, music, animation, etc. And the exploitation without compensation of electronic versions of stories and articles for magazines has become a source of bitter warfare between writers groups and newspaper and magazine publishers.

You might infer that I refuse to do business with the more exploitative of packagers and publishers, but that is not the case. Some of my clients are hungry, and occasionally some are desperate for any kind of work, and though I may judge certain packagers and publisher-packagers harshly, practically speaking I don't feel it is fair for me to turn down, out of hand, work for clients who might be grateful for a few thousand dollars and a job that gets them through a financial squeeze or crisis. It's easy for an agent to tell an author, "I'd rather see you starve than accept that deal"; it's not so easy for an author to agree with him. If, after a writer has weighed all aspects of a work-for-hire deal, he or she still wants the job, then the only thing an agent can do is negotiate what few safeguards he can, such as making sure the writer is not legally liable for changes or additions to his text rendered by the packager or publisher. The quality of help an agent can render in these cases is the equivalent of telling the tenant of an avaricious landlord, "You have two choices: sign the lease or don't sign the lease."

Because packagers prosper from a supply-and-demand dynamic that is clearly—at this time, anyway—in their favor, there is little that individual authors or agents can do to roll conditions back. It must be done through collective action. Sad to say, authors and literary agents are scarcely closer to effective collective activism than they were when I started advocating it in my column years ago. So if you've been holding your breath, let it out.

CHAPTER 12

Audio

I N CASE YOU'VE been in a coma for the last few years, a revolution has taken place in the audio and video fields. After a period of uncertainty following the technological refinement of Walkman-type audiocassette players, automobile audiocassette systems, and home videocassette recorders, the audio and video industries have found their legs. Consumer demand for audio and video electronics has permanently altered our nation's habits: people would no sooner leave their homes without their audio headphones than they would without their keys, and the videotape recorder has become an indispensable component of the television set that spawned it.

Because of the close relationship between these technologies and the book publishing business, many publishers have jumped into the creation, production, and distribution of audio- and videocassettes. Most of the publishers that are allied to entertainment complexes are taking advantage of the know-how, facilities, and product inventories of their affiliated companies to develop lines of book-record, book-cassette, and book-film tie-ins. Most bookstores of any appreciable size have departments devoted to selling audiocassettes, videocassettes, or both. And although the outlets for the sale or rental of videocassettes are at this time not always connected with bookstore chains, it is clear that in due time we will see a consolidation of the videocassette retail market and its eventual absorption into the bookstore chain system—or the other way around.

Just as political revolutions take a long time to affect the lives of rural people, the electronics revolution has only recently begun to filter down to the point where it affects the livelihood of the writers whose work is the basis for so much of the audio and video businesses. But the changes can now be palpably felt in the form of provisions in book contracts. Language over which very little fuss was made a few years ago is now being scrutinized and haggled over by publishers. For a while we experienced great uncertainty if not downright confusion about contractual standards. What is a good royalty on audio deals, anyway? Can one license the same property to two different audio companies? Should there be reserves against returns in audio as there are in the book business? However, some coherent trends have developed, and the time has come for authors to know what they are.

Provisions for audio and video have existed in publishing contracts for a very long time. It's just that the publishers didn't call the media "audio" or "video." Typical is a 1969 Doubleday contract in which the appropriate provisions are headed, "Sound Recording, Filmstrips, Teaching Machines, Microfilm":

> Author grants to Publisher the sole and exclusive right to sell the Work or parts of it for mechanical reproduction and transmission, including, but not by way of limitation (a) sound and picture recording or any other method hereafter known or devised; (b) filmstrips; (c) programs for machine teaching; (d) microfilm and photocopying (except motion picture), or any other method now or hereafter known or devised for information storage, reproduction, and retrieval.

Today, publishers' legal advisors are rewriting contracts with more precise definitions of "audio" and "video," definitions that painstakingly differentiate those media from such kinfolk as television, radio, stage, motion picture, computer software, records, and electronic publishing. And whereas those mechanical and electronic recording rights were as often as not ceded to publishers by authors and agents who didn't see much value in them, now those rights have become serious bones of contention, and often they are deal-breakers. Several publishers that are tied to entertainment companies insist on those rights as a matter of policy whether they have any real intention of exploiting them or not. And even when they don't have any such intention, they have proven highly uncooperative in licensing those rights to competitive companies. Some publishers that are not allied with entertainment companies nevertheless try to get a position on electronic rights just in case. One publisher, for instance, installed language in the boilerplate of its publishing contract stating that in the event the author controls any rights (such as movie or audio) "which the publisher has the capacity to exercise itself, the Author agrees to give the publisher the right of first refusal for the separate acquisition of such rights before licensing such rights elsewhere." In other words, if the owners of this publishing company buy or start a movie, audiotape, or videotape company, you would have to submit your book to that company before being free to make a movie, audio, or video deal with another firm.

Although we often talk about audio and video in the same breath, in terms of adaptation of your work, the two media are as far apart as their wavelengths are in the electromagnetic spectrum. As far as the immediate future is concerned, the chances are better that you will be dealing with audio than with video. By far, the predominant application of video right now is adaptation of motion pictures for use on home videocassette recorders. If your novel is adaptable to a dramatic medium, it will be acquired by a movie or television company, not a videotape one. If your book is nonfiction, the odds that it will be acquired by a videotape company are low unless it is a best-seller and has distinctive visual potential. There is a budding industry of making films originally on video, but the above remarks still stand.

Audio, on the other hand, is far cheaper to produce, requiring infinitely less technology, personnel, and capital to stimulate the listener's imagination than movies or video require to entertain the viewer. Therefore this chapter focuses on audio.

The terms for audio deals generally follow those for book deals—with some interesting exceptions. The tapes that are sold through bookstores are offered at discounts resembling those that apply to the book business—starting at 40 percent. But unlike the prevailing method of calculating book royalties on the list price, audio royalties for the most part are based on the net receipts after discount. If a tape package retailing for $50 is sold to a bookstore for 40 percent off, the licensor's royalty will be based on the $30 actually received by the tape company.

The royalty scale is generally in the area of 7 to 10 percent, and if you're weighing a royalty based on list price versus one based on net, in the above example you would be receiving $2.10 to $3.00 royalty per set instead of the $3.50 to $5.00 you'd get if your royalty was calculated on the list price. That's quite a difference!

Unlike book publishing, where royalties are accounted twice annually, audiotape royalties are accounted quarterly by many companies, and a few firms send statements and checks on a monthly basis. Tapes sold via mail order are usually not returnable, but those sold in stores are, and producers therefore hold a reserve of royalties against possible returns, as in the book business.

An even more interesting and important difference is that while book publishers insist on exclusive rights in their territories, many audiotape producers will consent to your selling the same material to their competitors for distribution in essentially the same, or at least in overlapping, markets. We recently made deals with no fewer than three different audio producers to adapt the same best-selling nonfiction book for audio sold in the retail, direct-mail, and subscription markets. Also, you can sometimes distinguish between an abridged audio version of your book and an unabridged one, and sell them to two different publishers.

When literary works are adapted to audio, the authors frequently ask to perform the reading themselves. Unless the author is a very big name and/or has a professionally trained voice, the producers prefer to employ professional actors or narrators to read or perform the adaptation. In cases where the producers do agree to let the author read his or her own work, there is usually no additional performance fee paid for the privilege though it's not unreasonable to have expenses paid by the producer if the author has to travel to the sound studio.

Advances at this writing are low compared to book prices—$5,000 or less for most properties—and there isn't that much leeway even for star authors of best-selling books. That's because the volume of sales on even popular audiotapes is lower than it is for popular books. A good sale of a single cassette is in the low to mid tens of thousands of units; a good sale of a six-cassette package is anything over seven thousand units.

Although the tape companies generally acquire or try to acquire world rights, translations are not much of a factor right now, and if you try to restrict the tape producer to worldwide English language rights only, or even U.S. and Canadian, reserving British and translation rights for yourself, you probably won't be jeopardizing your deal.

Because certain audio rights, such as exploitation of the soundtrack, are conveyed to a movie or television producer when you sell your work to one, you must be very careful when making an audio deal not to sell anything that might threaten a movie deal later on, or conflict with rights already conveyed to a movie producer. Straight reading of your book is usually okay, but when you venture into any kind of dramatization (even two different voices conducting a dialogue) you start to run the risk of treading on territory owned, or coveted, by a movie or television producer. So use the utmost caution when negotiating your audio deal, and consult your agent or lawyer about the appropriate language to be employed in the contract.

What sort of literary material is attractive to audio producers? One, of course, is fiction, in the form of either dramatizations or readings. Despite my warnings about selling dramatic audio rights, most novels are not suitable for acquisition by movies and television, because they aren't dramatic or visual enough. Those same books may well be adaptable to the audio medium, where much drama can be made out of little content, the listener's imagination furnishing the rest of the entertainment experience. Straight readings are also very popular, particularly if the narrator has an appealing voice. Children's audio is a very big market. Some genre fiction, such as romance, mysteries, westerns, and science fiction, has been successfully adapted, but audio publishers usually demand brand-name authors in those categories and turn their noses up at novels not published in hardcover and in big printings.

The other important category of material sought by audio producers is instructional: self-help, how-to, and the like. Video is great for many instructional topics that call for high visual content or activity such as cooking, exercise, sports instruction, and hobbies, but for topics that don't require visual stimulation, such as language instruction, business advice, or religious wisdom, audio is the perfect medium. A critical reason is the portability of audiotapes: they may be listened to while one is doing something else, like walking to work, jogging, or commuting. For most people these are not particularly pleasurable activities, and they feel they could be using their time to improve themselves intellectually, emotionally, or spiritually. The answer, obviously, is for them to listen to a tape.

The audio business is very young, and there are a great many companies fighting for a place in the sun. A couple of years ago there was a sort of feeding frenzy as these firms snapped up all sorts of literary properties in order to have something, anything, for their lists. But a slowdown ensued as the producers, distributors, and sales outlets paused to observe just what was selling. What they discovered was that audio buyers are not unlike book buyers: they look for the familiar name or the unique gimmick or premise.

One last but critically important criterion: audio publishers almost always insist on publishing their editions simultaneously with the first printing of the book. That means that as soon as you sell your book to a publisher, you must get cracking on submitting it to audio publishers. If your book publisher has the option to do the audio version, insist on a fast decision. If your publisher declines to do it, you can get it to other audio houses in time for them to get their edition out at the same time as publication date of the book.

CHAPTER 13

Multibook Deals

OR MANY WRITERS the term "multiple-book deal" conjures images of byzantine negotiations conducted in a smoke-filled conference room by a battery of literary agents, lawyers, accountants, and publishing executives, of telephone-number advances and thick contracts replete with state-of-the-art jargon about best-seller escalators, book club passthroughs, and topping privileges. The tyro author who would be overjoyed to get even a one-book contract must view such deals as relevant only to the gods in some literary Valhalla. What pertinence do these Ludlumian, Michenerian, Grishamian transactions have to the humble and brutish lives of nickel-a-word galley slaves?

The truth is that many more multiple-book contracts are proffered to writers than most people imagine, and most of them are no more complicated than one-book contracts. And their terms are substantially lower than those generally associated with Olympic-sized swimming pools on the grounds of Beverly Hills estates. In fact, if you write in any of the traditional genres the chances are that sooner or later you'll be offered a multiple-book contract. Whether your specialty is science fiction, mysteries, westerns, romances, male adventure, or even popular nonfiction, it is likely that a publisher will be interested in signing you up for more than one book at a time. You may have created a character in a novel whose exploits you or your publisher would like to extend to further books. Or your publisher may like your work well enough to ask you to write books in a series created "in the house," as it were. You would do well to understand the features of such deals, if for no other reason than that, after longing to have one offered to you, you might ultimately decide that they're not that hot after all and you'd be better off selling one book at a time.

When you think about it, a multiple-book deal is simply an elaborate extension of your option clause. In a traditional contract, the publisher usually gets an option on your next book at terms to be negotiated. In a multiple-book contract, the publisher makes a commitment to more than one book and specifies the terms and conditions for the acquisition of those books. The nature of those books is usually described in detail: "Books number 4, 5, and 6 in the adult western series featuring the hero Luke Starbuck," or "Four saga-length works of fiction set on and around a Savannah, Georgia, peanut farm during the American Civil War." The general terms—"boilerplate"—that characterize a contract for one book now cover two or three or more at a time. The warranties you agree to on book number one are identical to those on numbers two and three, for instance. A few boilerplate items may be altered to adjust for the multiplicity of books in the contract. The termination clause will have the phrase "on each work" in it or something along those lines in order to account for the probability that each book in the contract will go out of print at a different time.

One of the reasons publishers like multiple-book contracts, then, is simply that they are convenient. They enable publishers to prepare one contract for several books whose terms are pretty much identical. This may seem like insufficient reason to offer such deals to authors, and in truth it is. But when you realize how much time and labor goes into the preparation of even a routine book contract, you might feel less inclined to criticize publishers for wanting to speed up the flow of paperwork, which after all benefits authors too.

The principal object of multiple-book deals is security. Ideally, they should make publishers and authors feel equally secure (agents don't mind a little security either, by the way), but things don't always turn out that way, as we shall see.

The security comes in because all parties know where they stand with each other for the duration of the contract. The publisher knows that his author is not going to leave him after the next book or the book after that. The publisher also knows he won't be hit for a high price one or two books from now if the author gets hot tomorrow, because the prices for those future books will have been fixed at the outset, when the multiple-book contract was signed. The author, by the same token, knows there will be a home waiting for his next two or three books, and can count on a specific sum of money to be paid him when he delivers them. Even if the market for his kind of books collapses, his publisher is still contractually obligated to pay him for each delivered book, whereas if the author made contracts with his publisher on a book-by-book basis, the publisher could drop him as soon it became apparent that there was no more market for his stuff.

Another important factor is scheduling dependability. Where series or other related books are involved, success rests heavily on the timing of release of the books, and that timing can be set with certainty only if the publisher can absolutely count on reliable delivery of three or four or six books. By tying the author up for that many, the publisher knows (or at least hopes) that the author won't accept contracts with other publishers that will interfere with the delivery and publication rhythm of the series.

Of course, the big multiple-book deals that make front-page headlines incorporate all of the above factors plus very big front-money. These deals are designed to nail down a bestselling author for as long as possible, and in many cases there is little or no description of the books because nobody including the author knows what they're going to be about. Indeed, the publisher may not even care what they're about as long as it's guaranteed he'll get his mitts on them.

The publicity value of a multiple-book deal may outweigh its actual monetary value. The pages of publishing trade publications and writers' newsletters are filled with references to deals that make author and publisher look good but do not necessarily stand up to intense scrutiny. A "five-figure deal" might be for $99,000 or it might only be for $10,000. Or you may read about deals that "could bring the author $850,000 per book." They *could*, yes, if they sell like hotcakes, get picked up by major book clubs, go on the best-seller list for two years, and are made into major motion pictures. The actual guaranteed money in such deals might be quite modest, but the built-in escalators, bonuses, and similar features enable the publishers to wring the most publicity out of them.

And of course, deals that may seem relatively small to the public at large can be most impressive in the author's "hometown"—that is, the genre in which he writes. A three-book deal for a $75,000 advance might be sneezed at by the *New York Times,* but if the books are science fiction, romance, westerns, or some other genre, the writers and editors who read about such exploits in the trade papers will sit up and take notice.

Big deals or little, the underlying accounting principles are the same. Let's examine them.

There are several ways in which the accounting may be set up in a multiple-book contract. The first is to fix the advance for each title in the contract and to keep the royalty accounting on each book separate from that on the other books in the package. Thus you might have a three-book, $30,000 advance contract, with the advance per book pegged at $10,000. When book number one is published and earns more than $10,000 in royalties, the author will collect the overage in royalties even though the second book, say, has not yet earned back its $10,000 and the third book has not even been published.

The other way to structure a multiple-book deal is to "jointly account" the advances on each book. Joint accounting (also known as "basket accounting" and "cross-collateralization") creates a common royalty pool for the earnings of *all* books in the contract. This means that royalties earned over and above the advance on one book in the contract will not necessarily be paid to the author but will instead be applied to the unearned advances on other books in the contract. Until the total of advances in that contract has been earned out by royalties from any or all books in that contract, the author will not receive additional royalties. For instance, suppose we have that $30,000 advance deal for three books, but with joint accounting. Book number one is published and earns $15,000. Does the author receive royalties? No, because the three-book combination must earn a total of $30,000. Suppose, further, that the second book earns $15,000 too. Does the author now receive royalties? Again, no, because the two books have earned, together, no more than the $30,000 originally advanced to the author. Now book number three is published and earns $4,500 in royalties. Does the author now get anything? Yes, he gets $4,500, for the total royalties earned by the three books is $34,500, or $4,500 more than was originally advanced. Of course, it can work the other way around too. Suppose the first book in the package was a wild success and earned $35,000. The author would then collect $5,000 royalties on his three-book contract even though the second and third books weren't yet published. And when those books were published, all royalties they earned from the very first dollar would go to the author, because his $30,000 advance would have been earned out on the first book.

There are pitfalls for both author and publisher in multiple-book deals, for such deals are like long-term commodity investments. If you bet that a commodity will be worth X dollars one year from now, and between now and then the value soars far beyond what you estimated it would be, you will be left holding a considerably undervalued contract. Apply this to the case of an author who grabs a three-book contract for a $30,000 advance. The advance is paid in four equal installments of $7,500 apiece, the first on signing and the next three on delivery of each book. The first book is published and becomes a wild success: book club, reprint, movie, the whole bit. Now he delivers the second book and what does he get?—a mere $7,500. He may be mad at himself (to say nothing of his agent) for tying himself up for so long for so little. Of course, the difference between an author and a pork belly (and perhaps the only difference) is that the author at least has the opportunity to make up in royalties for the inadequate advance he negotiated two or three books ago when he was just another lowly writer in the crowd. Thus he may only collect $7,500 when he delivers book number two, but a few months later he may collect $50,000 in royalties earned on book one.

Bear in mind that by the same token the publisher stands to lose if the commodity—the author, his books, and the market—go short, that is, drop below what the publisher projected when he tied the author up for all those books. If a publisher signs you up for that four-novel peanut-plantation saga, and just around the time you're delivering the first one the market for plantation sagas collapses and your publisher can't give them away—well, there's going to be much rending of garments and maybe of jobs at that publisher's office.

So, it's a bit of a crapshoot both ways, and if you feel your books are going to be worth far more than the per-book advance you've been offered in a multiple-book deal, then turn that deal down. If the publisher doesn't agree with your appraisal of your future value, then he'll turn the deal down. Sometimes you can forge a compromise. If your publisher feels that the individual value of the books in a three-book deal is $10,000, and you feel it's $15,000, you can split the difference by structuring advances of $10,000 on the first book, $12,500 on the second, and $15,000 on the third. If the deal is jointly accounted, you'd simply add these advances up for a total advance of $37,500, but when you negotiate the next contract your price per book starts at $15,000.

Once a publisher has a good writer in his stable, he may be willing to pay high, even to overpay, to keep him there for a long, long time. I remember negotiating with a publisher for an author he coveted, and I fixed a price of $225,000 for a three book contract. He winced. "That's awfully high."

"What can I tell you?" I said with a shrug. "That's what I think he's worth, or will be by the time he writes his third book."

"Who knows how much he'll be worth two years from now?" the publisher sighed philosophically. "We could all be dead two years from now."

"That's true," I replied. "So why don't we just make a deal for one book and see how that one goes?"

The man sat bolt upright in his chair, a stricken look on his face. "Don't do me any favors." Alarmed at the prospect of having this rising young author for only one more book, the publisher quickly met my terms.

CHAPTER 14

Payout Schedules

W HILE THE SIZE of the advance is the criterion by which most authors measure the commercial value of their books, the size and timing of the installments in which the advance is paid are just as significant, and sometimes more so. Because the "payout schedule" directly affects the cash flow of publishers and authors, it is often a bone of bitter contention in negotiations, and many a player has walked away from an otherwise good deal because the payout schedule nullified advantages gained in the negotiation.

With few exceptions, advances are paid in installments. Part of the total money is payable upon signing the contract, the balance payable on acceptance of partial, complete, or revised manuscript; on certain calendar dates; on publication; and even after publication. Although the payout formula may be fairly simple when the advance is small, publishers and agents devote a great deal of attention to it when the stakes get high. The reason, of course, is the cost of money.

Until recently, when the inflation rate ground to a comfortably low single-digit crawl, it could be projected that the value of one thousand dollars deferred for one year was nine hundred dollars. At the same time, interest rates appreciated the value of that thousand dollars to something like twelve hundred in a year. Thus, between inflation and interest, a year's postponement of payout to an author meant a swing of some 20 percent in the value of that money. Both interest rates and inflation have, at this writing at any rate, stabilized at manageable levels, but for both publishers and authors, 5 or 10 percent per annum is worth fighting over and may indeed make a significant difference to their balance sheets.

Let's take a closer look at payout schedules installment by installment and sketch some ways authors may improve their position when the haggling begins.

- *Payment due on signing of the contract.* All contracts large and small require a consideration to be paid on signing, even if it be no more than one dollar, in order to bind the agreement. If the total advance is small enough, it may be payable in full upon signing. Most publishers today, however, have policies prohibiting payment in full on signing, and editors are ordered to defer some part of the advance in negotiations. Even if your book is a flawless gem requiring not a jot of revision, an editor may contrive to pay a second installment of your advance "upon acceptance of revisions" in order to satisfy company policy. Then, a week or two after vouchering the signature installment, the editor will put through the acceptance installment as well.

If the contract is for an unwritten book, the advance will be divided at least into an on-signing payment and an acceptance one to create an incentive for the author to deliver the work. The publisher may try to divide the advance even further, into installments payable on delivery of a partial manuscript or first draft.

You will have to do some solid reckoning before accepting too small an installment on signing, otherwise you'll run out of money before you turn in material qualifying you for the next installment. First you must subtract your agent's commission if any, then calculate the amount of time that will pass until you are entitled to the next payment. You then have to figure whether your living costs (including anticipated lump sum payments like school tuition, income taxes, or insurance premiums) during that period will be covered by what you collect when you sign your contract. A $50,000 advance may seem attractive to you, but if your publisher wants to pay you $10,000 on signing and it takes you six months to write the book, and your monthly nut is $3,000, you're going to be up the creek halfway through the writing of the book. So you must bargain hard for a down payment that will sustain you until you've turned your manuscript in.

- *Payment due on delivery of partial manuscript or first draft.* These installments are generically known in the book trade as "satisfactory progress" payments. To help bridge the gap between the on-signing and the acceptance checks, and to encourage or compel progress, publishers frequently negotiate installments payable when the author turns in part of the book. A typical deal might be structured: one third on signing the contract, one third on delivery of half the manuscript, and one third on delivery and acceptance of the complete manuscript.

Of the many ploys cooked up by publishers to stretch out their money, "satisfactory progress" is the least effective, and if it weren't so dangerous it would be just plain silly. At the very least, "satisfactory progress" is satisfactory neither to authors nor publishers, and the only thing it does for progress is halt it.

In a "satisfactory progress" situation, an author faces a number of choices, all of them terrible. He can turn in a rough draft, which is usually an embarrassing mess that will send most editors into respiratory arrest, or at least provoke them to request revisions that the author would ordinarily make on his own when tackling the final draft. Or he can stop work in the middle of the book, polish and retype what he's done so far, and turn a partial manuscript in. Either way, he will have to suspend work on his book until he has received some feedback from his editor. Even if his editor offers no feedback whatever, it may take weeks or longer to get that editorial reaction, and such delays are inevitably harmful to creativity and cash flow. If the editor does have criticisms, the author may be required to rework what he's turned in in order to get his hands on that money. To avoid all that hassle, therefore, an author may choose to forgo his "satisfactory progress" payment and forge ahead with the rest of the book, which defeats the purpose of such interim payments. Most authors do not polish chapters after drafting them, but prefer to finish a rough draft of the entire book and polish it in the final draft. Thus the time between the completion of a first draft and a final draft, or delivery of half the manuscript and all of it, may be so brief that the machinery for putting through the "satisfactory progress" installment will scarcely have begun turning when it will be time to put through the final acceptance payment. Furthermore, many editors feel it's silly to read a partial manuscript or first draft when the final product will be turned in a few weeks or a month later.

In short, "satisfactory progress" payments reflect little understanding of how authors work and pose a genuine threat to both the quality of a book and the timeliness of its delivery. Ultimately, this ends up hurting the publisher as badly as it hurts the author.

- *Payment due on acceptance of the manuscript.* Whenever possible, the balance of the advance on a commissioned book should be payable no later than upon acceptance. A number of contracts stipulate that a manuscript is deemed acceptable unless the publisher notifies the author to the contrary within a period of time, thirty days, sixty days, or thereabouts. This is a very desirable feature and one worth fighting for if it does not appear in the boilerplate of your contract.

In most contracts the definition of "acceptability" embraces revisions. If serious revisions are required by a publisher, the acceptance segment of the advance may be delayed until satisfactory revisions are turned in. If the revisions are minor, however, the publisher may often be prevailed upon to put through the acceptance money and take it on faith that the author will turn in acceptable revisions. There is an in-between state where revisions are necessary but the author cannot afford to do them without some sort of financial relief. In such cases the publisher may be persuaded to release some of the acceptance money to carry the author during the revision period.

I've expressed myself many times about the prevailing requirement in publishing contracts that an author must repay the on-signing installment of his advance if his manuscript is rejected. But in case you haven't read what I've said—well, I think it stinks. The on-signing advance should be regarded as a forfeitable investment, not a refundable loan. Needless to say, hard-headed (or hard-hearted) publishers see things quite differently.

- *Payments due on publication.* The purpose of publication installments is to enable publishers to start recouping what they've paid the author as soon as possible after disbursing his advance. Publication payments used to be the norm in American publishing. Then the rise of strong agents in the 1960s drove publication payments out of favor. But when money started to get expensive again in the 1970s (with double-digit inflation and interest rates), publishers pushed the agents back, and it is now common for publication installments to be paid. In some foreign countries such as England, the publication installment is still an article of faith.

The most common mistake authors make when agreeing to publication payments in a negotiation is failing to fix a time limit on them. Unacceptable language is, "$5,000 payable upon publication of the Work." Acceptable:"$5,000 payable upon publication of the Work or twelve months after acceptance, whichever date is sooner." The reason should become obvious if you think it through. Few contracts require publication of a book in less than twelve months after its acceptance, and many allow for publication in eighteen or even twenty-four months. Tacked on to these times are grace periods giving publishers an additional six months or more beyond the deadline to publish the work upon notification by the author that the deadline has passed. A publication payment may therefore not be due for as much as three years after a book has been accepted.

What is worse, publication of a book may be cancelled entirely for any of a number of reasons: staff changes, new policies, or events or trends that date that book. That means that the publication portion of the advance will not be payable at all, at least not according to the publisher's interpretation of the contract. I don't know if the point has been tested in court, but it can certainly be argued that if you sell a book to a publisher for $25,000, and the publisher cancels publication, you *still* sold the book for $25,000 even if some of that sum was to have been paid, for the publisher's convenience, on publication. Therefore, whenever you negotiate a publication advance, you should always stipulate that the installment will be due on publication or *X months after acceptance, whichever date comes first*. The X is negotiable, but should be no longer than the outside date by which the publisher is required to publish your book.

- *Postpublication payments.* Publishers have devised a fascinating array of gimmicks to postpone the day of reckoning to authors. Among these is the postpublication advance. Such installments may be payable on a specific date—X months after publication, say—or, in the case of a hardcover-softcover deal, one installment may be payable when the hardcover edition is published, another when the paperback edition is brought out. There are other creative variations on this theme, but because a book begins earning royalties from the date it's shipped, all postpublication advances amount to the same thing: paying authors with their own money.

Authors may want to try to negotiate payout schedules advantageous to their income tax status. An author who has already made a lot of money in a year may not want to receive a large on-signing payment that same year. A deal can be structured, therefore, so that only a token amount is paid on signing the contract and the balance of the on-signing advance is paid early in January of the following year. Not surprisingly, publishers like such setups, since they enable them to legitimately keep authors' money for several months. Literary agents, however, are not always thrilled to have their commissions deferred just because a client is enjoying a good year, so I don't feel your agent is out of line to request his commission on the full on-signing advance now, and to take no commission when the rest of your money comes in January.

If you do want to structure installments in a way that you feel is advantageous to you tax-wise, and your publisher is agreeable to the arrangement, the time to do it is when your contract is negotiated. If a contract is already in force and you ask your publisher to defer until next January a payment that is due this October because you don't want more money this year, the Internal Revenue Service may disallow it if you are audited and your publishing contract examined. The same holds true of requests to agents to hold money until the start of the next year.

The law makes it quite clear that money received by a fiduciary—a literary agent, for example—is construed to have been received by the author. This is not to say that publishers and agents do not hold money for authors in such circumstances, but getting away with it doesn't alter the statutes concerning "constructive receipt," and you may be liable for an adjustment in tax for that year plus interest and penalties.

Even if you are nothing more than a working-stiff type writer, it's still a good idea to get as much money up front as you can. A smart agent and a smart accountant will help you to structure your cash flow so that your hide is relatively intact every April 15. Don't let publishers earn interest on your money. Remember, the sooner you get your hands on it, the sooner you can start blowing it on stupid investments.

CHAPTER 15

Escalators

A TERM COMMONLY heard in discussions of book deals is "escalator." For instance, "Her book was bought for an advance that, *with escalators,* could exceed $1 million." Escalators are additional advance payments made by publishers to authors if and when certain contingencies occur. What are those contingencies? How much are they worth? And what, if anything, is their real value?

Escalators were created, among other reasons, to bridge the gap between author and publisher when negotiations reach an impasse. You strongly believe your book will be a best-seller or will be bought by a major book club or made into a motion picture, and you feel that your advance should reflect the same optimism on your publisher's part. Your publisher, on the other hand, hopes and prays you're right, but has seen many a slip 'twixt the cup and the lip. He cannot afford to overpay authors on the strength of hope alone. Of course, if your track record justifies it— if your last five books have soared to the top of the best-seller list, been main selections of major book clubs, and been made into hit movies—he will be greatly disposed to pay you a lot of money up front. But let us say, for the sake of argument, that this is not the case.

The answer is for the publisher to offer you escalators. These bind him to pay you scheduled sums of money if, and only if, your optimism turns out to be justified; if it doesn't, he owes you nothing beyond whatever royalties your book may earn over its original advance.

Although the terms "bonus" and "escalator" are used interchangeably in Publishingese, and I'll use them that way here as well, these extra payments are not really bonuses in the usual sense. They are always recoverable from royalties and subsidiary income generated by a book; they are, in other words, additional advances. If your original advance was $50,000, say, and your contract calls for a $10,000 escalator to be triggered by the release of a movie adaptation of your book, then your advance becomes $60,000. The $10,000 escalator is, in effect, a prepayment of royalties that your publisher hopes your book will earn as a result of the movie.

It would seem, then, that you are being paid with your own money, and in certain cases that is true. Suppose you sold your book to a publisher for a $25,000 advance, and your contract calls for a $10,000 escalator to be paid if your book is sold to a paperback reprint house for $100,000 or more. Further suppose that the book is auctioned off and sold to a reprinter for $150,000. If the traditional fifty-fifty split on reprint money applies, your share of the reprint money will come to $75,000.

Okay, the reprint deal triggers your $10,000 escalator. Now you've received a total of $35,000: your advance plus your escalator. But it is no hardship for your publisher to pay that escalator to you, because you are guaranteed $75,000 as your share of the reprint deal!

Other escalators are riskier for publishers and can end up losing money for them. Take another hypothetical case where you sell your book for a $100,000 advance, and the contract calls for a $25,000 bonus if a movie is made from your book. Let's say that both book and movie flop, and your book doesn't even earn back its original advance, let alone the advance plus the escalator. This is a case where the publisher was not paying you out of guaranteed monies, but is genuinely out of pocket.

Escalators fall into a number of categories. The most common is the best-seller bonus. The best-seller list usually used to determine escalators is the one in the book review section of the Sunday edition of the *New York Times,* though sometimes the one in *Publishers Weekly* is also used. There are several ways to structure best-seller bonuses. One is the length of time that a book is on the list, another is a book's position on the list. It is desirable for a book to be on the best-seller list for a long time, of course; it is also desirable for a book to be high on the best-seller list. Bonuses can be structured to reward length or position or both.

A long run on the list, even at the bottom, can be significant, both because it means the book is selling strongly over a long period of time, and because it enables the publisher to boast, " —— Weeks on the Best-seller List!"

Just as important is position on the list. The higher your book rises, the better it is, naturally. But the book that reaches the number one position causes a quantum leap in promotional value, even if it drops down or off the list the very next week. Therefore, many escalator schedules in book contracts are heavily weighted in favor of the number one slot.

The actual sums paid at the various stations of the list can vary widely. I have negotiated best-seller escalators for as little as a few thousand dollars and as much as high six figures.

There are a couple of other features of escalators I should mention. Almost all such provisions place a limit on the total extra money payable to the author, called a "ceiling." The other aspect is that escalators, or escalator installments, are payable within a short period of time after the event that triggers them. Thirty days is as long as it should take for most bonuses to be paid, otherwise the publisher will be taking back in interest what he owes you in bonus money. If a publisher waits until royalty time to pay you your escalators, that's not much of a bargain.

Another form of escalator is book club or paperback reprint, wherein your publisher agrees to pay you additional advance monies if a book club or paperback reprint deal on your book exceeds a certain amount of money. As we've seen, such escalators are almost invariably of the pay-you-with-your-own-money variety, because your publisher is guaranteed recoupment of the bonus out of the money he will eventually collect from the book club or reprinter. The only thing he loses is interest on the prepayment to you of money he would otherwise have paid in the normal six-month royalty cycle.

Then there are movie bonuses, which are usually payable upon national release by a major distributor of a theatrical motion picture based on your book. There's a mouthful of contingencies crammed into that sentence, so let's analyze it. First, the movie has to be released. Of course! you say, but many authors believe that a movie *deal* on their book ought to be enough to garner them a handsome bonus from their publishers. I'm sorry to tell you otherwise. Although there is some promotional value for a publisher to be able to boast, "Acquired for motion pictures by Universal," it scarcely does a thing for sales. Thus, escalators are usually not payable when movie rights to your book are optioned, or when the option is exercised. In fact, they are not even payable when your movie goes into production. Publishers have seen too many movie deals fall through to get excited when a star actor or producer takes an option on a book property. They have learned to their sorrow that many movies that go into production are not completed or released. So, in order to trigger that escalator, the film must be distributed.

And it must be distributed by one of the big distributors, Universal or Warner or MGM-UA and the like, rather than any one of the thousands of little ones that service the movie community. And finally, the movie must be released nationally, as opposed to locally or regionally. The premiere of a film, even a high-budget one made by a great director with superstar actors and actresses, is not going to boost sales of the book from which it is adapted if it's shown only at a few elite showcase theaters in New York and Los Angeles. In order for the film to have impact on mass market book sales, it must be shown at hundreds or thousands of theaters around the nation.

Again, the prices for movie escalators vary widely, from modest—in the low five figures—to very large in the case of authors with long track records in the area of books made into hit films.

Related to theatrical movie bonuses are television-movie escalators. But while the market for television adaptation of books is a very active one, the stimulus to book sales is usually minimal. Even though the exposure is tremendous, far greater than that of a theatrical movie, it is also ephemeral: an evening or two (repeated once, six months or a year later) and it's gone. For publishers this presents serious problems of distribution and promotion. The books must be in the stores precisely on the day of or the day after the airing of the film, and the film must be so heavily publicized that consumers will be motivated to buy the book at the time of the airing. This is expensive, inefficient, unpredictable, and usually, therefore, unsuccessful.

For a television movie to mean anything in terms of tie-in value, it must first of all be an event, one absorbing a minimum of four hours, but preferably spanning a whole week of evenings. It should also be based on a best-selling book such as *The Winds of War* or *North and South,* so that viewer recognition of both the book and movie stimulate each other: you've read the book, now see the television movie, you've seen the movie, now read the book. Because very few books are converted into television events on the magnitude of, say, *Shogun,* the prices for escalators in this medium are considerably lower than they are for release of a major theatrical film adaptation of your book. The conditions are that the TV film be of at least four hours, run on consecutive evenings, and be aired originally on a major television network.

There are other contingencies that may trigger escalator payments. Some contracts call for bonuses to be paid if a book wins a major prize or award that has promotional value: Pulitzer, National Book Award, and the like. In some science fiction book contracts, I have negotiated bonuses for winning Nebula or Hugo awards, and in a few cases I even worked in bonuses for *nominations* for those awards. To science fiction fans the words "Nebula" or "Hugo" on the cover of a book are powerful inducements to buy that book, even if the word "Nominee" is printed beside them.

Obviously, not all books are suitable for escalators. Midlist books, most genre books, and books in category series seldom have escalation provisions in their contracts. For the occasional *wunderbuch*, the midlist novel that becomes a word-of-mouth best-seller and gets made into a hit movie, the author who did not have escalators in his contract can nevertheless look forward to royalties in the usual course of things. Of course, the next contract he negotiates will, you can be sure, contain more escalators than Macy's department store.

There's no harm in your trying for escalators when you negotiate your next contract, because it's no skin off your publisher's nose to give them to you: he only has to pay them to you, as they say in Las Vegas, "on the come." So what the hell; go for it. That way, you too will be able to brag that you have sold your book—*with escalators*—for a million dollars.

CHAPTER 16

Acceptability

THE ACCEPTABILITY PROVISION of a book contract can be summarized as follows: A publisher engages an author to write a book, stipulating in the contract that if the manuscript is not acceptable in the publisher's sole discretion, the publisher may reject it and require the author to repay in full the advance he was paid on signing the contract. Until that advance is repaid, the publisher will not release the author from the contract, thus restricting the author from entering into a contract with another publisher for that (and perhaps any other) literary work.

Inherent in this provision are three potentially explosive elements. The first is that acceptability depends entirely on the arbitrary editorial judgment of the publisher. The second is that the author is required to repay every penny to his publisher when his manuscript is determined to be unacceptable. The third is that the author is restrained from selling his book to another publisher until his original publisher has been repaid, or at least until satisfactory provisions for repayment have been made. (And if there is an option clause in the original contract, the author may be prohibited from selling any other work to another publisher until satisfactory refund arrangements have been made with the publisher of the first part.)

This mixture has indeed exploded on numerous occasions, and with growing frequency as the stakes in our business have grown higher. But there is a qualitative difference between disputes over acceptability and those over most other items in publishing contracts. Whereas 99 percent of the quarrels that arise between authors and publishers end up being negotiated, settled, or compromised, those over acceptability often end up being litigated to final judgments. Now, publishers are loath to spend money on lawsuits, especially against authors, because it is expensive and makes for poor public relations. But when it comes to the question of acceptability, a publisher may be counted on to fight like the devil even though it looks lousy to dun and sue authors and the legal costs exceed the prospects of recovery of the money paid to the author. And authors who might otherwise shrink from the expense of prosecuting or defending a lawsuit have been known to dig in against all reason to wage war over the acceptability provision. Both sides seem anxious to make law on this issue. And when that happens, it usually means that a principle or precedent is involved that transcends money.

Authors frequently balk over the seeming right of life and death accorded in the provision that gives publishers the sole discretion to accept or reject a manuscript. But if the publisher doesn't have that right, who else should have it? The author? *Of course* a publisher is entitled to that right. As in any other business enterprise, the party that commissions a work is entitled to approval of the merchandise. It's only the potential to abuse the right that makes authors anxious, and there are enough instances of abuse to justify that anxiety.

In defense of publishers, it must be said that abuses occur less frequently than might be expected, and for two reasons. The first is that most publishers are extremely cautious about engaging authors to write books. Before contracting for an unwritten book a publisher will require ample evidence of the author's track record, writing skill, and reliability so as to minimize the possibility that the author will not deliver, will deliver late, or will deliver a problem manuscript.

The second reason is that most publishing companies today are run by committee. Just as the decision to hire a writer is not left to one editor, neither is the decision to accept or reject the finished product. Rather, the manuscript is circulated among members of the editorial board. This is particularly true when the sponsoring editor has doubts about the quality of the material. That editor's judgment is on the line, for he was responsible for advocating the company's investment in the project to begin with. If he rejects it, wasting his firm's time and raising the possibility that the money paid the author thus far won't be recovered, he loses face, prestige, and authority with his colleagues and employers. Sometimes he loses his job. Therefore, the editor who feels negatively about a delivered manuscript will seek backup from others on the editorial board, just as he solicited that backup when he acquired the book. And unless the manuscript is truly a stinker, the board may vote to go ahead with publication or revision despite its reservations. So there are fail-safe mechanisms operative at publishing companies that can reduce the potential for arbitrary rejection.

Nevertheless, abuses of "sole discretion" do occur. I can recall more than a few occasions when a publisher contracted for an unwritten book, then rejected the manuscript because the subject was no longer as timely or relevant as it was when the publisher signed up the author, or because the editor who commissioned the project was no longer there to lend support and enthusiasm to it. A notable example of this occurred when William Morrow rejected William Safire's manuscript of a book about Richard Nixon. Safire contended that the real reason Morrow found his book unsatisfactory was that between the time Morrow commissioned the book and the time Safire completed it, Richard Nixon had become persona non grata with the American public.

Agents and authors can cite numerous instances of publishers using the acceptability clause to renege on high-priced agreements. These publishers will agree to whatever terms it takes to get a hot author or property. Then, when the manuscript is turned in, the publisher may decide for any number of reasons that it overpaid. The publisher then threatens to reject the manuscript unless the author agrees to renegotiate the contract. The real reason for rejection may be that the publisher doesn't have, or doesn't want to spend, that much money. Thus far the courts have favored the publishers' argument that they should not be compelled to publish a book that they are certain is going to lose money.

It is extremely difficult for an aggrieved author to prove in a court of law that his publisher acted in bad faith in rejecting his manuscript. The parties cannot ask judge or jury to read the manuscript, because this involves matters of taste that are beyond a court's jurisdiction. So it's incumbent on authors and their lawyers to demonstrate that the publisher was motivated by bad faith, and I'm happy to note a trend toward admitting good and bad faith as factors in lawsuits over the acceptability clause. Admitting those factors in turn opens the door to questions of a publisher's editorial responsibilities, its obligations to furnish authors with editorial guidance, opportunities to rewrite, second opinions by other editors, arbitration and appeal, and other procedures designed to insure that authors are not placed totally at the mercy of publishers whose motives may be impure.

This also means that the stipulation requiring authors to repay their on-signing advance if the publisher rejects their manuscripts is coming under closer scrutiny by the courts. For if it can be shown that a publisher acted in bad faith when it turned a book down, a court may decide that the publisher is not entitled to a refund, no matter what the contract may call for. This very thing happened in a dispute between author Julia Whedon and Dell, in which the court supported Whedon's contention that Dell had acted in bad faith by rejecting her manuscript without affording her the benefit of editorial guidance, rewrite instructions, etc. The court not only allowed her to keep the advance Dell had paid her on signing the contract, but even ruled that she had not breached her contract when she sold the rejected manuscript to another publisher before being released from her Dell contract. In fact, the court ruled that when Dell failed to furnish Whedon with adequate editorial help, Dell breached its contract and at that point the author was released with no further obligation to repay her advance.

These developments are extremely promising from the viewpoint of authors even though, at this time, they still have to fight and even go to court to gain protection that should automatically devolve on them in the boilerplate of every publishing contract. At the same time, all this legal wrangling over sole discretion only serves to obscure the real issue in the war over acceptability: Is an advance a loan? *Or is it, rather, an investment?*

As things stand now, publishing contracts are nothing more than free options on an author's time, talent, and services. If, after the months or years it takes for an author to produce a book, the publisher turns the manuscript down, that publisher is entitled to get its money back in full. The only sum the publisher is out of pocket is the cost of the money—the interest, that is—that it "loaned" to the author while he was writing his book. Now, money-back guarantees are fine if you manufacture soup, soap, or spaghetti sauce. But it's quite something else if you write books. The principle of repayment on which the acceptability clause rests is a thoroughly odious one and deserves to be fought by any means at an author's disposal.

An advance is not a loan. It is a nonrecoverable investment, no different from an investment in a stock or bond issue, a mining or drilling operation, a Broadway show. A publisher reviews an author's "prospectus," his writing credits, sales records, reputation for reliability, and samples of the proposed work. If the publisher determines that a book by this author is a good investment, he puts money on it. As we have seen, the publisher truly examines book proposals as carefully as if they were "at risk" investments. Why should a publisher be entitled to get his money back while investors in every other type of offering stand to forfeit theirs? If for any reason the manuscript is disappointing to the publisher, the company has the right not to pay the balance of the advance due on delivery and acceptance. But the down payment must be forfeited and the author automatically released from his contract.

I realize that this is a hard line, but only by taking it will authors force publishers to demonstrate good faith when commissioning books. The publisher who knows he can recoup his full investment is going to have too many escape hatches when the book is delivered. He will have far fewer if he stands to lose money.

To a small degree, publishers have conceded the fairness of this position by modifying the requirement that the author promptly refund his down payment. Many houses now stipulate in their contracts that the refund may be paid out of the "first proceeds" received by the author from the sale of the rejected manuscript to another publisher. This is scarcely better than having to repay the advance at the time it's rejected. All it means is a postponement of the day of reckoning, an extension of the date when the publisher's "loan" must be repaid by the author.

BREAKING OUT

CHAPTER 17

Are Editors Necessary?

THERE'S BEEN A lot of talk lately about the decline of editing. These are fighting words.

The problem with evaluating this allegation is that everything editors do today is invidiously compared to the accomplishments of that quintessential master, Maxwell Perkins. Perkins practiced his art at the offices of Charles Scribner's Sons from 1914 until late in the 1940s and midwifed the masterpieces of such immortals as Hemingway, Fitzgerald, and Wolfe. "Where are today's Maxwell Perkinses?" is the plaintive cry of authors who discover horrifying grammatical, syntactical, factual, and typographical errors in their freshly minted books, or, worse, have them gleefully pointed out by friends and critics. Every such erratum is a rebuke to the hallowed memory of that figure who has been depicted as gracious, patient, erudite, nurturing, precise, demanding, polite, and modest, a man whose love of authors was exceeded only by his love of good and well-made books. Let's assume that he truly did possess all of the virtues ascribed to him, and more if you wish. I have no desire to desecrate either his memory or his achievements.

I just don't happen to think that "Where are today's Maxwell Perkinses?" is a very good question. It oversimplifies editing both then and now, and fails to take into account the fact that today's editors simply don't perform the same tasks that their forebears did. I know a number of great editors working today, but they're great in many significantly different ways from the great editors of yesteryear. Just about every aspect of publishing has changed since Perkins's era. The types of books published are different. Agents exert far more influence. The paperback industry has revolutionized the marketing of books. Computers and word processors have been created and refined. Bookstore chains have swept most independent bookshops out of business. Printing technology has improved immensely. Books today are not acquired, edited, produced, printed, or distributed the same way they were earlier in the twentieth century. They are not even written the same way.

We must also define "editors" before we apply the word irresponsibly. Editing is a highly complex set of functions, and no single individual is capable of exercising them with equal aplomb. The editor who wines and dines agents and charms authors may be a clumsy negotiator; the dynamic deal-maker may have no patience for the tedious and demanding word-by-word task of copyediting; the copyeditor who brilliantly brings a book to life word by word, line by line, may be completely at sixes and sevens when it comes to handling authors.

It is certainly easy to wax nostalgic about editing in the Good Old Days (which really ended only about twenty-five or thirty years ago). If accounts and memoirs of that era can be trusted, editors then were steeped in fine arts, philosophy, languages, and the classics. They were a breed of compulsively orderly and fanatically precise individuals who ruthlessly stalked and destroyed typos, solecisms, and factual inaccuracies, and who conducted prodigious debates with authors about linguistic nuances. Their pride in their labors matched—and sometimes exceeded—that of the authors themselves. And when it came to money, they placed literature high above crass commerce, and discussed author compensation with the same delicacy they reserved for childbearing.

Today's editor, industry critics claim, no longer has that pride and painstaking compulsiveness. Indeed, it has been contended, editors today do everything but edit. The nurturing of authors has given way to the acquisition of properties. Editorial taste and judgment have been replaced by the application of success formulas devised by editorial committees. Risk-taking, hunches, and commercial instincts have yielded to the conservative application of bottom-line buying policies dictated by bookstore chain managers and implemented by rigid computer programs. The new breed of editorial animal, it is asserted, looks down his or her nose at line editing and production details. The time and money pressures of today's monolithic and highly competitive publishing business have devalued good book-making. The result is books that fall apart, prematurely yellow with age, and are scandalously rife with typos.

Unquestionably, a shift has taken place in the role of trade book editors from what is generally characterized as line functions to that of acquisitions. The earlier role, the one that we most sentimentalize, combined nurturing parent and stern taskmaster, a person who could get a great book out of an author, then groom and curry the text until it virtually sparkled. Although editors then, as now, worked for publishers whose profit agenda seldom coincided with that of their authors, the editor was thought of as the author's friend, protector, and advocate.

The emphasis today on the acquisition role of editors places them in a more adversarial role with authors. Negotiation often pits them against each other, and the residue of resentment and distrust that remains after the bargain is sealed makes it difficult for authors to feel completely comfortable with their editors.

The paternalistic treatment of authors by editors in earlier times, however, produced its own set of inequities, for publishers took advantage of many authors who were too ignorant, shy, or well-bred to demand good terms of their editors. Knowing that most authors write for love, publishers tended to assume that they didn't need to write for money.

Resentment toward publishers over their exploitation of authors created the conditions for the rise to power of literary agents, and though new authors today are still at a disadvantage, the balance eventually shifts when they engage agents and become more successful. Good agents often insist on a large measure of control over the author–editor relationship, holding authors at arm's length from their editors to protect them from being taken advantage of. And what has happened in the four or five decades since this transformation occurred is that the agents have begun to take over the role formerly played by editors. Today's agents nurture authors, work closely with them in the development of their work, perform a great many editorial tasks, and lend strong emotional and psychological support. And, perhaps most important of all, in a turbulent world of publishing mergers and takeovers and editorial musical chairs, agents have become the islands of stability and reliability that were once the province of editors. So, if the importance of editors in this respect has diminished, the loss has not necessarily affected authors for the worse.

Or, take the tasks of copyediting manuscripts and proofreading galleys.

Although these still fall upon the employees of publishing companies, the high costs of running businesses have caused a shift from in-house line editing to freelance work done at home. Many copyeditors are former employees of publishers who have managed to adapt their responsibilities to their domestic schedules. But the pressures of producing large numbers of books annually have forced publishers to overload editors with work or to seek less experienced people to do these highly demanding jobs. Some publishers just can't afford the time or expense to train copyeditors, supervise them closely, review their work, and instill in them a grasp of house style, a knowledge of company tradition, and a sense of pride. English is not even the first language for many copyeditors. And those who are fluent in English may not have the patience, precision, and skill to be good editors.

Whether we like it or not, the responsibility for well-edited books is shifting to authors. Actually, they have always borne much of that burden. In hardcover publishing particularly, most authors are given the opportunity (if not the contractual right) to review copyedited manuscripts and to proofread galleys, and if an author doesn't care enough to double-check every fact, every dubious grammatical construction and spelling, indeed every word of his manuscript and galleys, he has no one to blame but himself for a flawed product.

It is harder for authors to control errors in paperback originals and reprints, however, because tight publication schedules often make it prohibitive for publishers to furnish galleys for review by authors. Also, authors rarely get to see galleys of paperback reprints of their hardcover books. But authors and their agents can and often do demand the right to examine galleys in exchange for a promise to turn them around promptly. Thus, even paperback authors have a chance to bring out unblemished books.

The development of computerized editing and word processing hardware and software promises to eliminate many problems for authors and editors. Although numerous technical, financial, labor, and other obstacles have impeded the automation of some important editorial functions, I'm reasonably certain that these will be overcome in the foreseeable future, making clean copy in both manuscript and galley an everyday occurrence. The same is true for style, design, composition, and other aspects of the publishing process that are now in the hands of a diminishing number of expert craftspeople. In short, emerging technology will replace a good deal of the mental and manual labor involved in producing books.

What do all these changes leave for editors to do? The answer is, just about everything. Unlike those of the older generation, today's editors must master an entire gamut of disciplines including production, marketing, negotiation, promotion, advertising, publicity, accounting, salesmanship, psychology, politics, diplomacy, and—well, editing. But into that last designation goes a bewildering variety of activities, many only remotely connected with the stereotyped one of sitting in a monastic office hunting for typos.

The dizzying pace and complexity of modern publishing makes it neither possible nor desirable for editors to sit all day reading or conversing with authors. They must be worldly and sophisticated, capable of shepherding the projects they sponsor through a gauntlet of technical, financial, political, and other hazards. Though editors are often criticized for being corporate animals, in this respect at least we should thank our stars that they are. For they and they alone understand how to work their systems, to maneuver, coax, and sometimes ram their beloved books—*our* beloved books!—through the corporate obstacle course. Today's editors are professional company men and women, and if they don't have a problem with that characterization, I don't see why we should.

There are many editorial qualities that are irreplaceable. Among them are taste, discrimination, personal emotional response, a sense of order and organization, determination, devotion, pride, and tender loving care. In these respects, no one has discovered anyone or anything that can remotely take the place of an editor. Agents can't do it because they're outsiders. Computers can't do it because they're heartless.

But none of those virtues means anything if editors are lacking in courage. The biggest threat to the health of our industry is not mergers and acquisitions. It is failure of nerve on the part of its editors. The evolution of publishing from a profession run by individuals to a business managed by committees has created a population of editors preoccupied with holding their jobs. The pressures they live under are constantly forcing them to lower the common denominator when selecting the projects they wish to sponsor. This means that it is easier to say no than yes.

The way that this attitude manifests itself for me is editors' resistance to acquiring books that are even slightly flawed. It was not long ago that the prevailing attitude among editors was, "This book has some problems,

but the author is so talented that I'd like to buy it and work with him."
Today such words are rarely heard. A book with problems is a book
rejected, and more and more one hears editors say, "Let the author revise
it, then we'll decide if we want to buy it." Many of them have confided in
me that they would love to buy the book, but the prospect of bucking the
system is simply too daunting.

When I asked an agent colleague of mine whether she thought editors
were necessary, she quipped, "Of course they are. Who else can take
agents to lunch?" If editors are to remain more than entertaining luncheon hosts, if they are to be not merely necessary but indispensable, they
will have to continue resisting the pressures toward homogeneity
and mediocrity that are arrayed against them by the monolith of Big
Publishing.

Maxwell Perkins would understand that.

CHAPTER 18

Sales Conference

TWICE EVERY YEAR, around mid-May and mid-December, a curious lull befalls the frenzied lives of literary agents, like those abrupt silences that occasionally muffle a party when everybody, inexplicably, stops talking at exactly the same time. I've experienced enough of these semiannual brownouts that I ought to expect them by now. Yet they always take me by surprise, and I can predictably be heard at these times barking to my staff, "Is there something wrong with our phones? Is this a mail holiday or what?" At length it occurs to me: it's sales conference season. I then take advantage of this hiatus to catch up on paperwork.

Sales conference is the time when a publisher's list of forthcoming books is introduced to the company's commissioned sales representatives, who then go forth to the stores in their territories and line up orders. Since this is the point where the editorial process interfaces with marketing and distribution processes, it may literally be said that the fate of your book, and possibly your career, is cast at sales conference.

For the people who work at publishing houses, these convocations are red-letter days, major events in their corporate lives. For the past six months they have been sweating, suffering, beating their breasts, and rending their garments over the books they have acquired. Now they are going to pitch them to the folks who actually get them into the stores. This is a time of intense anxiety, for the presentation of the list is by no means a matter of handing the sales reps a set of proofs and saying, "Read it, it's terrific." Indeed, it's uncommon for the reps to read any but the most important books on their publishers' lists. Nor is it necessary.

If they don't need the book itself, however, they do need information about it, and in the weeks leading up to the conference editors scurry frantically about the halls of their companies, rounding up cover proofs, advertising copy, promotional notes, author-tour itineraries, and anything else that will make their books look and sound irresistibly tempting to sales people, store buyers and distributors, and ultimately to consumers.

The conferences are held in different locations around the country. Many companies hold their winter conferences in Florida, Puerto Rico, and other tropical climes, giving participants a chance to relax in the sun after work sessions and making the event in part a paid vacation. Other publishers hold conferences closer to home, in resort hotels within easy driving radius of New York City. Some publishers conduct them in the city itself. The more distant the conference, the fewer employees may be permitted to attend due to the costs of airfare and accommodations, and therefore the privilege of attendance is one of the ways an editor's status at a publishing company is determined. Conferences held in New York City enable all staff members to participate. From the viewpoint of sales reps these may be great fun, entitling them to a week in the Big Apple with a publisher picking up the tab. But for the publishers themselves, New York City-held conferences are harder work, as there is little letup from the grueling labors of conferring and ingratiating themselves with the sales representatives.

Each publisher has its own style, format, and strategy for sales conferences, but typically the days are divided into morning and afternoon sessions. At these, the editors sponsoring the books, or perhaps the heads of editorial divisions, present each title with a brief description of the contents and salient sales features. What successes have the author's previous books enjoyed? Is the book tied into some trend or fad, some event such as an election, opening of the baseball season, a disaster, a war, a trial, a scandal? Is there a movie or television adaptation in the works? Are author appearances planned? Is the author engaging, promotable, famous?

The editor's spiel is fortified by a variety of supplementary material: cover proofs, bound proofs of the book itself or excerpts or condensed portions, inside illustrations, an agenda of the author's tour, posters or mock-ups of advertising copy, plugs by famous authors or other celeb-rities, trailers from movie or television tie-ins, slide shows, audiocassettes, and all manner of gimmicks such as buttons, pens, and bookmarks. Sometimes the publisher will stage a real dog-and-pony show, with professional entertainment, elaborate skits written and performed by the publishing staff, and even cameo appearances by star authors.

If the publisher's list is a big and multifarious one, the work sessions may be broken down into specialized seminars in which the sales reps, distributors, or chain store buyers may educate themselves as to the nature of such categories as science fiction, westerns, or romances, or focus on strategies for one or two blockbuster lead titles.

All of this activity is designed to impress and enlighten the sales reps, help them to understand the publisher's aims and problems, give them an opportunity to offer feedback garnered from experiences in their territories, and inspire them to get behind the publisher's list with every fiber of their being.

What makes these sessions so critical to the success or failure of your book is that they bear directly on the number of copies that will be printed and distributed, and on the energy that will be expended on the mar-keting. Thus, sales conference is the week of reckoning for the list, during which time it is inscribed which books shall fly and which shall bomb, which shall be raised up to the best-seller list and which cast down to the remainder bins, which shall be stacked near the cash registers in pyramids of pharaonic magnitude, and which secreted spine-out in quantities of two or three in the wrong department of a bookstore.

Broadly speaking, there are two ways in which printings are deter-mined by the activities at a sales conference. At the one extreme are those books for which printings and sales goals are somewhat nebulous in the publisher's mind. These books are presented as vigorously as possible in the hopes the sales reps will get turned on and bring in a surprisingly large number of orders. At the other end of the spectrum are those titles for which the publisher has set specific sales goals and the sales are expected to fill their quotas.

Most of the books on any given list fall somewhere between these two approaches, and not all the books get fair shrift. This is particularly true of first novels, midlist books, experimental works, and books that are part of a series. There is only so much you can say about a first novel, or about the latest Regency romance, or a book about costumes of Colonial Virginia, and there's no sense in trying to tell these highly sophisticated sales people that such books are going to leap off the shelves by the score. On the other hand, as there is a steady market for such books, it can be expected that a minimum number of copies will sell without undue effort on the publisher's part. Still, it's easy to see how the best-seller mentality can affect your book in a sales conference situation as it does in the editorial boardroom, the review media, and in the bookstores.

Armed with all this information, with press kits, cover proofs, promotional gimmicks, and inspiration, the sales reps go forth to the stores and sell, sell, sell. Although the publisher may have outlined a sales strategy for the list, the handling of sales is largely left to the discretion of the reps. Conditions in each territory vary widely: Consumers may buy westerns by the truckload in the southwestern region, but the same books will lie in great untouched stacks like dead fish in the bookstores of the Northeast. They may adore Ludlum in Cleveland and ignore him in Topeka. A book on the hottest new rock group may march out of California stores in regiment strength, but in Bible Belt bookstores, will molder in unopened cartons.

The sales reps servicing these territories understand the tastes of the readers there, and know how to "play" the books in their sales kits like so many cards in a rummy game. Like authors, agents, and publishers, the salesman or woman makes the most profit on best-sellers, and so these titles may be expected to muscle out the rest of the list. The salesperson may make all sorts of bargains to induce store buyers to take that quota of the big book: special discounts, relaxation of strict return policies, a little coaxing here, a little coercing there, and some trading off of little books for big ones elsewhere. Among the little ones may be your book. Or maybe it's the other way around, and you're the lucky author whose big book will push the little ones off the boards. This is, you must realize, a jungle, however civilized the product being sold. Someone once said that the wise man never looks too closely at what goes into his laws or his sausages; perhaps best-selling books should be added to that list.

Although business is not conducted around the clock at sales conference, it is never far away at breakfast, lunch, or dinner, at cocktail time, out on the beach or the golf links, or in the evening at the theater or floor show. Sales conference is a time for everybody to get to know everybody else a little better, creating a sense of teamwork and harmony. Many editors tell me they come away from these occasions with an enhanced sense of "family" about the people they work and deal with. You may know next to nothing about someone in an office down the hall from you, but in the relaxed informality of a resort setting, that person may tell you something about himself or reveal aspects of his character that have been held in tight check by the requirements of office decorum and the hurly-burly of the business day.

Sales conference is the place where an editor can bestow a personal touch on a sales campaign, and that can make the difference to a book's success. "I know books like this don't ordinarily work in your region," an editor might say to a sales rep he or she has buttonholed at the bar, "but this particular novel has some aspects that will appeal to the stores you service." It works the other way around, too. Sales reps, knowing their particular market a lot better than the publishers do, will pull an editor or sales manager aside and say, "My customers can't keep science fiction in their stores; are you going to increase the number you publish?" Or, "Everybody in my territory wants to know when the next book in the Hieronymus Bosch detective series is coming out." Or, "Dell and Berkley are doing really well with a certain kind of romance, so how about our starting a similar line?" In short, sales conference is the time and place for important dialogues among staff members of publishing houses, among sales people, and between publishers and sales reps, distributors, or bookstore and chain store personnel.

Is there any place for authors at sales conference? Except for the very biggest names, authors are seldom invited to the ones held outside New York City, and because of the expense of bringing authors to New York, any that are invited to the conferences held in the city are usually people who live in or near the city to begin with. Invitations are not automatic, however, as few authors are dynamic, attractive, and promotable enough to make a strong positive impression on the sales reps. There is still much you can do, though, to cooperate with your editor in furnishing him or her with information and sales features about your book, anything and everything that will enable your editor to highlight your book when the presentation is made.

Maybe, then, you too should become aware of the onset of sales conference season, and instead of writing it off as a period of downtime in your calendar, get yourself involved in the preparations. It need not cost you a lot of money. One of my clients, the author of a tragic romance novel, bought a small carton of tissue packets for her editor and urged her to hand them to the sales reps with the other material in the promo kit for her book. "Tell them to have a good cry," the author said. It proved quite effective.

Perhaps you can think of something equally creative. After all, why on earth would you want to go to a tropical resort, all expenses paid by your publisher, anyway?

CHAPTER 19

"P & L"

ONE OF THE LEAST pleasant duties that agents are obliged to perform is explaining to their clients why their books have flopped. And there is no dearth of reasons: the editor was fired, the company was taken over by a conglomerate, the salesmen didn't understand the book, someone stuck a lousy title on it, they didn't advertise it, they didn't advertise it enough, they underprinted it, they brought it out too soon, they brought it out too late, there was an Act of God, there was an Act of Satan—an agent's files are a veritable Grand Guignol of publishing horror stories.

The one thing it does not always occur to agents to tell their clients, however, is that their books have not really flopped, at least not from the publisher's viewpoint. Maybe your book wasn't a best-seller, but that's not to say your publisher didn't make money on it. Most authors and a great many agents tend to equate the earning-out of an author's advance with the recoupment of a publisher's investment. It's an understandable misconception, for to authors, royalties are profits. If their books start earning profits, they assume the publisher has started making profits too; and conversely, they figure, if the advance doesn't earn out, the publisher must have lost money on the book.

Seldom is this equation true. Although royalties are a gauge of success or failure for an author, publishers use an entirely different system to determine how well or badly a book has done for them. In that system, authors' royalties are only one element of the profit picture, and it is entirely possible for a publisher to make a big profit on a book whose advance has not earned out, or to lose money on a book whose advance has earned out.

Because I have never worked for a publishing company, it took me a long time to grasp this distinction. But because it's a terribly important one, explaining as it does why publishers often seem to be doing everything they can to lose money on their books, I've tried to educate myself in basic publishing economics and would like to share my findings with you.

In most cases today, publishers prepare profit-and-loss projections for books that they are considering acquiring. The calculations differ widely from company to company, from type of book to type of book, and even from book to book. The database for an illustrated book is quite different from that of a hardcover novel, which in turn differs from a paperback novel; and even within the genus paperback novel are such species as lead novel, category novel, movie tie-in, etc.

Many staff members may be involved in producing these estimates: editors, production people, sales managers, sub-rights directors, advertising and promotion personnel, the company comptroller, art director, and so on. Each tries to factor into the profit-and-loss worksheet the best-case and worst-case numbers that will help their firm formulate as accurate a picture of a book's potential as is possible in our unpredictable business. The worksheets are really a tool, and their data may be manipulated and negotiated so that costs trimmed from one area may be applied to another in the hopes that enthusiasm for the book will not be dampened by discouraging figures from one or two precincts. If, however, all or most of the committee members come in with poor profit projections, it's unlikely that hearts will prevail over heads when the votes are cast at the editorial meeting.

I may be romanticizing the past, but these complex formulations don't seem to be much of an improvement over the intuitive judgments reached by the founders of such illustrious houses as Knopf, Harper, Scribner, Random House, and Simon and Schuster. Be that as it may, publishing decisions today are reached by computers, consensus, and committee, and we may consider ourselves lucky if someone remembers the love factor when the bottom line is being examined.

Love aside, what are the elements of a profit-and-loss projection? What kind of "P & L" figures are resting at your editor's elbow when he phones you or your agent to commence negotiations on your book?

The key figure on the positive side of the ledger is revenue to be realized from sales of the book. You get this by multiplying the number of copies sold by the wholesale price of the book, that is, the actual price received by your publisher after he discounts it to the book trade. If the list price of the book is $20, and the average discount offered by your publisher to the stores is 40 percent, the actual price received by your publisher will be $12 per copy.

"Copies sold," remember, means net sales after returns, for in the publishing business books are sold on a returnable basis. So, if a publisher prints and distributes 25,000 copies of a book but 30 percent of them are returned, the actual number of copies sold (what publishers call the "sell-through") will be 17,500. Multiply that 17,500 by the $12 per copy that your publisher is getting and you get the publisher's gross sale. In this example, that comes to $210,000.

To this figure is added the publisher's anticipated share of subsidiary revenue: book club, paperback reprint, first or second serial, foreign rights, etc. Depending on how liberal or conservative the firm's fiscal policy is, these numbers range from wishful thinking on the one hand to zero if the publisher doesn't want to count on income that is not absolutely guaranteed at the time the book is acquired. More and more publishers tend to take a highly conservative position in prognosticating sub-rights income. For one thing, agents have grown tougher over the last few decades about permitting publishers to participate in that income; and for another, the collapse of the paperback reprint market early in the 1980s forced hardcover publishers to count on nothing but hardcover sales when preparing their projections. These are significant factors in the driving-out of midlist books from the hardcover marketplace.

Another source of revenue for publishers derives from the sale of remainders. If the undistributed or returned copies of a book, such as the 7,500 copies in the above example, are sold to remainder jobbers they will bring in a few thousand dollars for the publishers, and that goes into the plus side of the P & L.

Now for the minus side. From the income generated by sales of the book, remainders, and sub-rights income, your publisher subtracts his costs. These fall into several categories that are reckoned by formulas drawn from company and industry experience and the counsel of the firm's financial officers and accountants. One category is plant costs: typesetting, color separations for the cover or for color illustrations, preparation of halftones for black-and-white illustrations, and all other procedures up to the actual printing of the book.

The second category is manufacturing costs, lumped together as "PPB": printing, paper, and binding.

A third is overhead. Included here are rent or mortgage payments on the publisher's offices, electricity, salaries, telephone, office supplies, the cost of money, warehousing, sales commissions, insurance, and the many other expenses required to run a business. Because each publisher includes or excludes different items when calculating overhead, the fluctuations in overhead allocations differ widely from one publisher to the next. A safe guess is that most houses allocate between 30 and 40 percent of gross sales.

The next category is author's royalty. This figure is fixed by contract. Royalties represent a big chunk of a publisher's costs. An 8 percent royalty on a $3.95 paperback comes to about 32 cents. But remember that the publisher sells that book to the trade at a discount. If the discount is 50 percent, or $2.00 a copy, the royalty will absorb about 16 percent of that revenue.

Then there are some miscellaneous costs such as outside design, cover art, copyediting, indexing, illustrations, and the cost of free and review copies.

And, finally, there is the cost of advertising and promotion.

As I mentioned, accounting practices vary widely when it comes to allocating costs to specific books on a list. Should the publisher allocate the same share of his total costs to every book regardless of its importance, profitability, and actual share of the company's investment? Or should big books carry a proportionately larger share of the cost load than routine ones?

Because publishers don't agree on the fairest way to deal with the question, their allocation formulas vary widely, and a good example of this is advertising and promotion. Some publishers simply average out the cost of advertising and promotion for all books on their list and add some percentage points to the overhead charge on each book. For other publishers, it makes no sense to allocate to a routine book a percentage of the enormous cost of pushing a best-seller. These publishers therefore "break out" the advertising and promotional cost of each book and show it on their profit-and-loss worksheets as a separate item from overhead.

Okay, we're ready to do some calculations. Take the gross sales of your book, add remainder income and anticipated subsidiary rights revenue, and you have an income projection. From this you deduct your plant and manufacturing costs, overhead, royalties, advertising and promotion, and miscellaneous costs. What you end up with is projected profit or loss.

The final figures are educated approximations, of course, and don't take into account many factors on both the income and outgo sides of the ledgers, such as corporate taxes, inflation, damaged copies, losses due to strikes, fire, and flood, interest earned on royalties banked between semiannual royalty periods and on reserves against returns, and much, much more. Still, on the average, paperback publishers earn something like 15 to 20 percent pretax profit on routine books. And, because unit costs go down and sales volume goes up on best-sellers, the profit on major books is even higher.

What do the numbers tell us? For some of us, they only bear out our worst paranoid fantasies that publishers are battening on the lifeblood of authors. These fantasies are fueled by the facts that publishers do not share their profit-and-loss projections with authors, conceal vital sales information when reporting royalties, and, because most publishers are owned by larger corporate entities and are not, therefore, required to disclose financial information to stockholders or the public. One of my western-writer clients says writers are like mushrooms: "They're fed a lot of horseshit and kept in the dark."

Others among us may realize that publishing is a tough, unpredictable, and treacherous business, and perhaps the people who play for such high stakes deserve a handsome profit for the risks they take and the capital they invest (though it must be said in all fairness that 15 or 20 percent is not exactly a windfall profit). I don't know the answer. But I can safely say that the profit-and-loss worksheets of most authors I know are a lot more depressing than anything I've seen from publishers.

⌁

CHAPTER 20

Pub Date

F EW EVENTS IN the life of a book are as thoroughly invested with magic and mystery as its publication date. Although the season, month, and day of publication are, as often as not, selected merely to satisfy the expediencies of a publisher's schedule, many authors and even some publishers assign cabalistic value to pub dates, and a great deal of myth and nonsense has come to surround the process. One hears such platitudes as, "January is a lousy month to bring out a book," or, "Nobody buys books in August," or "Can you believe they released my book on Friday the thirteenth?"

As some fifty thousand books are published annually, you may safely assume that a day does not go by without a book being officially launched somewhere. I know of no records correlating the success or failure of books with their pub dates, but I daresay that if someone were crazy enough to trace the fates of best-sellers back to the dates on which they were published, it would be demonstrated that successful books debut on just about every date on the calendar—including Friday the thirteenth. It would also be discovered, I'm sure, that just as many books flop as triumph whose pub dates are agonized over and deliberately selected for maximum impact.

A few words about the differences between hardcover and paperback distribution might be pertinent here. Hardcover books are for the most part shipped directly from publisher to bookstore (though the advent of powerful hardcover wholesalers and jobbers is changing this, it should be noted). Hardcovers can be, and are, shipped on any date, but traditionally they are categorized by season: spring and fall. Sometimes Christmas is designated a third "season." Hardcover publishers hold spring and fall sales conferences to introduce books scheduled for the following season, and they issue spring and fall catalogues. A hardcover published in July will probably be considered a spring book; one published in February, a fall book.

The rise of the paperback industry created a very different distribution rhythm. Until relatively recently, when the great bookstore chains made direct distribution of paperbacks a significant factor in the publishing industry, paperback books were carried only by the same distributors who stock magazines in newsstands and drugstores, and this form of distribution is still the dominant mode in the paperback industry. But because distribution of magazines follows a monthly cycle, the scheduling of paperback books became a monthly affair. Catalogues issued by mass market publishers are for the most part monthly, and, unlike their hardcover counterparts, paperback editors refer to pub dates by month, not by season. And while it is impractical to conduct a sales conference every month, paperback publishers do consult with sales staff and distributors on a monthly basis far more extensively than hardcover publishers do. The lingo of paperback distribution is closer to magazines, too: hardcover books are published, but paperbacks are *released* or *issued*.

In an earlier era when novels and general nonfiction were affordable only by a wealthier segment of society, the summer was undoubtedly a dead time for booksellers as the carriage trade fled the cities for favorite rural watering spots. A book published in July or August could very well die, and it's easy to see where the notion arose that August publication is the kiss of death. In September the affluent returned to the city, presumably hungry for good books to read and mindful of the impending Christmas holiday, when books make excellent gifts. That is why fall has always been considered the best time to launch a book, and for the most part that remains true, because a book that goes on the best-seller list in the fall has a good chance of carrying into the Christmas buying season. And if January is considered a lousy time to publish, it's because bookstore owners are preoccupied with postholiday returns, budget deficits, and winter vacations to recover from the intense business of the previous few months.

Mass market publishing and marketing have smoothed out many of the hills and valleys of bookselling, making the business a year-round enterprise. The capital required to feed a mass market maw allows for no downtime. Every month must carry its share of the annual business, and every book, whatever its publication date, must be considered a source of maximum profit potential. "People used to say things like 'July is a good month for publishing but August is bad'," Robert A. Gottlieb, former president of Alfred A. Knopf said in a *New York Times* article. "All those maxims are true until books come along that disprove them, then the opposite is true." Gottlieb added that Knopf published most of its books "at the first rational moment," and I would say that many of his colleagues do the same.

Some books definitely do have seasonal pertinence. Sports novels or nonfiction books come to mind, for they are often dependent on the start of playing seasons or tournaments. It makes common sense to bring a base-ball book out in March and a football book in August. And sometimes there are excellent strategic reasons for publishing a book in a specific month.

The scheduling of books for publication on a specific calendar date is usually aimed more at gratifying whim or superstition—publisher's or author's—than at achieving any significant commercial advantage. It is flattering for an author to have his book published on his birthday, but from that day forward the book is on its own. It seems logical to bring out a biography of Lincoln on Lincoln's Birthday, or an account of the attack on Pearl Harbor on December 7, or a study of the John F. Kennedy assassination on November 22, for these dates possess a certain degree of promotional cachet. But that's as far as it goes.

Quite clearly, a book's publication date is nowhere nearly as important as some other factors on which publishers spend a great deal of time and energy during scheduling meetings. Possibly the key one is what the competition is doing. If, for instance, Simon & Schuster knows that Crown is going to be publishing a new novel in September by its blockbuster author, S&S might well think twice about scheduling its own fall leader around the same time. Information about the pub dates of major books is usually available from a variety of sources such as publishers' catalogues, *Publishers Weekly,* and the free exchange of information among friendly competitors. And occasionally, when the exchange of information is not so free, friendly competitors have been known to resort to subterfuge.

If, however, two lead books scheduled for the same time are not really competitive—a literary novel, say, versus an international thriller—the publishers might not be afraid to go head to head, because two different audiences can support both books and simultaneously boost them onto the best-seller list.

Publishers may not be so gentlemanly if they get caught up in a race to be first out with a book on a hot subject. Dramatic news events will occasion rivalries that are anything but friendly, for now the competing publishers are committing a great deal of capital to getting their books into the stores first. In some cases both books do well, but on many occasions the second book across the line suffers grievous losses.

You can see, then, that unlucky pub dates can occur on any given page of the calendar, and the circumstances attending the birth of your book are far more auspicious or inauspicious than the date. Any day is Friday the thirteenth for the author whose publisher goes bankrupt on his pub date, or the one who finds himself on pub date without a sponsoring editor because the one who originally acquired his book left six months ago to take another job, or the one whose pub date was unheralded by a single ad because the whole advertising budget for that month was allocated to a blockbuster on the same list.

~&

CHAPTER 21

Great Expectations: Advertising and Publicity

I F THE DISCONTENT of authors could be likened to a pie, the largest slice by far would represent resentment about the failure of publishers to advertise, publicize, and promote their books. Although I'm fairly articulate when it comes to explaining to my clients why publishers do or don't do certain things, I'm all too often at a loss for an answer when they ask me such questions as, "Why would my publisher spend $25,000 to acquire my book and then only $1.25 to advertise it?" Or, "How could they spend $100,000 to advertise that dreadful piece of pornography and not a dime on my book about nuclear disarmament?" Or, "Why is my book the best kept secret since the Manhattan Project?"

We live in a world in which it is universally acknowledged that the most effective way to move merchandise is to hype it to consumers. In the publishing industry, however, most of the product goes un- or under-advertised, and even books that publishing people consider to be heavily pushed are ridiculously underboosted by the standards of most other business enterprises. A few years ago, I handled a book by a leading business executive, and one day I proudly announced to him that his publisher had decided to allocate $75,000 for advertising and publicity for his book. "Great!" he exclaimed. "And how much are they going to spend on the second day?" In his field, $75,000 could be thrown casually into a single-page ad in a magazine. Something is definitely out of whack here. In defense against author complaints, publishers respond that writers cherish unrealistic expectations, that even modest promotional campaigns are too expensive, that many books sell themselves without any publicity whatsoever, that many investments in this sector are unproductive or actually counterproductive, and that authors are not always aware of the efforts their publishers make to promote their books.

I don't think it's unreasonable for authors to hope that their publishers will try to stimulate consumer interest in their books. Nor is it unrealistic to suggest that publishers might benefit as much as authors from the publicizing of their products. But after countless discussions with publishers on this issue (not all conducted sotto voce, you may rightly guess), I have to admit that it is more complicated than we may think. Before you rush to judgment, listen to what your publisher has to say.

- *Some types of books are going to sell whether we push them or not.* A great many routine paperbacks sell and sell well with little or no help from their publishers. The reason is that paperback publishers have learned that there is a hard-core audience for romance, science fiction, western, horror, and other genres. These readers will buy just about any book in their favorite category whether it is good, bad, or indifferent. In certain male sectors like action-adventure or traditional cowboy novels, for example, a paperback publisher can anticipate 25,000 guaranteed customers, and he would have to work very hard to sell fewer copies than that.

But, you ask, don't publishers want to sell more than this minimum? You'll be surprised to learn that the answer is: not necessarily. The cost of stimulating sales beyond the minimum support level may not be balanced by the profits. Some publishers are content to take a small profit on each title, rather than risk a loss going for the bigger profit.

Paperback publishers have also discovered that popular authors will naturally separate from the pack as a result of such factors as word of mouth, good reviews, feature stories in the press, and consumer demand in bookstores and other points of purchase—all with little or no money spent to create that demand. When those sales figures begin drifting upward, a wise publisher will consider ways to elevate that author even further. At that point advertising and publicity may come into play. Which leads to a second truism that publishers hold dear:

- *Advertising can't make a book successful; it can only keep it successful.* The fate of most books is sealed long before they are released to the public. The critical period is when the sales staff solicits orders from bookstore buyers and distributors. The enthusiasm or lack of it will determine the print run, and if the support is feeble, as likely as not little or nothing will be spent to advertise. Nor will ads necessarily send buyers flocking to the stores, even assuming the publisher feels that ads are a wise investment. If, however, a book meets with high popular demand, publishers may spend money on advertising and publicity to reinforce that demand. A new book by a popular author will probably get advertised, even if it's a lousy book. A new book by an unknown will probably not get advertised, even if it's great. Which leads to the very next rule of thumb, to wit:

- *Very little midlist fiction benefits from heavy investment in advertising and promotion.* Publishers are, understandably, reluctant to invest a lot of money to push serious, literary, experimental, and first novels. With hardcover sales projected in the low thousands, and with no guarantee of book club or paperback reprint revenue to underwrite the cost of publishing such midlist books, publishers prefer to let them make their own way on the strength of free advertising such as reviews and feature stories or word-of-mouth praise, or low-cost advertising such as catalogue announcements, publicity releases, or house ads that tout many of the publisher's books at once. As we've seen, though, there is some reason to believe that even if publishers spent heavily on ads for midlist fiction, it wouldn't compel consumers to buy, because the authors' names are not familiar to most of them.

As for promoting the authors themselves, it almost never works for midlist fiction, and for a very simple reason: it is extremely hard to express effectively the virtues of a work of fiction on a radio or television program.

- *Star authors, as usual, are exempted from all of the above rules.* If midlist fiction is so hard to promote on talk shows, how come best-selling authors show up on them all the time? One reason is that the subjects of their novels may be discussed as if they were nonfiction.

While the plot of a novel is impossible to summarize entertainingly and the characters are too complex to capture in a pithy one-liner, there is usually something in the subject itself that serves as an excellent launching pad for stimulating discussion. "Tell us who your drug-crazed starlet heroine is in real life . . ."

Even more significantly, in the world of best-sellers, people are often more interested in the authors than in the books themselves. Best-selling authors are celebrities like movie and sports stars. Publishers who promote them stress the charms of the writer as much as they do the charms of the writer's work. If you'll listen carefully when a star author appears on radio or television, you'll notice how superficially the book itself is discussed. Attention focuses on such questions as: "Where did the idea for your novel come from? Did anything unusual happen to you when you were researching your novel? How much money did you get for your book? Is it true you're: getting married, getting divorced, having a baby, having another baby, buying a yacht, buying a castle, buying a nation?" These are precisely the same questions that might be asked of a film star hyping his or her latest movie.

Best-selling authors are also exceptions to the rule that print advertising can't make books successful. While ads seldom make consumers visit a bookstore to buy a midlist novel, they will attract them in droves to purchase a new novel by Stephen King, Danielle Steele, Janet Dailey, or John Grisham. Why? Because these fans are predisposed to buy the books to begin with.

- *Nonfiction authors are easier to promote than novelists.* The subjects of many nonfiction books are, as we've seen, much more appropriate topics of conversation than the themes of novels. Nor must the author enjoy immense celebrity to quality for an invitation to a talk show. An interesting subject about which you feel passionately and speak articulately is often good enough to score a hit on radio or television. Terrific buns, big bazooms, and doe eyes are not necessary to furnish an entertaining fifteen or twenty minute chat about the current state of bioengineering or the destiny of wildlife on Alaska's North Slope.

I don't suppose they do any harm, though.

↝

CHAPTER 22

Brand Names

WHEN I FIRST entered the publishing business early in the 1960s the paperback revolution was in full swing, and among the innovations introduced at the time was the insertion of ads in paperbacks (other than ads for other books on the publishers' lists). Although a number of products were tried out, the ones I most vividly remember were cigarettes. There was debate on both Publishers' Row and Madison Avenue about propriety and economics, and I don't recall that I cared much either way; it was fine with me if people wanted to run ads in books, and fine with me if they didn't. The ads didn't inspire me to buy the product, but few ads do anyway. Nor did I find them a desecration of literature, mainly because the books they ran in were pretty much desecrations of literature already. Still, some authors did not like it, and others worried that the insertion of an ad for Marlboros in *The Attack of the Hydrangea People* today could lead to one for Desenex Foot Powder in *War and Peace* tomorrow.

I doubt if such ethical considerations would have prevailed if the economics of carrying advertising in books were sound, but they apparently were not. In addition, the susceptibility of book buyers to such ads was not terribly high. Publishers and advertisers might, given enough time, have overcome these problems had not, the story goes, some publisher run some cigarette ads in a book about the dangers of smoking (the story may be apocryphal, but it's too good to resist). The incident pointed up the dire possibilities, and so it came to pass that many authors and agents demanded specific language in their contracts stipulating that no ads would be run in their books (except, as I said, for other books published by the publisher) without their express consent.

Ads in books are not very cost-effective ways of conveying a sales message. If the average distribution of a run-of-the-mill paperback original is 50,000 copies (it's often less), of which perhaps half will be returned, you're talking about 25,000 exposures of the ad, maybe a few more if the book is circulated beyond the original purchasers. That's not a great many exposures compared to the hundreds of thousands or millions an advertiser can get in national magazines, and its a pittance compared to the effectiveness of advertising on network television. But, you say, doesn't the advertiser pay less to run ads in books than in magazines or on television to compensate for the difference in exposures? He certainly does; so much less, in fact, as to make it scarcely worthwhile for the publisher to sell the space.

There are other problems as well. Despite the commercialization of the publishing industry many publishers do have ethical compunctions about mingling ads with the texts of books, and although they may have few reservations about publishing books depicting human depravity in all its hideous glory, they draw the line at disposable razors and smokeless tobacco. You figure it out. Another problem is consumer resistance to ads in books. While most buyers of literature don't think twice about ads that appear in magazines, they find the same ads discomfiting in books. This may relate to the disposability of magazines; books are to keep, and book buyers may feel that their possessions are contaminated by ads.

The most serious of all objections has nothing to do with cost-effectiveness, ethics, or the proclivities of book buyers. It has to do with the U.S. Postal Service, for running ads in books jeopardizes the cheap rates the post office charges for books shipped via special fourth class. Today, routine shipments of books go this way, as opposed to the more expensive Parcel Post or third class rates, or truck or United Parcel Service. It's a (relatively) inexpensive rate and one that publishers continually lobby postal authorities to maintain. If, however, books begin carrying advertising, they cross the line into the territory occupied by magazines, thus running athwart of the postal authorities eager to collect the higher revenues generated by the mailing of periodical literature. If the profits from such advertising don't offset the higher postal expenses, the publishers will obviously have made an expensive mistake.

It may well be that the postal obstacle is fatal to any scheme for reviving the idea of running advertising in books. But if we accept the truism that where there's a will there's a way, then we may be able to find creative ways around the problem. First, however, authors have to acknowledge that advertising in books does not necessarily spell the twilight of western culture as we have known it. Perhaps they would have an easier time doing so if they thought there was something in it for themselves.

What's in it for publishers, we all know: money. Advertising defrays costs and enhances profits, worthy goals for any business. But authors do not benefit from advertising revenue, nor do I think many of them feel entitled to do so. But surely, if they consider the rates paid to contributing authors by such ad-rich publications as the *New Yorker* or *Playboy*, it should be clear to them that there is a distinct relationship. Without meaning to sound overly cynical, it's easier to imagine authors accepting ads in their books for disposable razors and smokeless tobacco if they're paid advances twice the size of those they're now getting. Maybe the time has come, then, for authors to rethink their hostility to the notion.

It may well be that, for the reasons I've given, it's an unfeasible one. Nevertheless, it does raise a related issue having to do with the relationship between book publishing and other commercial enterprises. You might call it brand-name sponsorship of books, and though our industry is awakening to its potential, there's still a lot of fuzzy thinking in this area.

Our society is heavily dependent on brand names for the selection of consumer goods, and the consumer of books is no different from the consumer of soap powder. Publishers are confronted by a serious problem in this respect, however, because when it comes to selecting books, the "brand name" of the publisher means nothing to the consumer. Oh sure, the average bookbuyer is probably more familiar with the names of Random House, Doubleday, and Simon & Schuster than he is with firms like M. Evans, W. W. Norton, or David Godine, but he does not prefer Random House books to Norton ones. The book buyer has no brand name loyalty, and little brand name recognition: I warrant 90 percent of all readers (except perhaps readers of romances, who seem to know their Silhouettes from their Loveswepts) cannot tell you the names of the publishers of the books they are currently reading, including the one you hold in your hands at this very moment. Readers who loved a recent Putnam book could not care less about Putnam books in general, and if the author moved to Viking, his readers would buy his Viking books as avidly as they bought his Putnam ones.

Readers, as I say, are as brand-name conscious as anybody else, but for them the brand names are favorite authors; authoritative titles, such as M.D., Ph.D., President, or Director; and brand names in other fields of endeavor, such as the *New York Times* (for, say, cookbooks) or the National Football League (for official player guides and statistical books). As far as the first two classifications are concerned, publishers already do as much as they can to acquire and promote popular authors and titled authorities. But I'm constantly surprised at how little advantage publishers have taken of the availability of brand-name companies to sponsor books—sponsor them, that is, the way product manufacturers sponsor radio and television programs. Yet, almost invariably, such sponsorship has resulted in big sales and often best-sellerdom. It's easy to understand why. The Procter and Gambles, General Foods, and Ford Motor Companies of the world are loaded with money and spend stupendous sums on advertising and promotion. The sums necessary to back a book and put it on the best-seller list are pathetically low compared to what must be spent to achieve consumer acceptance of some new product or model: we're talking about perhaps a hundred thousand dollars or a little more, the cost of one or two magazine ads for soap products or automobiles or cigarettes. For another thing, these companies are in a position to buy books—lots of them, for use as premiums given away or sold at high discount to purchasers of their products.

Many writers who are not names may have wonderful ideas for books and superb expertise to bring to them. They will probably not get very far, however, because good ideas and extensive knowledge are unfortunately not enough to interest publishers in commissioning books. I cannot tell you how many worthy proposals are turned down annually by agents and publishers because the authors lack "credentials." When I see such proposals, I often suggest that the author try to link up with a brand-name company in that field and try to interest the firm in sponsoring his book. The same principle might wed brand-name sponsors to whole lines of books. Cosmetic or fragrance manufacturers could be persuaded to back lines of romance novels, or a jeans manufacturer to lend its name to a line of western novels, for example.

There is gold mine potential in this area known as licensing, and, because it means more work for authors (and possibly lucrative deals for them if authors and their agents play their cards right), far more attention ought to be paid to bringing sponsoring companies onto the publishing scene.

Some purists will attack this notion as another form of subsidy publishing, and that, unquestionably, is what it is. But an industry subsidized by Marlboro cigarettes, Kellogg's corn flakes, and Alpo dog food is still preferable to the present system subsidized by authors.

ॐ

CHAPTER 23

Book Clubs

OOK CLUBS ARE such solid fixtures in the lives of authors, agents, and publishers that we take them for granted, like enormous monuments that we no longer notice on our way to work every day. How impoverished our environment would be without book clubs can easily be grasped when you realize that some 7 million Americans subscribe to them. And because changes in pricing, reader tastes, distribution, marketing, and other trends have drawn new attention to the functions of book clubs, this is a particularly good time to examine this phenomenon.

Book clubs are an outgrowth of attempts to reach a larger segment of the reading population than was then being served by bookstores. Experiments like department store book clubs (there were Macy's, Gimbel's, and Bloomingdale's clubs among others) and tie-ins of cheap editions of books with the sale of products (a tobacco company included miniature volumes of Shakespeare plays in its cigarette packs) inspired an enterprising merchandiser named Harry Scherman to found the Book-of-the-Month Club in 1926. He perceived that an enormous potential audience, particularly in rural areas, had inadequate access to bookstores in towns and cities. Mail order, which worked so successfully for many other products purveyed to rural people, ought to work with books, too, Scherman reasoned. But he put a twist on this concept that made it a dramatic departure from the Sears, Roebuck approach. It's called the "negative option," meaning that unless members expressly indicate that they do not want the latest selection, the club will assume they do want it and will send it to them. Scherman's insight into human nature was almost diabolically shrewd. Perhaps he didn't trust that members would buy books simply because they were good, and he counted on such human foibles as laziness, guilt, and confusion to make members default on their obligation to return their cards in time to prevent clubs from shipping selections to them.

Whatever the motives of Scherman and subsequent book club entre-preneurs, the clubs caught on fast and hard, sweeping the country and, in the process, revealing some serious flaws in the way that books in this country are distributed and promoted. One publisher observed that "the clubs advertised books extensively and nationally, sold them regularly to people who had previously been only occasional book buyers and, most importantly, fostered the habit of regular reading," according to John Tebbel in his excellent book about American publishing, *Between Covers*. Tebbel cites book clubs for professionals such as businesspeople, engi-neers, and the like as particularly effective in reaching audiences that conventional bookstore marketing simply cannot touch.

Not unexpectedly, the creation of the clubs provoked a great outcry among retail bookstore owners, who felt gravely threatened by them, particularly when the Literary Guild added the wrinkle of offering books for prices below retail. Many retailers accused publishers who dealt with clubs of collaborating with the enemy. Harder to comprehend was the opposition by publishers, who after all did stand to profit from book club revenue. Their contention, however, was that book clubs represented an element of crass mercantilism and cynical exploitation of the hallowed spirit of literature (publishers believed the oddest things in those days!). *The Bookman* asserted that book club members were "too feeble-minded, too lazy, or too busy to make their own choices." But book clubs were an idea whose time had come, and after consolidating their gains during the Great Depression of the 1930s (reading being one of the few affordable pleasures of that grim era), they became the institution we revere today.

With few exceptions, the basic idea concocted by Scherman has not changed. A lot of other things have, however, forcing Book-of-the-Month Club and its imitators and competitors to take measures to keep up with changing times, tastes, and conditions.

One of these is the shrinking of rural America, making bookstores accessible to people in all but the remotest reaches of the nation. Fortunately for the clubs, accessibility of bookstores is not by any means the most important factor for potential book buyers. Indeed, urban members constitute a large portion of the clubs' memberships. A far more important element is price. Book clubs offer discounts on the list prices of books, starting at around 10 percent, and additionally offer free bonus books plus sign-up inducements such as free sets of books.

As long as a wide gap existed between bookstore and book club prices for books, clubs could hope to continue doing a healthy business. The critical test came when the paperback revolution took hold, making paperback originals and reprints available for prices far below those offered by clubs to their members. But the clubs came through the test unbowed, revealing how solidly the convenience factor figured in the thinking of book buyers.

Most recently, the clubs found themselves under intensive fire from their old enemies the bookstores following the explosive expansion of such chains as Crown and Barnes & Noble. Not only did these chains reach deeply into rural territories that had been big profit targets for book clubs, but they started discounting books at or below the prices offered by the clubs. And when you added postage and handling charges to the prices members paid for book club selections, the allure of the stores became very compelling. Fortunately for the clubs, the stores could not sustain the narrow profit margins generated by "deep discounting," and although discounts are still offered on certain books by chain stores, the threat to the clubs from that source seems to have been averted.

It would appear that no matter what weapons the enemies of book clubs throw at them, the clubs survive because they possess one advantage the stores cannot overcome: selectivity. For readers too busy or uncertain to sort out the welter of new books, clubs proffer the recommendations of a panel of experts who have screened the candidates and distilled the very best. Furthermore, many book clubs cater to specialized tastes. Book buyers interested in subjects ranging from dance to war, mysteries to science fiction, nostalgia to travel, sailing to nursing, business to computers can satisfy their predilections by joining clubs aimed at those specific interests.

Most book clubs make their selections in pretty much the same way. Publishers submit books at an early stage, in manuscript or proofs, accompanied by promotional material and any other information about book and author that the publisher may feel will make the book more attractive to club members. (On occasion, a book will be chosen by a club after publication.) The submission is assigned by the club's editorial board to a reader, hopefully one who will give it an informed and sympathetic reading. Recommended works are then circulated to the rest of the editorial committee and are discussed, rated, and voted on. The club then negotiates deals with publishers on the books they wish to acquire. The club either guarantees to purchase a quantity of copies of the publisher's edition or, if the club has its own printing facility, licenses the right to publish its own edition. In either case, most clubs pay an advance against a royalty, though some smaller clubs pay a flat fee for a fixed, one-time printing. After the deal is struck, the clubs solicit orders from their membership. Except for the clubs that do their own printing, most clubs earn their profit from the difference between the cost of copies purchased from publishers and the price received from subscribers.

Although most clubs allow members to pick and choose selections, the Reader's Digest Book Club operates by requiring its members to take each and every volume offered during their term of subscription. The RDBC selects several titles to go into each monthly release, then condenses and edits them for both length and taste. In keeping with Reader's Digest's editorial policy, there are strictures against excessive sex and violence, hard-to-identify-with characters, and slow-moving or excessively philosophical, controversial, or experimental books.

Book clubs are a major source of book sales, the largest clubs reaching hundreds of thousands of subscribers, and one of them, the Reader's Digest, boasting approximately 1.5 million members. While condensation and/or expurgation of your book (and sharing of your royalties with companion authors in the same volume) may not thrill you, sale of your book to RDBC is a handsome score, with advances starting around $25,000.

For the biggest literary stars the advances paid by book clubs can be mind-boggling, such as the $1.75 million reportedly paid by the Literary Guild for James Michener's *The Covenant* after a bidding war with the Book-of-the-Month Club. BOMC's advance for a less-blockbusting main selection is still nothing to sniff at, around $80,000 on the average if there is bidding competition by other clubs. If, however, there are no bidders to bump up the action, book clubs may offer as little as they can get away with. In any event the advances paid by most clubs are usually below $10,000. Often, however, publishers can sell the same book to more than one club. Royalties usually range from 5 to 10 percent of the book club's price.

The money paid to publishers by book clubs is, with almost no exceptions, split equally between publisher and author, and in a great many cases the club income makes the difference between profit and loss for a publisher on a given book. Indeed, a former head of Book-of-the-Month Club told a gathering of literary agents that she considers book clubs the saviors of midlist books. It can certainly be argued that in an era of increasing attention to frontlist books, book clubs keep a great many books in print far longer than publishers themselves are able to do.

Although the key interface with book clubs is the book publisher, agents often cultivate book club executives in order to give them early notice of publication deals on books that might be hot prospects for the clubs. Some time ago, my agency performed the equivalent of passing a camel through the eye of a needle when we submitted an unsold manuscript directly to the Reader's Digest Book Club and secured a commitment from the Club to buy the book if we could find a publisher for it. We had failed up to then to sell this lovely family-type story that seemed to be too tame for the editors who had read it. But it was right up the RDBC's alley, and armed with a five-figure book club offer, we easily attracted a publisher for the book. But this was a rare event and we just happened to have the right book in the right place at the right time.

It's hard to imagine authors failing to be delighted by book club sales, but there have been a few. Willa Cather's arm had to be twisted to accept book club selection of *Shadows on the Rock* because she considered it crass exploitation of her work (authors had the oddest ideas in those days, too!). More recently, a number of authors, notably Stephen King, have objected to book club acquisition of their books on the grounds that club sales cut into sales of hardcover and even of paperback editions of the same book, losing them both readers and money.

Their reasoning is by no means without merit. Take a big-name author such as King whose book is published by a hardcover-paperback company that pays him, we can assume, a full royalty on both editions of his book. Suppose the hardcover edition sells for $25 and the paperback for $7. One thousand copies of the hardcover edition might bring in about $3,000 in royalties. One thousand copies of the paperback edition might bring in about $700. Now, suppose one thousand copies of the book club edition are sold at a 20 percent discount to subscribers, or $20. The royalty on those thousand copies will be about $1,300. But that money must be split fifty-fifty with the author's publisher, netting the author $650. Thus the book club's revenues are about 25 percent of what the author will get for the same number of copies sold in hardcover, and even a little lower than the royalties for the same number of paperback copies sold. Although it can be argued that the same thousand people who might buy the book through a book club wouldn't necessarily buy it in stores if it weren't carried by the club, you can nevertheless see how authors like King might view sales of their works to book clubs as losing propositions. The war between bookstores and book clubs still smolders, sixty years after the opening volley.

CHAPTER 24

Bookstore Buyers: The Book Stops Here

THE BOOKSTORE BUYER is the last link in the chain connecting author to reader. Or perhaps we should say he is the last obstacle between them, for as we track the life of a book from the time the author turns it in, we may well be put in mind of the upstream battle of a salmon against rapids, waterfalls, submerged rocks and trees, and a host of predators. Many perish before they reach the quiet headwaters, and most that make it are doomed as well. A book must struggle against all manner of challenges: the hazards of editorial judgment, the treacheries of corporate politics, the uncertainties of the economy, a host of human failings, and a congeries of unlucky or providential events.

The final, and perhaps most brutal, stretch in the obstacle course occurs when the publisher's sales representatives attempt to interest bookstore buyers in their forthcoming lists. These hardy men and women will have attended their publishers' sales conference, where scheduled books are introduced to them by the firms' editorial staffs. As we've seen, editors presenting their books accompany their pitches with pertinent information and sales aids: the author's track record, advertising and promotional plans, news of movie or magazine or foreign deals, anything, in short, that makes the book stand out from its partners on the publisher's list, or from the competition on the lists of other publishers. Then, bearing proofs, catalogues, covers or dust jackets, sales information, press kits, and novelty items such as buttons or bookmarks, the sales people make appointments to visit the buyers in their territories.

Before the advent of bookstore chains, these sales reps (or "travellers," as they were then known) visited individual bookshops and pitched their lists to each store owner or purchasing manager. The dialogue between buyer and sales rep reflected their joint interest in matching consumer reading tastes with the current and past lists of titles offered by each publisher. Although bookstore chains have been around for a long time, until recently these were not a significant factor in buying patterns, and the relationship between sales rep and store buyer was a highly personal one emphasizing local values.

The rise of the chains has revolutionized every aspect of book merchandising, not the least of which is that special bond between publisher and bookseller. The impact of this change cannot possibly be understated. The buying power of the chains is so highly concentrated and leveraged that even a modest order per store, multiplied by the number of stores in any given chain, can easily make the difference between success or failure for a given book; a larger order can put a book on the best-seller list or extend its stay on it for a long time. Indeed, some chains have their own best-seller lists on which publishers heavily rely in assessing sales activity of their books. To a disturbingly increasing degree, chain store buyers are being consulted by publishers about whether or not to acquire certain types of books, placing the buyer in effect on the editorial boards of some publishers.

The same power that can exalt a book can cast it down if the chain store buyers withhold their blessing. Thus, publishers are concentrating an ever-increasing portion of their time, energy, human and financial resources to currying favor with the chains at the expense of the independent bookstore. Not unexpectedly, this has resulted in the near-demise of the old-fashioned bookshop. These beloved emporia, with their casual atmosphere and library-like hush, with the visual and tactile delights of wonderful and interesting books everywhere the eye settles, with the varied stock reflecting the eclectic tastes of both owner and clientele— these are yielding one by one to the march of progress represented by clean, tidy, bland, efficient, convenient chain store branches with their homogenized stock, distinctly unbookish sales staffs, and computerized record-keeping and purchasing programs.

Individually owned shops cannot hope to compete with the discounted prices offered on frontlist books by the chains, nor can their low-volume turnover generate the kind of capital necessary to meet the rents in high-traffic urban and suburban shopping centers. Over the last few years, an association of small booksellers in northern California litigated with a publisher, Avon Books, alleging that Avon offered preferential discounts to book chains, a practice that the small stores maintain is widespread through the publishing industry. The store owners simply did not have the funds to prosecute their suit to the bitter end and were compelled at length to settle, leaving the issue unresolved but guaranteeing that preferential discounting in favor of the chains will continue to drive nails into the coffins of the small bookstores. At this writing, similar litigations are creeping through the courts.

Although they differ from one another in buying policies and patterns, discounting practices, and many other respects, fundamentally all chains function in much the same way. Their buying staffs receive sales representatives of publishers or publishing groups and listen to their spiels about forthcoming titles. The buyers then consult their records and sales data, review the information and material furnished by the publisher, and yes, they even read the books. After taking everything into consideration, the buyers put in their orders: some in large quantity, some in small. And sometimes, they don't buy any quantity at all.

How is business transacted in a typical buying office? Well, for one thing, you may safely believe that the publishers' reps talk fast. Given the large size of many publishers' lists, sales people have precious little time to give speeches. It has been estimated that they have between thirty and sixty seconds per title to get their message across. I suppose that if you divided their publisher's list precisely by the number of minutes granted to the rep for this interview, that estimate would be accurate. In fact, it doesn't quite work that way.

For one thing, there are some kinds of books that require little or no salesmanship: certain backlist books, for example. When the stock of Dr. Spock's *Baby and Child Care* or *The Random House Dictionary* falls below a certain number, it is usually reordered automatically. The latest novel in a long-running series may not call for extensive discussion. Some other types of books, such as most first novels, will seldom fetch large orders even if the sales rep talks himself blue in the face, unless it's something on the order of *The Hunt for Red October* by Tom Clancy. That is because the buying policies of the chain, or the parameters of the computer's purchasing program (more about this presently) simply prohibit a large order for first novels, and the experienced sales rep has learned to save his breath for pitching books for which there is more latitude (and potential for commissions). "Don't waste my time in the 'gimmes,'" one buyer is fond of saying. "Just tell me about your featured books." He is referring to such "product" as celebrity biographies, new books by best-selling authors, timely or controversial nonfiction books, and other books that the publisher believes will have "legs." On these the sales rep may soliloquize to his heart's content: he will invariably find an attentive listener.

What are the things that chain store buyers look and listen for when sales reps go into their routines? Bear in mind that salesmen are salesmen the world over, and whatever they are hawking there is usually a per-centage of blarney mingled with the truth. Astute buyers have learned to detect it, and because they are powerful and have at their disposal the best information-gathering capability this side of the Russian embassy, wise sales reps seldom bluff, bullshit, or soft-pedal the truth. "Don't tell me my market," another buyer told me he frequently says to sales reps.

The thing buyers most want to hear is, how much is the publisher getting behind the big books on its next list? A sales rep will boast of enormous "in-house" enthusiasm for a book, may show the buyer a fancy bound proof specially printed to impress the book trade, may inundate the buyer with tie-in gimmicks of all sorts, may tender to the buyer an invitation to publication party in a swank restaurant. Few of these induce-ments turn the buyer's head as much as a commitment by a publisher to advertising, publicity, and promotion. In particular, as one buyer reported to me, bookstore people are most impressed by plans for co-op adver-tising. As opposed to advertising that carries only the name of a book's publisher, co-op ads show the book's cover along with the name of the store: "Available at all XYZ Bookstores," such an ad might read. The cost of the ad is borne by both publisher and bookstore, and the publisher's commitment in hard dollars guarantees that the company will be getting strongly behind its product.

One of the most unsettling aspects of chain store buying practices is the use of computers to make decisions. As in so many other applications, the computer is both an invaluable tool and a frightening menace. It provides the book-buying office with highly detailed information about sales patterns on a book-by-book, author-by-author, store-by-store, region-by-region, publisher-by-publisher, basis, and the data are available instantly. Track records of previous books by any given author may be summoned by the touch of a finger or two on a computer keyboard, providing the buyer with all the input he needs to make his decision.

Some chains depend more heavily on computer data than others, and in many instances purchase orders are rigidly programmed: "If we bought 10,000 copies of that author's last book, we cannot buy more than 10 percent more copies of his next one, so put us down for 11,000." It is here that the greatest danger to literature may lie, for obviously this slavish devotion to ordering programs simply does not take into account such critical factors as a buyer's common sense, his instincts, and his personal enthusiasms. Most of all, it does not take into account the quality of the book in question, for even if an author's book is a quantum leap in quality over its predecessor, the buyer who has not read it—or even one who has—may be compelled by his own computer program to order the same number he would if the book were no better than the last.

It was comforting for me to learn, as I prepared this chapter, that there are still buyers, even in chain store offices, who care about books and authors and maintain a personal rapport both with publishers and consumers. The best buyers recognize the computer for the tool it is, but understand that a time comes when you have to walk away from the computer screen and go out among the customers.

Spencer Gale, a former executive of Doubleday Book Shops and of the Waldenbooks chain, believes that the vital information harvested by computers must be balanced by a humanistic approach to book ordering. "Computers don't read books and computers don't buy them," he told me. Doubleday Book Shops is a relatively small chain and its buying staff is small, too. Nevertheless, its buyers are presented all of the books that the larger chains are shown. These buyers must of necessity have a broader range of interests than those of their specialist counterparts in the giant chain offices. The staff constantly discusses books with each other, creating a sense of teamwork that makes Doubleday Book Shops' batting average—its ratio of sales to purchases—a respectable one. If one buyer says he just doesn't have a feel for a certain type of book or a specific author, he may defer to someone else in the office. One buyer for another store told me she conducts informal but highly accurate market surveys by showing new women's novels to her mother and highly touted young adult books to her teenage daughter. Good buyers look beyond their own predilections: "You are not buying for your taste alone," Gale expressed it.

Nevertheless, one gets the uneasy feeling that the noose around the throats of all who love literature is tightening with each step toward the consolidation and computerization of the publishing industry. The acquisition of B. Dalton by Barnes & Noble and the chain's move to New York City forge another massive link binding seller and buyer together. The intimacy between the publishing and bookstore businesses is now all but visible and palpable. It may legitimately be wondered what use sales reps will be in the future if there no longer is any distance for the "traveller" to travel. A phone call, a lunch date, a stroll across town, and the fate of a book could be sealed even before its acquisition by a publisher.

CHAPTER 25

Audits

OST BOOK PUBLISHERS' contracts have provisions granting authors the right to examine the books and records of their publishers under certain conditions: i.e., the examination must take place on the premises of the publisher during normal business hours; no more than two audits may be conducted in any given year; an audit must be commenced within a reasonable time after the issuance of the royalty statement in question; the records on any given book shall not be examined more than once; the publisher is not required to keep records on a book for more than a certain period of time, etc.

Although, I am told by one accountant, examinations of publishers' accounts are on the rise, invariably these have been conducted by authors with lucrative contracts. I can say with certainty that the vast majority of authors has only the vaguest notion of what is involved in an audit. Perhaps we can rectify that problem here. Harder to rectify is the somewhat bovine attitude on the part of many authors that their contracts are too small to merit auditing, and the royalties to be liberated by an examination of a publisher's books would not be worth the cost, which can run to a thousand dollars a day or more.

These assumptions are not necessarily correct. While a publisher's profits from midlist and category books are indisputably smaller than those from best-sellers, the *total* profits from the former can be immense by virtue of the fact that there are so many more of them on publishers' lists than there are best-sellers. And because most best-sellers are by established big-name authors, the huge royalties they earn are usually paid in advance, giving publishers little leeway to reserve royalties, whereas publishers commonly hold at least half the royalties collected on midlist and category books for which modest advances are paid.

If collective audits of such routine books could be undertaken, thus spreading the cost per author, they might well yield a surprisingly good return on the authors' investment in an accounting firm. More important, such group audits would keep publishers honest by exposing questionable accounting practices. It is therefore heartening to note that some author and agent organizations are sponsoring such group audits or making funds available for them. Because your book, or books similar to yours, might be spotlighted by an audit, you might want to tag along with the C.P.A. for a visit to a publisher's ledgers.

Before we embark, we ought to discuss just what gives us the right to audit a publisher, anyway. As I said at the outset, many publishers grant that right in the boilerplate language of their contracts. Certainly, every author or agent negotiating a book contract should insist on an audit provision. But if it is absent from a contract through oversight or design, or if a publisher refuses to grant that right to an author, does that necessarily rule out the possibility of an audit? Not according to the attorneys and accountants I have spoken to. They maintain that any licensor whose contract calls for royalties is entitled to examine the statements and supporting data of the licensee. Therefore, whether your contracts stipulate that right or not—indeed, even if you've been so foolish as to waive that right—your publisher cannot legally prohibit you from auditing his books. He can make it extremely difficult: he can postpone and stall, he can "misplace" and "lose" documents, he can subject your accountant to unpleasant conditions—a monastic cell with a hard chair, rickety table, and one flickering taper. But he must, ultimately, let your accountant go over the books.

Within recent memory there were some shady publishers who did that sort of thing, but happily they were driven out of business by their legitimate competitors. Today, while some publishers are frugal with their hospitality toward accountants, many shrug and say, "Come on in, we have nothing to hide."

Assuming your publisher is cooperative, the first step is for the accounting firm to make an appointment. The accountants will have examined the author's contract and all royalty statements from publication date to the present and will use these as the jumping-off point for their investigation. They will then request the printer's affidavits stating how many copies of the book were run off, along with information about damaged or destroyed copies. They will, of course, expect affidavits for all printings of the book. If there has been more than one printing, the accountants will want to know if the cover price of the book was raised.

Then the accountants will examine the records pertaining to distribution of the books, either to wholesalers or directly to book chains. The number of copies distributed plus the number of copies left in the warehouse plus the number of copies damaged, destroyed, or given away for free should add up to the number of copies printed. If they don't, suspicion will certainly be aroused that the publisher printed copies he has not reported.

The next critical source of information is copies returned. In hardcover publishing, the books themselves are returned to the publisher for credit, and counting these, while tedious, is not as stupefying a task as counting returned paperbacks, for the dimensions of hardcover printings and distributions are nowhere near those of paperback. In paperback publishing, however, returns are usually effected simply by stripping the covers off the bound books and returning the covers to the publisher's warehouse, saving the substantial cost of shipping whole books back whence they came.

Obviously, the job of counting paperback covers, which even for a modest-sized publisher number in the hundreds of thousands each month, is impossible to do by hand. Modern paperback houses handle the problem by printing product codes, those black-and-white coded bars similar to those you see on canned and packaged goods at your grocery store, on the backs of their book covers. The stripped covers are fed through machines that read the codes and compute title, author, list price, number of copies returned, and other data.

We now have all the information we need: number of copies printed, number of copies distributed, and number of copies returned. But there is still a gap between what the author feels is owed him and the actual amount of royalties he has been paid. That gap is the royalty on the number of copies the publisher has reserved against returns. As most authors now know, publishers create such reserves in order to give credit to distributors and stores that might return copies of books in the future. The reserve is determined by the executives who run the publishing company, and while it is to be hoped that these individuals will base their judgments on experience, reasonable evaluations of market conditions, and common sense, the existence of this tempting pool of undisbursed money has a tendency to cloud executive judgment, particularly in the pressure cooker of corporate bottom-line expectations.

Here, then, is the answer to the commonly asked question, "Is it possible for print, distribution, and return figures to be falsified?" The answer is, not without enormous difficulty, for it is neither safe nor practical to do so. For that to happen, the entire publishing organization—the clerks who document the printing and distribution information and count the returned covers, the bookkeeping and accounting departments of the publishing company, and the staffs of the printer and distributor—would have to be in on the conspiracy and sworn to secrecy. That is plainly preposterous: there simply isn't enough profit in the publishing business to make such wide-scale corruption worthwhile.

It is also completely unnecessary, because the same results are achieved by the decision of a handful of publishing officers to fix reserves against returns at an excessively high level. And it's all perfectly up-and-up from the publisher's viewpoint, because the establishment of reserves is a business judgment that may be argued but cannot be cited as fraudulent—unless one takes the position that the entire system is a license for publishers to earn interest at the expense of authors.

No, my observation is that print, distribution, and return information are not falsified, at least not in a way that could be described as deliberate and systematic. It would be closer to the truth to say that publishing bookkeeping is subject to the same goofs as the bookkeeping of any other industry. And though it may seem that the errors always fall in favor of publishers, the accountants I've spoken to state that as many fall in the authors' favor. Thanks in good measure to the consignment method of selling books, publishing bookkeeping is far, far more complex than it has to be, and that makes it a breeding ground for error.

One of the standard provisions of every audit clause in book contracts is that if errors of more than a certain amount, usually 10 percent of the sum stipulated in the publisher's royalty statement, are found by auditors, the publisher pays for the cost of the audit. Such a provision might make it tempting for authors who feel shortchanged by their publishers to hire an accountant, figuring the accountant will certainly be successful in detecting an excessive reserve against returns and get at least 10 percent of that reserve released. Thus the publisher would be required to pay for the audit, right?

Wrong. A high reserve against returns may not be considered an error. It's merely—in the publisher's eyes at least—a judgment call, a prediction or anticipation that a certain number of copies will be returned. Anybody contemplating an audit of his publisher's records should therefore be prepared not to recoup his accountant's fees from the publisher. Released royalties might defray or pay for the audit, but the publisher will stoutly maintain that no bookkeeping error was made.

Is there some alternative to hiring an accountant to find out whether your publisher is giving honest weight? Well, if you can prevail on your publishers to furnish you with information about the number of copies printed, distributed, and returned, you need nothing but a pencil and paper and a grade-school math education to figure out whether you have collected everything that is due you, and what the reserve against returns is. Then it's simply a matter of arguing with your publisher over the propriety of holding so much reserve money, or holding it for such a long time. The problem is getting that information: if publishers wanted you to have it, they'd put it up front routinely in their royalty statements. With persistence, however, you or your agent or your lawyer will be able to secure the information.

After reviewing it, however, you may feel in your bones or have other reason to believe that the figures furnished to you are incorrect, that your publisher printed or distributed more copies than he's told you, or took in fewer returns. You will then have to hire a professional accountant to examine the publisher's books, as the job is too complex and time consuming for untrained individuals. This is especially true if there is reprint, book club, foreign translation, or other subsidiary rights revenue— another very common source of bookkeeping errors among publishers but one that space prohibits me from analyzing in detail.

Some agents are able to build into book contracts provisions requiring publishers to furnish details of printing, distribution, returns, and reserves against returns in royalty statements, or copies of contracts and statements from sublicensees, such as book clubs and reprinters. For many agents and authors, however, it is futile to attempt to make publishers comply with such demands. This can only be achieved by collective action on the part of a determined, organized, and fearless cadre of professional writers or agents.

CHAPTERS 26

Never the Twain

M OST AUTHORS HAVE a simplistic notion about how books are marketed and sold to the movies. Their impression is that their literary agent, operating alone or with a Hollywood co-agent, submits a book to producers until he finds one who likes it enough to make an offer, the same way that book agents submit manuscripts to publishers. In truth the process is maddeningly complicated and confused and can daunt many otherwise sophisticated New York literary agents. And while some agents have better movie and television track records than others, none has formulated a single and satisfying solution to the challenge of efficiently finding the right producer for movie or television adaptations of books.

The film business is by no means a monolithic industry where purchases are made by only a handful of companies. Completely to the contrary, the world we know under the umbrella term "Hollywood" is kaleidoscopically fragmented. Countless producers, bankrollers, screenwriters, actors and actresses, directors, agents, studio and network executives, and coattail riders scramble endlessly to assemble "packages" that will stay still long enough to get a property purchased, developed, produced, and released.

The New York literary agent, faced with this jumble of elements and claims, is all too often at a loss to know with any certainty what is genuine and what is dross, particularly because, as one learns after even brief exposure, the lingua franca of the movie business is insincerity. Unlike the publishing business, where if somebody says he owns the rights to a book you may be fairly certain he's telling the truth, Hollywood swarms with people selling things they do not own. I call it the Hollywood Hustle, and I can name on the knuckles of one finger the people out there who do not practice it in some form. Hey, it's not that hard. Suppose you want to make a movie, and the only things you need are a book, a screenwriter, a director, a cast, a distributor, and $20 million. You start the ball rolling by, let's say, asking the agent of a famous movie star if the star would be interested in a certain book if a deal could be put together for it. Of course, the agent is going to say maybe. That's good enough for you. You now go to a screenwriter, show him the book, and ask him if he'd like to adapt it, and of course, the screenwriter is going to say, sure, why not, if the price is right, who have you got to star in the movie? And you say, you're negotiating with this star. And if you have just enough of a track record so that anyone bothering to check your background doesn't reveal a complete fraud, and if you talk fast and knowledgeably, you just may be able to line up enough interested parties so that one or two actually sign. You can then make the rounds clutching that contract and get the others to sign as well. Congratulations! You've just gotten full screen credit as a producer!

The reason it's hard for a New York agent, even one possessed of highly sensitive baloney detectors, to sort out the truth is that the movie and television businesses are characterized by an ever-shifting flow of power, capital, and influence, and it is labor enough to keep up with the scramble of musical chairs in the publishing field, let alone that of movies and television. New York agents respond in any of a number of ways: they employ a movie and television specialist to operate out of their New York City offices; they engage independent specialists based in New York City; or they engage West Coast movie agencies.

It would seem that the last choice is far and away the best solution. That may have been so ten or twenty years ago, but I do not believe it is necessarily so today.

When I first came into publishing, the movie industry was still something of a definable, organic entity. A handful of powerful studios controlled the assembly of movie packages, and three networks controlled television programming. And because the field was more orderly, the role of the West Coast agent was, too. West Coast agents did in fact do for movie rights what East Coast agents do for book rights: they offered novels or original screenplays to movie producers and studio story departments, negotiated deals, took a commission, and remitted payment to the author or the author's literary agent.

As the 1960s and 1970s progressed, however, and the unified studio system gave way to one based on independent producers, artists, and sources of finance, the West Coast agents' approach shifted. They began accepting "talent," such as producers, directors, and actors, for representation. These clients sought the agents' help in negotiating their fees and acquiring literary or screenplay properties that they could produce, direct, or star in. Quite clearly, these agents were sailing into uncharted and very dangerous waters, for they no longer represented sellers only; they now also represented buyers as well, and in a growing number of instances they represented both the buyer and the seller of the same property or service. This is clearly a conflict of interest, because representation of buyer and seller makes it impossible for an agency to handle a negotiation at arm's length, as the legal phrase is.

The creature emerging from this broth was the agent-packager, a breed that assembles movie and television deals out of client components within each agency's own client list. The dilemma of which client to take the commission from—the buyer or the seller—was resolved by creating a "packaging fee" that is negotiated off the top of the total money available to finance the package deal. The net money after deduction of the packaging fee is then distributed according to the formula negotiated by the agent-packager with each client.

Students of power dynamics will realize that the distribution of these net monies, including those paid to authors for the rights to their literary properties, may be manipulated if not arbitrarily assigned by a shrewd agent (and West Coast agents are nothing if not shrewd). Indeed, the function of the West Coast agent-packagers seems to be identical to that of the old-time movie studios, with the exception that the agent-packagers do not actually distribute movies or air the television programs they package. To put it succinctly, the West Coast agent no longer represents the seller vis-à-vis the buyer; he *is* the buyer!

The New York literary agent surveying the West Coast scene sees arrayed before him a growing number of agent-packager-producers, and in due time it may dawn on him that these outfits are in competition with each other. Each West Coast agency has its own client list out of which the components for a deal are selected, and although those agencies do work out deals with one another in order to obtain the services of each other's clients, it can safely be stated that the desirable route is to cull the package entirely out of the agency's own stable.

What this means for authors and their New York literary agents is that West Coast agents are no longer as capable of thoroughly covering the movie and television markets, as they used to be. If you or your agent engage a West Coast agent to sell movie or television rights to your book or story, you should be aware that that agent may not be accepting the mandate with clean hands, to use another legal phrase.

Another reason New York agents don't always like to turn their properties over to West Coast agencies is that it means splitting a commission with them. On the average, New York agents charge 15 percent commissions on movie and television deals. If they let a West Coast agency make a deal for them, they'll have to give that agency at least half of their commission, and maybe more than half: some West Coast agents feel that because they do most of the work on such deals, they should get a higher percentage of the commission.

While many New York agents reason that 5 percent or 7.5 percent of something is better than 15 percent of nothing, the big numbers paid for movie and television rights can make an agent excusably greedy, and many therefore try to handle those rights themselves. It is not an easy task, for they must keep up with ever-changing industry buying patterns, personnel changes, news, and gossip, and in the movie business even more than in books, timing is critically important: you have to be there with the right property at the right time, and know the right person to call. Frequent trips to California may be necessary to meet and deal with the movers and shakers out there.

The fact that the movie studios, networks, and many major producers have New York offices, story departments, and scouts makes it seem easier for a New York literary agent to conduct movie and television business in Manhattan. To a degree that is true, but not to a sufficient degree. The New York offices of West Coast firms are good for expediting the submission of literary properties (and they're great for extending screening invitations to literary agents), but almost none has the authority to purchase or negotiate. Furthermore, it is not always desirable to give early looks at upcoming hot properties to New York scouts and story departments. In fact, it is often important not to let them get their hands on those properties. There is only a small number of studios and networks, and if they all "pass" on a property—turn it down—it will effectively be dead. A commonly held view of the people who read and screen properties for studios and networks is that they are not notable for their vision and imagination, and that they operate on the bureaucratic principle that it is safer to say no than yes.

Many New York agents therefore feel that it is much better to offer their properties to producers who can visualize a work's cinematic values and who have at their command the financing and industry connections to put together an impressive package that they can bring to studio and network brass. But which producers to offer those properties to? Aye, my friends, there's the rub, and it brings us right back to the desirability of going through West Coast agencies.

There simply doesn't seem to be a satisfactory answer, and perhaps the best that can be said for agents on the opposite coast is what is often said about people of the opposite sex: You can't live with 'em, and you can't live without 'em.

CHAPTER 27

Books into Movies

I

T'S OFTEN SAID that they're not making movies the way they used to. That's a matter of opinion (it happens to be mine), but if it's true, the decline can be attributed to the fact that they're not adapting books the way they used to. Since the golden age of filmmaking in the 1930s, the ratio of theatrical films based on books to those made from original screenplays has been steadily shifting to the latter. Today the odds that your novel will be made into a movie are distressingly low, even if your novel becomes a best-seller.

I can't believe there are fewer adaptable books today than there have been in the past. Why, then, aren't they making books into movies anymore?

One reason facetiously offered by book people is that nobody in Hollywood reads. Relying on my own experience, I'd have to say that's untrue. What is probably closer to the mark is that movie people don't have a lot of time to read, but then, neither do book people. Most of us are so busy reading manuscripts for business that we can't spare a moment to read for pleasure. While I, like so many of my colleagues, can read three or four book-length manuscripts in one evening, I have been plodding through a published biography, at a rate of a few pages a week for over two years; it's taking me longer to read that sucker than it took the author to write it!

At any rate, what little reading time movie people have is usually spent reading screenplays. Books are synopsized for them by readers, and only if a reader's recommendation makes the book sound as if it has strong movie potential will a producer read the book itself. And sometimes not even then.

The downward trend in film adaptations follows the decline of the studio system and the corresponding rise of one revolving around independent producers. Under the old arrangement, all-powerful studios acquired best-sellers and other literary properties and adapted them for producers, directors, and stars belonging to the studio "family." The studios were self-contained entities possessing financing, production facilities, and distribution capability—the three elements essential to making commercial films. After World War II, however, producers, writers, actors, and others challenged the studios in a bid for more artistic independence and a bigger piece of the profit pie. They succeeded to a degree in weakening the studios' absolute power and control, but at a high cost: the loss of efficiency. Today's producers cannot simply scoop up all the talent they need from one studio pool, but instead have to assemble "packages" out of a fiendishly complex and far-flung tangle of artists, agents, lawyers, unions, guilds, financiers, smaller distributors, and other elements.

This radical change has taken its toll on adaptations of books. Let's see how.

The hardest part of getting a movie made is raising the money. It is easier to raise a sunken treasure galleon than to raise money for a movie. These days a film budgeted at $20 million is considered a home movie; indeed, $20 million is now the salary of a superstar. Still, it's a lot of money, and anyone furnishing it to a filmmaker expects either an excessive participation in profits or an excessive say in the way the movie is made, both of which are abhorrent to a producer. Studios are not disposed to back films until all elements of the package are in place, or at least a "bankable" star or director has made a commitment.

In short, few independent producers have any money. Not long ago—twenty or twenty-five years—we used to see a number of outright purchases of books for movies. Though an outright purchase doesn't guarantee a movie will be made, the size of the outlay, often hundreds of thousands of dollars, certainly guaranteed an earnest effort would be made to recoup the investment. Today, one seldom hears about outright sales. Everything is optioned. When independent producers start piecing together a movie deal, the item on which they least want to spend what little money they possess is the book; for them, the key item is the screenplay.

The screenplay opens the doors to securing financing by stimulating the interest of stars and their agents, and then to assembling the rest of the elements. Once these all come together and the money has been put up to make the film, the author can be paid. Until then the author is in effect asked to subsidize the writing of the screenplay by being moderate in his asking price for the option. In many cases authors are asked to give producers a free or nominal option against a big purchase price and share of the profits. These strangely unbalanced deals—often options of a few hundred dollars against purchase prices of hundreds of thousands—result from the fact that the option money has to come out of the producer's own pocket, whereas the purchase money comes out of someone else's.

Although there is a lot of activity in options of books for the movies, it can be argued that the option system is actually harmful to a book's chances of being made into a movie. Options are usually purchased in six- or twelve-month increments, but are renewable at the producer's option for several more six- or twelve-month periods with the payment of additional option money. The process can tie up a book for eighteen months, two years, or longer while the producer frantically tries to juggle screenplay, financing, distribution, director, and stars in the hopes of getting them to sign a contract. Nobody wants to sign a contract until he has a guarantee. The financiers may want a distribution commitment before they fork over their money; the director may want a particular star to agree to appear in the film; the star may want a terrific screenplay; the screenplay writer may want a huge fee; the studio may want the book to be on the best-seller list.

Since the odds against everyone signing are so high, it's likely that when the option or renewal lapses, your book will have been shopped all over the movie business. Though you'll then have an opportunity to market the rights again and pursue those who might have been interested in your book a year or two ago, the book will probably have the smell of death clinging to it, and you'll be unable to revive it.

Clearly, it's a lot cheaper and easier for a modestly heeled producer to option or commission an original screenplay than to get involved with books. But with the kinds of movies that are pulling in big bucks at the box office these days, it may reasonably be asked, "What do producers need books for, anyway?" So many of these films are youth-oriented, exploitive, devoid of ideas, predictably plotted, action-packed, and populated with stick-figure characters. A producer contemplating making one of these teenage fantasy films is certainly not going to seek those values in books. Indeed, he would have to search far and wide to find books dumb enough to make into today's hit movies.

Interestingly, the one area in the entertainment industry where books are still welcome, and in fact welcome as never before, is television, and the immense appetite of the networks and cable companies does not threaten to diminish in the foreseeable future. Publishers' lists are combed furiously by producers seeking movie-of-the-week or miniseries candidates, and because of network commitments to air scores of these films annually, the search has become intensely competitive. Many of the properties optioned or acquired are novels, but television producers, unlike theatrical film producers, plunder short stories, articles, and nonfiction books as well as novels in their quest for adaptable material.

Ironically, the quality of television movies now often exceeds that of many theatrical films. Once characterized as a vast wasteland, television has discovered ideas and begun to develop them into vehicles that are often intelligent, sensitive, moving, and controversial, touching on themes that the movies used to portray but seldom do any more. Out-of-wedlock children, incest, senility, spouse or child abuse, drug addiction, kidnapping, and physical disability are some of the themes that have been woven into recent original television movies, and few who have watched them can claim that they are inferior to most theatrical films made today or that they are not the equal of many made in the past.

From the viewpoint of the author with a book to sell, this change is of major importance, for it no longer is smart to disdain television deals while holding out for a theatrical one. It is likelier that an option will be exercised for a TV movie than for a theatrical one, and the price gap between the two media has begun to close. And, from the viewpoint of pride of authorship, the chances are better than ever that an author's vision will be preserved intact in a television adaptation. For all these reasons I recommend that if you or your agent are approached by producers interested in adapting your work for television, and the terms are comparable to what you might get from a movie-movie producer, don't hesitate to make that deal.

Here are some other suggestions for improving your chances of making a movie or television sale in today's market.

- *Prepare an extremely brief—no more than two pages—synopsis of your book to show to interested producers.* It should be a highly compressed summary of the theme, story, and characters, and should read like a jacket blurb except that the emphasis should be on the cinematic values rather than the literary ones. Potential buyers will want to see the manuscript, proof, or printed copy anyway, but if they have time to read nothing else they will read your summary, and a well-written one will enable them to visualize the film the way you yourself visualize it.

- *Give no free options, even of a few weeks' duration.* Inevitably you will be approached by would-be producers claiming they know exactly the right studio or network executive who will buy your book, and all they need is a couple of weeks to make a deal, and could you let them have just this one shot free of charge because by the time the papers are drawn up it will be too late, etc. Most agents who have dealt with movie and television people have heard this line before and shut the door on it; they've learned that people don't respect properties they get for nothing. An investment in an option guarantees a certain amount of commitment and responsibility. You don't have to draw up a complete movie contract for such a modest deal, but a deal memorandum synopsizing the highlights of the negotiation, such as option price, purchase price, profit percentages if any, duration of option and renewals, reserved rights, credits, and so forth, is a must.

As for that claim that the producer needs only a few weeks, don't believe it. Everything in the movie business takes six times longer than you would imagine it should. I have seldom seen a movie option exercised after six months, and indeed have seen producers dig themselves into an awful hole by paying too much money for too brief an option, necessitating their renewing the option for too much money again for yet another brief option. The author who finds himself in the position of dealing with such a producer enjoys the rare pleasure of being in the driver's seat, so if someone wants a short option, give it to him, but make him pay for it.

- *Renewals of a producer's option on your work should be more expensive than the original option and should not be deductible from the purchase price of the rights.* The initial option is usually applicable against the purchase price, but thereafter the producer is in effect paying rent on your property. If you allow him to deduct renewal fees from the purchase price, he is in effect not renting your property but buying it from you in installments, and relatively painless installments at that. You'll want that lump sum due upon exercise of the option to hang over the producer's head like some ominous cloud. And, by making renewals more expensive than the original option, you are telling the producer that tying your property up for such a long time is an inconvenience, and one that is not mitigated by the money he's paying you to extend your option.

- *If you option your book before publication, try to negotiate the deal in such a way that the option expires around your publication date and is not renewable beyond that date.* Your property will probably never be hotter to movie people than before it's published, when it will not have been exposed to the entire industry or shopped all over town. Thus anyone taking an option before publication is getting your work at its ripest moment. If, by the time the book is published, your producer has not been able to make a deal, his option should expire, and expire without hope of renewal. If your book then goes on to get good reviews and/or hits the best-seller list, you have a second lease on life.

↝

CHAPTER 28

Take This Job and Shove It

MOST WRITERS DREAM of leaving their day jobs (some have night jobs as well) and launching careers as full-time freelancers. In their eagerness to realize that goal, many of them quit as soon as they've made a few sales. This decision invariably turns out to be ill-advised if not catastrophic after the author discovers that he did not properly reckon the cost of independence, project the size and flow of earnings, or prepare himself psychologically. Even an author lucky enough to strike it rich on his first book should use the utmost restraint before quitting his job to become a writer. By the time he realizes he doesn't know what to write for an encore, he may have raised his lifestyle to an unsupportably high plateau.

The questions of whether and when writers should go full-time are among the most common and vexing that agents have to deal with, and if an agent ever had a notion to play God, here is his opportunity. The responsibility for this decision is awesome and demands ten times the prudence required to advise authors about such matters as selecting the right publisher for their books. The number of factors is large and their complexity intimidating. It's the kind of decision that should be reviewed with a great many people to collect as much input as possible.

An excellent idea is to make a list of pluses and minuses, what you stand to gain and what to lose. Often the right choice will jump out at you when you review this list. The secret is to make sure you have enumerated all the factors. Then you must be brutally honest with yourself. You do not want to subject yourself and your family to needless suffering because you erred on the side of wishful thinking when you drew up your scenario.

My first rule of thumb is to determine whether you have enough work lined up *under contract* to guarantee employment for one to two years; that probably means you have reached a level of skill and reliability your publisher can count on. I seldom permit an author to include in his expectations income that is not absolutely guaranteed—royalties, foreign rights sales, movie deals, and the like—unless there is a solid history of such windfalls in his track record. If you've never sold British rights to your previous books, if you only *hope* your next book will earn royalties, if your father-in-law *thinks* your book is a natural for the movies, I toss these items out of the equation, because they are only fodder for self-delusion and disappointment.

I do, however, include in the equation the renewal of current contracts after you have fulfilled them, particularly if you are a genre writer. If you have a three-book contract in an ongoing series, I tend to consider it a likelihood that you'll be given another contract at the expiration of this one. If you're an established mainstream writer with three or four books under your belt and a potful of good ideas for new ones, I'm disposed to take for granted that you'll land a new contract when you complete your present book.

The renewal of contracts means money payable on signature of those agreements, so that when you look down the road for money to be earned after fulfillment of your present commitments, you should be able to count on income from new deals. It is also reasonable to figure that you'll get more money per book than you're getting now, because it's likely the publisher will feel you're a better writer and there'll be more of a sales record to justify raises. There is also a tendency among publishers to give raises to their regular writers if for no other reasons than inflation, longevity, loyalty, faith in the future, and humane motivations. You have to ask for these raises, but there's a good chance that if you don't push it too hard, your publisher will give you a little more the next time around just because you're a nice person.

Another important factor I weigh when discussing with authors the decision to go full-time is increased productivity.

At present, because you're only able to devote an hour or two to your writing in the evenings, and maybe twice that much on the weekends, you are not capable of turning out more than two books, say, per year. But if you launch a full-time writing career, you may be able to double or triple your annual output, meaning double or triple the revenue. There is also, I've observed, a tendency for writers to improve the quality of their work after they become full-timers, because they're exercising their skills to a greater degree, and (domestic distractions notwithstanding) their concentration increases. And if you do become a better, faster writer, the prospects for raises in pay from your publishers become even better. The process, in due time, becomes self-perpetuating.

Having painted the future in broad, and slightly rose-tinted, strokes, it's time to focus on the hard realities of budgeting your money after you make The Big Move. Get out that legal pad and set up two columns, Income and Expenditures. So far, so good. Unfortunately, that's about the only straightforward thing about setting up a budget, because when you start to analyze each item, you quickly see that simple concepts and definitions are elusive.

When you work for "the man," you most likely receive a regular paycheck from which certain mandatory deductions are withheld. Among these are federal and state income taxes, sometimes municipal ones as well. Social security contributions are also compulsory. Then there may also be deductions for disability insurance, worker's compensation, medical insurance, union dues, stock option purchases, pension contributions, and donations to the boss's pet charity. Your net take-home income has been 20, 40, even 50 percent or more of your gross salary.

When you become a full-time writer, however, you suddenly find yourself in the position of "taking home" a "paycheck" from which nothing (except commissions, if you have an agent) has been deducted. At first glance that's great. At second and third glances, you realize that the heavy burden of responsibility for many of those obligations, formerly taken care of by your boss, now rests on your own shoulders. You will have to set aside enough money to pay income taxes, social security, and other taxes such as unincorporated business taxes, occupancy taxes on your business property (your office, that is); medical and/or disability insurance premiums; pension contributions (you may now qualify for a Keogh

Plan savings account); and whatever other "benefits" you wish to continue enjoying as carryovers from your erstwhile job. So, the $50,000 per annum that you project taking home when you go full-time may translate into less than $25,000 of disposable income after you set aside all the obligations your employer used to pay on your behalf.

To your projections of income from your writing, add income from your spouse's job if any, investment dividends and savings interest, and other sources of guaranteed revenue such as teaching, lecturing, or consulting income. And you must not rule out your savings as a potential source of income. Because delays are more the rule than the exception in the publishing game, it is entirely possible that you will have to tap the principal in your savings account or liquidate a long-term investment in order to tide yourself over between checks.

Because many major expenses are payable quarterly (such as estimated federal taxes), semiannually, or even annually, you might consider opening a savings account for those obligations only. You can then earn a little interest on the money you have set aside to pay those bills. Needless to say, you must never invest that money in speculative ventures.

When you try to tote up the "expenditures" side of your projections, you once again discover that nothing is as simple as it seemed to be when your boss took care of things. You will immediately see how costly medical insurance is, particularly when you are no longer participating in a group health care plan. The social security rate for self-employed people is higher than for those in "respectable" jobs (writing has not been a respectable job for twenty-five years).

And then there are those "bennies" and perks you took for granted when you worked for that company. If you had an expense account, you will now have to absorb that portion of the benefit that was formerly spent on yourself, in particular travel and entertainment. No longer can you charge the firm for your spouse's meal when you take clients or customers to dinner; no longer can you bill your boss for mileage incurred on that side visit to Disneyland during your business trip to Los Angeles. And because current tax law permits you to deduct only a percentage of legitimate entertainment expenses, you've also lost that part that your company absorbed in tax on the undeductible part. Say good-bye to the free use of the postage machine when you mailed off your personal bills; to the telephone from which you called your publisher, your agent, your kid in college, your mother in Florida; to the photocopying machine on which you ran off copies of your manuscript after everyone had gone home; and to the office word processor, computer, coffee maker. Say good-bye to the paid vacation. You want a vacation, you now can take fifty-two weeks a year if you want, only you have to pay for them out of your own pocket. Say good-bye to sick days on salary. Say good-bye to the company car and the company jet and the company dining room. Buy your own car and jet and dining room.

I am not saying there aren't also many hidden benefits to leaving our job for a full-time writing career. But somehow, the savings on carfare or on the expensive wardrobe you're trading in for the freelancer's uniform of jeans and T-shirts don't seem to balance the hidden costs. And not everybody fervently believes that getting to see more of one's spouse or kids is a hidden benefit.

The biggest challenge to the newly independent is the large lump-sum payments due with unforgiving regularity throughout the year. Among these, as I've said, are quarterly estimated federal income and social security taxes, but there are also state and local taxes and estimates and medical insurance premiums. This is not to mention those other lump sums you have to pay whether you are self-employed or not, such as automobile and home insurance, private school or college tuition, summer camp fees, repair contracts on major appliances, and the like. And these all have a way of going up. Add to them the cost of occasional but inevitable contingencies, the kind that always seem to rear their heads hours after your warranties expire and moments after you have served notice to your boss of your intention to leave his employ; washing machines giving up the ghost, television picture tubes burning out, automobile engines seizing, wisdom teeth impacting.

Aside from being fiscally unprepared to deal with these aggravations, you may not be emotionally able to cope with them. This is by far the graver problem, for while you can often juggle your accounts or hustle up some money to cover short-term deficits, it is much, much harder to find the psychological resources for dealing with that condition of perpetual anxiety about money that is the lot of most freelance people.

The truth is that not everybody is constitutionally cut out to work for him- or herself. There are those who are incapable of preparing a budget or of staying within its rigid boundaries. There are those who cannot handle the loneliness of freelancing and the loss of the social support that comes from working with others. There are those who lack self-discipline, those who, after years of punching in and out at a time clock, reporting to a boss or supervisor, adhering to rules and regulations and work orders, are at a loss to structure their own time. There are those who cannot set short- and long-term goals or keep to them. There are those who cannot live with the distractions of full-time domesticity. There are those who go to pieces at the prospect of drawing on their savings or selling off an investment to cover an unexpected expense. There are those who indulge their newfound freedom by tackling that Great American Novel they've always dreamed of, instead of doing the commercial projects that have to be done to keep their finances on a steady course.

Having tried the freelance life for several years in my twenties, I can testify to having flunked most of the above tests. Though I did produce a goodly number of books during that period, and earned a decent living, I found the loneliness and isolation very hard to bear, and the budgeting of money impossible. I had some savings salted away, but having been raised to think of drawing money out of savings as tantamount to filing for bankruptcy, I suffered woefully. Every month, when the time came to pay my bills, I developed all sorts of neurasthenic symptoms ranging from vapors to hysterical pregnancy. So, be as candid with yourself as you can be when you contemplate making this critical career decision, and ask your spouse, your best friend, your accountant, your attorney, your shrink, and your agent to be so, too. If they vote yes, then all you'll need is a ream of paper, a pair of jeans, and a few T-shirts, and you're in business.

Oh yes—don't forget $100,000 worth of book contracts!

CHAPTER 29

Breakout Books

FROM TIME TO TIME a writer bursts upon the literary scene with a first novel of astonishing accomplishment, and the world gasps as if witnessing the genesis of a supernova out of a hitherto undetected star. Critics poring over the author's pedigree for clues to his development usually find only such banal biographical facts as that he was a reporter for his high school yearbook or a bridge columnist for some obscure midwestern newspaper. But this author had apparently been struck to his knees by a sublime inspiration and spewed the work out of his soul in one volcanic eruption. One thinks of *Catch-22, The Naked and the Dead, Gone with the Wind,* or *Raintree County.* In some cases the author never again rises to the height of his first book, and in not a few the author never writes another book at all. But that first book is enough to make the author's name a household one forever after.

Professional writers often greet such events with mixed emotions. On the one hand they cannot help but join in the outpouring of adulation. On the other, if they are honest with themselves they will probably confess to intense envy. For, this . . . this *amateur* has somehow hit a grand slam home run on his very first time at bat, has achieved in one stroke something that most writers may never achieve in their lifetime, or may achieve only after decades of struggle and sacrifice: a breakout novel.

It is always instructive to examine a society's underlying assumptions, and it seems to me that the big breakout has become an article of faith for everybody involved in the world of books, from publisher to critic to consumer. What disturbs me is that it has also become an article of faith for writers. But before I elaborate on that statement, let's see if we can define a breakout book.

Implicit in the term is that there is something to break out from. In many cases it is a body of work in a genre, such as romance, science fiction, mystery, or western. Or it may simply be what is opprobriously termed the "midlist," that purgatorial place between success and failure occupied by books that are good but not good enough, bad but not that bad, promising, interesting, nice, pleasant, okay, and a lot of other less-than-hyperbolic adjectives, books that are profitable enough to tantalize or not unprofitable enough to discourage.

The world of genre and midlist books is populated by writers whose fates are still being fashioned by the gods. Some of them will remain in their comfortable niches forever, content with nonhyperbolic work and relieved that there is always a buyer for their books. Others will hang in long enough to see their books hailed as venerable classics, probably after it is too late for them to appreciate it. Still others will drop (or be driven) out. And others still will break (or be broken) out.

The breakout process occurs in a number of ways. An influential critic "discovers" an author and proclaims his greatness to the world. This happened with William Kennedy (*Ironweed*) and John Irving (*The World According to Garp*). Thriller writer John D. MacDonald awoke one Sunday morning after toiling for decades to find his latest Travis McGee detective novel hailed on the front page of the influential *New York Times Book Review*. Or perhaps an army of loyal readers will storm the bookstores and cast a favorite into the pantheon by popular acclaim, as happened to Alice Walker and *The Color Purple*. Sometimes reading tastes veer unpredictably, exalting a cult figure into the mainstream, such as John Barth whose *The Sotweed Factor* was a college classic for a generation but until recently a well-kept secret from mass audiences. And finally there is the author who, by dint of Herculean effort, catapults himself (with the help of a substantial capital investment by his publisher) into the front rank with a work that shatters the mold of his former creations. It is this type that most publishing people mean when they talk about breaking out. So let's look at it a little more closely.

The breakout book marks a departure in quantity and quality. Often it is actually, physically, larger than previous works. Genre paperbacks range from fifty thousand to one hundred thousand words, generally speaking, and midlist hardcover fiction is seldom longer than, say, eighty-five thousand words. In order to justify the higher price that publishers charge for lead fiction, they look for works of at least one hundred thousand words, and in many cases the books run far longer. Recent best-sellers by some famous denizens of best-seller list summits are over one thousand printed hardcover pages long, extending to as much as half a million words between covers. Although these works can't be defined as breakout books, since the authors have long and successful track records, they do illustrate the difference between best-selling authors, who are encouraged to write thick books, and midlist authors who are importuned to keep the length down. Although you may be able to break out with a gemlike Slim Little Volume, the tendency among star authors is definitely toward heft, for heft is equated, for better or worse, with importance.

Naturally, I don't mean merely padding a hundred-thousand-word novel with fifty or a hundred thousand more words. The plot must be proportionately more complex, the time span longer, the characters more numerous and treated in greater depth, the mise-en-scène more elaborate, the details of time and place portrayed with greater attention. And even with all these elements, unless the author has breathed life into the work, it will not fly.

It's hard to say just what it is that makes the difference. It's not necessarily the writing, for horribly written books are exalted onto the best-seller lists all the time, and if you've been a bad writer all your life, it's not likely your breakout book will be better written than anything else you've ever done. But there is certainly a departure in quality that marks the breakout book. Publishing people sometimes refer to it as the author "finding his voice," meaning that he has fused a large, original, worthy subject and well-honed skills with the flame of inspiration and love.

And so, while the book may belong in a superficial sense to a category, it will amalgamate traditional category elements and formulas with that unique viewpoint, theme, style, passion—with that "voice"—to create something entirely new and grand and wonderful. The whole will be larger than its parts, so that it is not merely a super-romance or a super-mystery, a super-western or a super-science fiction novel. In a sense it will be a new genre. For example, occult and horror fiction were here long before Stephen King, but he transmuted the genre and stamped his name on it, as did Louis L'Amour with westerns, Georgette Heyer with period romances, Danielle Steele with contemporary romances, and Ray Bradbury, Arthur C. Clarke, and Robert Heinlein with science fiction.

Implicit in the breakout event is the sense that the author's metamorphosis is permanent, and that henceforth he or she may be counted on to produce a consistent body of work in the same vein as the book that broke out. Reading the work of today's best-selling authors, you get a strong impression that they're not merely striving to repeat a winning combination, but rather have discovered their true identities in their books. James Michener with his geographical sagas, Harold Robbins, Judith Krantz, and Barbara Taylor Bradford with their sex-and-power fantasies of the super-rich, John Jakes with his American historicals mingling fictional and factual characters, Sidney Sheldon with his tales of lust and vengeance—you might well wonder if in these instances soul, style, and story have not been blended into one entity.

As I'm drifting treacherously close to the metaphysical, let me bring you back to earth with a simple definition: you know an author has broken out when publishers start commissioning imitations, referring to the authors as if they were registered brand names. "I want a western family saga a la Louis L'Amour's *Sacketts,* or maybe a little sexier like Janet Dailey's *Calders,*" one might hear at the luncheon table. Or, "I'm looking for a writer to do England the way John Jakes has done America." Or, "Do you have a client who can portray Madison Avenue the way Judith Krantz did Rodeo Drive?"

The big breakout requires, of course, the complete commitment of the publisher. But though you might think publishers are dying to push a ton of chips behind anything faintly resembling a breakout book, in truth they feel rather ambivalent about the process. For one thing, obviously, it costs an awful lot of money, and the premature launch of an unripened author, or a misjudgment about the "breakoutability" of a book, can create catastrophic losses and profound embarrassment followed by the sound of rolling heads. Publishers often therefore err on the side of caution, preferring to launch their breakout campaign only after the "numbers" on previous books by that author are immense, rather than hype somebody who has not built a broad audience. But by the time the publisher reaches the conclusion that the author's moment has come, the author may be gone: his agent will have found a publisher that wasn't so ambivalent.

From time to time, readers will actually be ahead of a publisher in the creation of a breakout. Publishers sometimes underestimate an author's popularity and the demand for his work. In due time, the groundswell of demand for an author will be felt in a publisher's office, thanks to reports by the salesmen out in the field, and if the publisher is smart he'll ship as many copies of the next book as the traffic will bear. But if he is not alert, he'll lose the author to a house that is. This happened when thriller writer Dick Francis switched from Harper and Row to Putnam, where he now enjoys best-selling hardcover sales of every new book. Putnam knew the potential was there and detected the clamor that Francis's previous publisher failed to hear.

I sometimes wonder whether writers shouldn't step back and question whether breaking out is all it's cracked up to be. While success has been a goal in all ages, I don't think I am romanticizing the past in stating that the pressure to succeed has never been more intense for writers than it is now. Thirty-five years ago when I came into this business, there was among writers some sense that a life of quiet literary accomplishment book after book, the appreciation of a small but discriminating audience, and an income sufficient to support a middle-class lifestyle were worthy ideals. It was joy enough to be read; the heart swelled to see somebody reading one's book on the subway or to come across it in a library (remember libraries?).

Today such goals seem not merely unattainable to most writers, but inconceivable. Although the shift in thinking has been evolutionary, for many writers the realization impacted in the late 1960s and early 1970s, when a series of blockbusters starting with *The Godfather* altered our thinking. No longer was it enough for a book to be read: it had to be experienced by the Global Village, had to become an international mass market multimedia event, in order for the author to feel fulfilled. Such feelings are promulgated and perpetuated by publishers and the press in the form of the "blockbuster mentality," adding to the conviction most writers today have that they are faced with but two options: go for the jackpot or become a janitor. The anxiety generated by these forces is enormous. Authors no longer feel that they have time to patiently develop craftsmanship, to build an audience, to attract the attention of critics— in short, to become professional writers. Instead they feel they must come roaring off the blocks with a spectacular work.

❧

Section Four

SINS OF
COMMISSION

CHAPTER 30

Publishing Spoken Here

I'VE OFTEN THOUGHT that one of the critical roles literary agents play is that of translator. We perform the task on several levels. The most obvious and fundamental is explaining the nomenclature of publishing to the uninitiated author. The writer who sells his first book to a publisher and reads his first contract is plunged into a sea of words that may be totally unfamiliar to him, or that are used in a totally unfamiliar way. "Force majeure," "net proceeds," "matching option," "warranty," "discount"—these need to be defined for the novice author. There are many difficult concepts to be grasped, such as "advance sale," "midlist," "fair use," "reserve against returns," "pass-through," and "hard-soft deals." The language has its own slang, too, and our initiate hears bewildering references to who handles the "sub-rights," what is the tentative "pub date," and what happens when the book is "o.p.'d."

Agents patiently try to demystify these terms, but it may take many years of experience before our clients are completely at ease with them. It may well be true that what distinguishes professional authors from their amateur brothers and sisters is that the pros have undergone this linguistic rite of passage, and are now able to sling around "pre-empts," "first proceeds," and "escalators" with the best of 'em.

But there is another, and profoundly more important, job for the agent-translator to perform beyond explaining to his clients the terminology of the book industry. I'm talking about using language to forge and strengthen the bonds between authors and publishers. For, while the goals of both may ultimately be identical, they are usually achievable only after many conflicting viewpoints and interests have been reconciled. Sometimes those conflicts become intense, and if allowed to go unresolved can cause serious if not fatal breakdowns in the relationship. An agent, standing between these potential adversaries, must find common ground for them to stand on, else all—including his commission—is lost. And though their differences may be genuine, sometimes they are semantic, and if an agent can pinpoint and settle the linguistic problems, perhaps the more substantive ones will not seem quite so insuperable. Although it's a stimulating challenge, not all of us enjoy sticking our heads up in this no-man's land.

You must not think, however, that editors cannot be seriously wounded. And it is important to know that fact, because a hurt editor (or art director or royalty bookkeeper) may not want to work as hard for an author who has irked him or her as for one who has been supportive, tolerant, and forgiving. This is not to say that editors are so thin-skinned they fold the first time someone criticizes them. But I do know that if an author or agent injures an editor's feelings seriously enough, it can undercut his or her initiative, and that may eventually redound to an author's detriment. Some years ago I phoned a bookkeeper who had been verbally abused by an author a few months earlier. This author was owed another check, and I wanted to know where it was. "Funny thing about that check," she said, deadpan, "it keeps falling to the bottom of my pile."

It is therefore vital that editors and their colleagues in other departments of publishing companies be handled with a certain degree of diplomacy, and it is in the language of that diplomacy that most agents are adept. We have learned that "a soft answer turneth away wrath." And most of the time, we are able to rephrase or paraphrase the blunt demands, the raw needs, the hard feelings, the hostile remarks, of our clients into gracious packages of civility that convey everything the author intended without damaging the fragile sensibilities of the person at whom they were directed.

I've been keeping some notes about discussions recently conducted with editors and am happy to offer herewith a few examples of this process in action. Some of them are tongue in cheek, others are deliberately exaggerated. Still others will sound stilted, and that is because, unfortunately, that is the way I speak.

175

Let's take one of the commonest problems in our business, that of getting editors to make up their minds about submissions. Editors are burdened with a great many tasks that curtail their reading time. They may be inundated with manuscripts to read. They may be on the fence about a submission and wish to postpone a decision for a while. They may be soliciting opinions or sales estimates from colleagues in their company. They have many legitimate reasons for taking a long time to read submissions.

At the same time, some editors seem to have a considerably dimmer sense of the passage of time than people in other fields, such as airline management or television programming. So, one of the first lessons one learns in the agenting profession is how to translate an editor's promises about time. "I'll read it overnight" too often means, "I'll get around to it in a week." "I'll read it in a week" means, "I'll be back to you in a month." And "I'll read it in a month" may well mean that the manuscript is lost.

In order to reasonably hold editors to their promised schedules, agents use the elegant phraseology of coercion. "As I'm loath to keep manuscripts out of circulation," I might say or write, "may I trouble you for a decision?" If this fails to yield a reply, I might escalate to something more pointed, like, "My client is getting restless," or, "I'm under some pressure to determine where we stand."

Sometimes a humorous approach is in order. I'm a great believer in the power of teasing to accomplish that which solemnity cannot, and I'm not above a little sarcasm under the appropriate circumstances: "When I submitted that manuscript to you, the oceans were two inches lower."

If an editor has sat on a submission for an unconscionably long time, I will invariably get a phone call from my client saying, "You tell that sonofabitch that if we don't have a decision by Friday, I'm personally gonna come down there and rearrange his prefrontal lobes with an ax haft!"

Justified though that ultimatum may be, it is couched in language this is terminally infelicitous. By the time I'm through modifying it, it may sound something closer to this: "As you don't seem able to make up your mind, suppose we say that if I haven't heard from you by Friday, I'll put another copy of the manuscript into play elsewhere, and you may take as much time thereafter as you wish." And sometimes I'll put a finer point on my message with this veiled warning: "Do let me know when your work load is down to a more reasonable size so that I can resume submitting books to you."

I'm certain that you must be saying to yourself, "How is an editor going to get these messages if the agent pussyfoots around that way?" The answer is, editors get these messages loudly and clearly, for unless one is incredibly dense, he will have little doubt that a knife has been placed against his throat.

Another common problem for agents is, of course, overdue checks. Authors are remarkably articulate when it comes to expressing the discomforts of financial deprivation and to depicting the character and ancestry of those who conspire to keep them in that condition. Unfortunately, most editors would go through the roof if exposed to the authors' invective. Enter the honey-tongued agent, and though that agent might love nothing better than to say, "Pay up our we'll vaporize you," it's more likely he or she will say something a bit more subdued. Perhaps a subtle form of extortion: "It would be to your advantage to remit payment promptly so as to avoid scheduling delays." In plain English, this informs the editor that unless his company ponies up the dough, the agent isn't going to deliver certain manuscripts that the publisher desperately needs to put into production. Because a late manuscript can wreck a production schedule at fearful cost to a publisher, the wise editor will undoubtedly give the check-processing machinery an extra-hard spin when he gets a message like that from an agent.

I can think of lots of other ways that agents refine the harsh language of their clients without sacrificing effectiveness. For instance, though we may be thinking, "My client just turned in a real turkey," what we are telling an editor is that, "My client thought you might like to see a first draft of his book before he starts polishing it."

Or, "My client is going to sue you into Rice Krispie–sized pieces" becomes, "My client is contemplating contacting his attorney, at which point the matter will be outside of my control."

Or, "My client thinks your editor is so incompetent, he couldn't spell "cat" if you spotted him the C and the T!" becomes, "I'm not certain that the author's and editor's views about the book are entirely compatible."

"My client is so upset he's taking big bites out of his living room sofa" translates into, "My client is finding it hard to understand why . . ."

"You'll use that cover on my client's book over his dead body!" may be altered to, "My client is pretty determined."

Here's a brief glossary of other agently euphemisms commonly employed when tempers start to overheat:

- You: "I'm thoroughly disgusted with those people."
  Agent: "My client is somewhat disenchanted."
- You: "If I had that editor's throat in my hands ..."
  Agent: "I'm not sure my client is completely comfortable working with you."
- You: "They're lying and cheating."
  Agent: "My client feels he may have detected some discrepancies."
- You: "What a crummy deal!"
  Agent: "Some of the terms leave something to be desired."
- You: "I wouldn't sell another book to that butcher if he were the last editor on earth."
  Agent: "Let's have lunch."

The transmutation of hurtful language works the other way around, too, so that when we have to tell a client that his publishers hate his book so much they want to manure a cornfield with it, we may say something like, "It didn't live up to their expectations," or, "They found it lacking in certain respects." Or an editor's remark to the effect that a certain author couldn't write his way out of a trash can liner becomes, "They don't feel you've reached your potential quite yet."

Here are a few others.

- Editor: "This material is simply lousy."
  Agent: "Your editor is disappointed."
- Editor: "What language is your client writing in, anyway?"
  Agent: "Your editor pointed out some obscure passages."
- Editor: "Your client is the rudest person I've ever had the misfortune to work with."
  Agent: "Your editor seems to have overreacted to what he perceives as a slight."
- Editor: "Is your client crazy, or what?"
  Agent: "I'm not sure your editor appreciates your sense of humor."

Of course, not all agents approach matters as delicately as this. Some of us are in fact quite plainspoken, and even the most tactful among us realizes that there are unavoidable occasions when we must unsheath a steel fist from the velvet glove. Still, it is gratifying to know that at least when it comes to the language one may still find reminders of the time when publishing was a profession for civilized ladies and gentlemen.

CHAPTER 31

Timing

OKAY, HOTSHOT, WE all know you're smarter than your agent. At least, that's what you're always telling your friends. So let's see how well you can do at second-guessing him or her in a few hypothetical situations. For every correct answer, you get a free power lunch in the Grill Room of the Four Seasons with any publisher of your choice; for every one you get wrong, same prize but you treat.

- Your client has had twelve genre novels published in paperback. They've sold about fifty thousand copies each. She thinks the time has come to be published in hardcover. You tell her:
  a) She's absolutely right and you're getting on the phone at once.
  b) She should write another dozen paperbacks that sell fifty thousand copies each, then you'll move her.
  c) Wait till her paperbacks start selling in the hundreds of thousands of copies each.
  d) She's crazy to want to be published in hardcover.
- Your client has just turned in the manuscript of a book that has good film possibilities. The time to start contacting producers is:
  a) When the book is in bound proofs.
  b) When finished copies come off the presses.
  c) When the book starts getting good reviews.
  d) Yesterday.
- You recently sold a client's first novel to a publisher for $5,000. The

client has an idea for a new novel that he thinks has big money potential, and he wants a much bigger advance. The best time to ask for it is:

a) Now.

b) Six months from now.

c) Around the time the first novel is published.

d) A year after the first novel has been published.

In case you haven't noticed, all the questions in this quiz have to do with timing. Few authors realize it, but one of the most important reasons for hiring agents is that they have a superior sense of timing. "Timing is everything" might almost be called the agent's motto ("Patience is every-thing else" might be considered the agent's second motto). The most successful agents are those who understand that there is a season to push and a season to ease up, a season to fight and a season to turn the back, a season to watch and wait and a season to strike. Sometimes the moment presents itself on a platter; sometimes it has to be worked with brute force like steel on a smithy's anvil. And there are times when, for all an agent's scheming, for all his exertions, for all his manipulations, he simply cannot make the thing happen. (That's usually a signal for me to go shopping.)

Most authors are impatient. It's a forgivable character trait, for it often goes hand in hand with ambition. But because authors cannot possibly be as objective about the progress of their careers as their agents are, their impatience can make them their own worst enemies. A goodly part of an agent's day is spent restraining authors.

Although we usually associate timing with the moment when an agent pulls off some million-dollar coup, many of its applications are far more prosaic. A couple of years ago a literary agent wrote a piece for *Publishers Weekly* complaining about rude editors who do not return agents' phone calls. Her broadside elicited a chorus of cheers from fellow agents, and from writers who'd had similarly unpleasant experiences.

I had a different reaction, though. Her article made me wonder wheth-er the telephone is not greatly overused by agents, and whether there are many occasions when a note would do instead of a call. This is parti-cularly true in the conduct of routine business such as inquiries about submissions, contracts, and checks. Editors are usually harried with paperwork, urgent business, and other phone calls, and so there is an odds-on probability that a scribbled note taken down during a phone call will presently be buried beneath the day's alluvial deposit of letters, internal memos, manuscripts, catalogues, contracts, and junk mail. I've noticed, however, that editors seem to place more significance upon written inquiries, and they move on them more promptly. More importantly, underuse of the phone by an agent may motivate editors to take his calls when he really needs to get through. If an editor doesn't want to talk to an agent because the editor thinks the agent is calling about that overdue check, when actually the agent is calling to pitch a hot new property, a vital opportunity will have been missed for both of them.

The preceding is not a particularly glamorous example of timing, but in the last analysis it's the daily employment of wise timing that makes a good agent effective.

But then there is that dramatic application that makes an agent feel he's been waiting all his life to yank the ripcord, and the decisive moment has come. Not long ago a fellow agent called me for consultation on a particularly delicate timing problem involving a star author. This author had a very big book scheduled for publication about nine months from that time, but because he was very unhappy with his publisher, he had asked his agent to seek another one. His agent had done so and lined up a terrific deal. In order to get out of his option with his current publisher, the author merely had to submit an outline and reject whatever was offered. When to do that—that was the problem.

The new publisher was pressing the agent to finalize their deal. Publishers get very nervous about leaving big offers open for too long, since agents have been known to use those offers to solicit even higher ones. Despite the possibility that the offer would be withdrawn, the agent was dragging his heels. By breaking with the current publisher too early, the agent could demoralize the sales people and cause the company to pull some of its advertising and promotional money from the upcoming book; a publisher that is losing an author may not work as hard for him as one that looks forward to a long association.

What did I advise my colleague to do? I'll let you brood about it for a minute or two in the security of your armchair, but remember that in this real-life situation, millions of dollars, the agent's relationship with his client, the agent's relationship with two publishers, the fate of a book on which the author had spent a year, the fate of many books to come, and a lot of egos and reputations were on the line. Perhaps you would understand it better if you got out of your armchair and read the rest of this chapter while standing on a rickety stool with a hangman's noose around your neck.

Although I have tried to demystify the publishing business for you, I have to confess that the instincts governing the sense of timing, including my own, are wonderfully and impenetrably mysterious to me. I am fairly certain that they are of a piece with artistic inspiration. Most of the time, if you ask me to articulate the reasons why I chose a certain moment to demand a dramatic raise in an author's pay, or to go from a book-by-book arrangement to a multibook package deal, or to move a client out of paperback originals and into hardcover, I can express them fairly coherently. But then there are those inexplicable revelations, blazing across the mind when one least expects it, that illuminate a situation with dazzling clarity and put one in touch with some very profound impulses.

I take pride in handling most business matters expeditiously, but occasionally something will come along that I frankly don't know what to do about. It will sit on my desk glowering at me, mocking me, demanding attention but eluding solution. I gaze back at it, mutter an oath, but am paralyzed with uncertainty. You might call the condition "agent's block." The client and the publisher are pressing for a decision. I offer feeble excuses that sound very much like procrastination or, worse, timidity. In truth, I'm simply waiting for the green light to go on in my brain. Inevitably it switches on, but when I least anticipate it, such as awaking from a nap or glomming a midnight snack. The answer is suddenly printed in bright headlines before me, and what was so difficult suddenly becomes ridiculously easy. The time, at last, has come.

Lest I start to sound as if agenting is a variety of religious experience, allow me to let you in on a little secret. Some of the things agents do that authors think are brilliantly timed are in truth matters of dumb luck. An author writes a book and I sell it to precisely the right editor and it goes on to become a best-seller. I would love for you to think that I selected that editor the way a handicapper selects a winning horse. And perhaps I did. But sometimes, finding the perfect editor for a book is a matter of who is not out to lunch, in a meeting, or in the bathroom when an agent starts making phone calls.

Now, about that quiz.

Situation Number 1: The paperback author who wants to be published in hardcover. Despite the evidence that you can make a much better living writing original paperbacks than you can hardcover books, most authors feel an uneasy sense of illegitimacy about paperbacks. And it is true that hardcover books have a better chance of being reviewed (negatively as well as favorably, don't forget) and selling to the movies. But if an author's paperbacks are selling in routine numbers, as in this example, the time may not be propitious for the leap into hardcover, for the author hasn't built an audience prepared to follow her into the more prestigious and expensive format. On many occasions a premature debut in hardcover can be catastrophic and the author may forever lose the opportunity to be published in boards again.

Situation Number 2: What is the best time to start soliciting movie rights to a book with promising film potential? The answer is, immediately if not sooner. Movie and television people need to feel they are getting in on something hot. By the time a book is published it will have been circulated among all the key studios, networks, and producers owing to Hollywood's highly efficient system for obtaining early looks at anything that sounds interesting. "A published book," the late producer David Susskind once said to me, "is very dead meat." There are of course exceptions to this rule, and examples of books made into successful movies decades after publication. But if you have a hot movie property, there's not a moment to lose. And remember, it's a good idea to prepare a brief synopsis of the book, highlighting its cinematic qualities, to accompany the submission for those in Hollywood who don't have the time (or the ability) to read.

Situation Number 3: When is it appropriate to ask for a higher advance? The answer is, it's always appropriate to ask, but not always appropriate to expect. For new authors, the period of time between the sale of the first novel and publication is an extremely perilous one. Assuming an author is of average productivity, he will have ideas, outlines, or even completed manuscripts of new works long before that first book has been published. *Until* that first book has been published, however, the publisher will have no basis for calculating the value of the author's work and will therefore resist offering him more than a token raise in price. Indeed, because publishers don't formulate a clear picture of a book's sales for about a year after publication, owing to the time it takes for unsold copies to be returned, it may be two or three years from the time you sell your first book before you are justified in requesting prices bigger than starting pay. So if you answered (d) on the quiz you may have been closest to the truth.

You can't, of course, afford to sit around for several years waiting for the results on your first book, so there are several strategies for bridging the gap. One is to become more prolific (including writing books under pseudonyms for other publishers if your first publisher can't absorb your entire output). Another is to write your second, third, and even fourth novel on speculation rather than trying to line up contracts for them on the basis of outlines or portions-and-outlines. As I've said before, publishers are able to make much faster judgments about finished books than partial ones, and usually pay higher prices.

Finally, we return to the quandary of the agent torn between responsibility for his client's forthcoming book and eagerness to nail down a deal with another publisher before the first publisher backs out. The situation was, as I pointed out, quite treacherous, but I advised the agent to wait until the very last moment, a few weeks before publication of the book, before informing the current publishers that they weren't going to get the author's next book. By that time the advertising was set, the author's tour locked in, the books were in the stores, and the publishers were committed to doing everything possible to make it a success and recover their investment.

As for the publishers threatening to withdraw their offer if the agent delayed, the agent visited the head of the company and persuaded him to leave his offer on the table. "Look," said my friend, "you have my word of honor that I will not use your offer to seek other bids. I cannot afford to offend a rich and powerful publisher like you. Please bear in mind that if we announce the author's decision too soon, the other publisher may pull its advertising and promotion and their book will flop. And that will make it much harder for you to sell the author's next book." Happily, the publisher saw the wisdom of this argument and held his offer open. It all worked out happily, even for the publisher who lost the big-name author. Oh, the publisher was sore for a few weeks, but then the agent phoned him and told him that another client was unhappy with her publisher and wanted to move to another house. "Interested?" he asked. Of course he was interested!

Now, that's what I call an agent with an exquisite sense of timing.

‒ి

CHAPTER 32

Is Life Too Short?

I N THE LAST chapter we discussed one of the most important qualities a literary agent can bring to his job: good timing. I've been thinking about another virtue that most good agents possess, and that's patience. If timing is the art of "when to," patience might be said to be the art of "when not to." In many cases, that means when not to knock your head against a wall, when not to wring a client's throat, or when not to hop in a taxi, race over to a publisher's office, and trash his desk.

Although some people are born patient, for most of us it's an acquired quality. We attain it only with experience, and it may be the only significant benefit of aging.

If you are constitutionally incapable of practicing patience, you are definitely not cut out to become a literary agent. Despite the appearance of furious activity, and notwithstanding such timesaving innovations as multiple submissions, word processors, laser printers, electronic mail, high-speed presses, overnight mail, instant books, and quickie releases, the truth is that just about anything of importance that happens in our industry happens slowly. Good books are written at a snail's pace, submissions take ages, negotiations drag on, money flows like cold lard, and the building of an author's career from first sale to best-selling masterpiece is about as dramatic as watching a lake evaporate. Difficult publishers test our patience, as do difficult authors. If agents seem to have a higher per capita ratio of weekend homes than other professionals, have pity on them: they must have a place to go to chop wood, bay at the moon, and otherwise relieve the strain of holding their natural impulses in check during the other five days a week.

I do not own a weekend home, but I do have a set of molars that have been ground down close to the nerve endings from restraining the desire to commit a variety of felonies in order to make things move faster. Behind a demeanor that one of my clients once described as "judicious," seethes a cauldron of emotions, energy, grievances, and heroic fantasies. I smile, I speak moderately, I behave politely, I move deliberately. I polish my buckler and hone my sword, my ear cocked for the call to arms. It may come in the form of a letter, a phone call, an offer, an opportunity, an insult. But I am ready for action (see "Timing"). Meanwhile, I wait.

I wait, for instance, for you to finish your book. Because my agency does a lot of business in paperback original series, I have to wait only a month or two for many books. For most mainstream ones, however, I have to wait nine months, a year, or longer. The potential in these books presses heavily upon my consciousness; I'm dying to wheel and deal. But with few exceptions there is little to be done to convert that potential until the manuscript has been turned in. However much I am dying to go into action with that book, I cannot advance the calendar by one day, the clock by one minute. I grind my teeth and wait.

I wait for publishers to make up their minds about my submissions. Decisions on manuscripts can be forced by means of the auction, and when agents have to move fast they can elicit decisions virtually overnight. But most material does not command that kind of attention. The more conventional approach of one submission at a time, or at best two or three simultaneously, is what is usually called for. Like most agencies, we have a reminder calendar and regularly write or phone publishers prodding them to keep the property in question at the top of the pile.

Despite every measure taken to make editors respond to submissions promptly, it is unrealistic to expect decisions in less than six weeks, and quite realistic to expect none in less than three months. If a work isn't placed on the first or second round of submissions, therefore, a year or more can pass with relatively few submissions to show for all the investment of time. So we wait.

We wait to make deals. Deals can be struck in a matter of minutes, but many negotiations take days, weeks, or even months to unfold. With the evolution of publishing from an individual entrepreneurial enterprise to a bureaucratized corporate one, seldom do agents end up negotiating with the principals of a publishing company. Instead we take up terms with editors, who refer them to superior officers or editorial boards. Several weeks may pass if the appropriate executives are not available to formulate offers or counteroffers. Often, figures have to be worked up by a variety of departments to help the company determine its negotiating strategy. During which time we wait.

We wait for contracts. The people who work in the contract departments of most publishing houses are among the most professional in our industry. Nevertheless, it is seldom possible for them to produce contracts for signature in less than six or eight weeks. After the editor reaches agreement with the author or agent, he prepares a deal memo summarizing the terms of the contract, for approval by the head of the company. After approval has been rendered, the deal memo goes to the contract department where it serves as the basis for the formal agreement. This agreement is reviewed by the acquiring editor and an officer of the company, then returned to the contract department for issuance to the author or agent. After signed contracts are returned to the publisher, they are circulated for signature and a voucher is issued directing the accounts payable department to prepare the check. We now wait for the check.

We wait a long time for the check because in many cases the accounts payable department is not in the same building or even the same state as the contracts department. After receiving the voucher from the contracts department, accounts payable prepares a check that must be reviewed and signed by the controller or other officer of the company. It is then forwarded to the contracts department to be issued with the contracts, or sent to the payee directly from the accounts payable office.

If form follows function, publishers could not conceive of a better structure for attenuating the time it takes to release money. Even with all hands working at maximum efficiency—not a very desirable state, you must realize, when there is interest to be earned—I figure two to three months is now the industry average for payout from the time check vouchers are issued. Agents who have managed to map and penetrate the system can keep things moving with phone calls to various departments along the paperwork routes goading delinquent clerks to press on with their tasks. Nevertheless, we wait. We wait for books to be published.

Well, you get the idea; just about everything concerning publishing is a test of an agent's patience. And that includes authors.

One of my colleagues has created, with tongue somewhat in cheek I suspect, an index for rating his clients; he calls it the PITA factor. PITA stands for "Pain In The Ass." He assigns his client a rating from one to ten, depending on such factors as how often they ask him for advances, how many times they call him at home at six o'clock on Sunday mornings, how many editors they insult, and in general how much maintenance they require beyond routine care and feeding. Their PITA factor is then divided into the commissions realized on their sales. Applying his criteria, an author who earns only $1,000 annually in commissions but who is a model client is as valuable to his agent as one who earns $10,000 in commissions but is a raving lunatic. "Life," says my friend, "is too short to have to deal with pains in the ass."

Well, I don't know. As I said at the beginning of this chapter, if you do feel that way, the literary agent's trade is not for you and you should go into something less aggravating, like commodity trading or hospital emergency room administration. When it comes to dealing with artists, irritating behavior comes with the territory. And, far more important, think of what they have to put up with. With the rare exception of the author whose first book stuns the critics, sweeps the public off its feet, and soars to the top of the best-seller list, success for most writers is won only after decades of economic struggle, mental anguish, crushing obscurity, and the consumption of murderous doses of pride. They spend a lifetime practicing patience, and if they do not always practice it very well, if they are difficult when they're starting out, difficult when they begin to make it, and difficult when they finally arrive, a larger degree of tolerance is called for on the part of those who serve them, particularly if they've never tried that life themselves.

A PITA scale that does not factor in the emotional satisfactions of midwifing an author's first book, of nurturing his career as he gains in skill and confidence and stretches to grasp his vision, and of attending his graduation ceremony featuring smashing reviews and sales by the trainload, requires some serious rethinking.

Life is not too short if an agent's patience is rewarded with such satisfactions as these.

❧

CHAPTER 33

To Fee? Or Not to Fee?

To FEE? Or not to fee? That is the question.

And for many literary agents, reading fees are a hot question indeed. In the eyes of many writers, publishers, and even other agents, the charging of fees for agents to review the work of aspiring writers is unethical at the very least. Some feel it is downright fraudulent.

There is a lot of evidence to support the detractors of this practice, I regret to say. But it may also satisfy some very important needs, and, if rendered ethically and responsibly, it can create opportunities for developing writers that are no longer available to them through traditional channels. Let's examine the conditions and problems confronting literary agents that often give rise to the necessity of charging fees.

Until the post-World War II era, the responsibility for discovering new writers belonged almost entirely to publishers. Although literary agents have existed since the nineteenth century, their emergence as a decisive force in the publishing process had not yet commenced, and authors almost invariably submitted their work directly to publishers. As the number of would-be authors was not overwhelming, publishers were able to sort through submissions in a relatively reasonable time. And though the ratio of unsuitable to suitable submissions was undoubtedly as high as it is today, the lower volume of manuscripts made it economical for publishers to retain editors on staff whose task was to find good material in what has come, lamentably, to be called the "slush pile." In short, the profits realized from successful books pulled out of the slush pile out-weighed the cost of reading the rest of the material.

All of this changed as the century wore on. The publishing business became more competitive and expensive, forcing publishers to look harder and harder at their bottom lines. One of the items that didn't fare very well under scrutiny was the cost of reading slush. The chances of finding a best-seller there were about as good as discovering a diamond tiara in a corn flakes box. Several years ago, Viking Press vigorously publicized its discovery in the slush pile of Judith Guest's *Ordinary People*, a big best-seller that was then made into an enormously successful movie. But it was the first unsolicited novel bought by the company in twenty-seven years!

How many editors had worked how many hours at how much salary to haul that prize fish out of the sea of submissions? A little number-crunching might suggest some answers. I have it on the authority of several editors that unsolicited submissions received by the average publishing company number some ten thousand or more annually. If you figure that a reasonably intelligent editor can read between five and ten of these a day (assuming he or she has nothing else to do but read), he or she will be able to polish off approximately one to two thousand sub-missions in a year. Even assuming the higher figure, it means that a minimum of five editors is required just to read so-called over-the-transom submissions.

Starting salaries in publishing these days are approximately $20,000 annually; with fringe benefits and employer contributions to social security, it's probably closer to $25,000. Thus, the cost of retaining a staff strictly to read slush is at least $125,000 per year, not counting the cost of handling and postage for rejected material. Or the cost of the time that senior editors spend reading those manuscripts that may be recom-mended by the slush pile editors. All things considered, it probably costs close to $200,000 for a publisher to keep its doors open to unsolicited material—and that's every year. It would probably cost that much to publish works that are discovered there. And then there's a little matter of making a profit. In brief, a publisher would probably have to sell close to half a million dollars' worth of books discovered in its slush pile in order to justify the existence of a well-managed program dedicated to finding good books there. That's every year, chum.

Clearly, the game is not worth the candle; at least, not when publishers know that it is infinitely more cost-effective to acquire material from literary agents.

As the twentieth century progressed, agents grew more and more influential, and publishers increasingly relied on them for quality material. In due time, trade publishers began to neglect their slush piles, and ultimately, most of them abandoned them altogether. Today, most large trade publishers return unsolicited manuscripts unread or scarcely glanced at. Some houses, however, particularly paperback ones that publish a lot of genre material, do manage to read unsolicited books, at least books that seem at first glance to have merit. But, at a cost of between $25 and $40 per manuscript, which is the going rate for outside readers, the toll can be high. One editor told me his monthly nut for outside readers runs well over $1,000.

Publishers that refuse to read slush generally return manuscripts with printed notices stating that the firm reviews only submissions made by literary agents. In effect, agents have become the slush pile readers for the publishing industry. In certain respects, this task is not as burdensome for agents as it is for publishers, for agents' slush piles are excellent sources of potential new clients. Publishers offer narrower windows of opportunity to authors than agents do. A publisher seeks books to fill its own list only, but an agent seeks them to fill many lists. An author submitting a novel to a publisher that publishes only nonfiction will be wasting that publisher's time. But if he sends that same novel to a literary agent he won't necessarily waste that agent's time, because the agent knows of lots of houses that do publish fiction.

In another respect, the shift in responsibility for discovering and developing new talent has placed a heavy burden on agents, for along with the benefits go the expenses. After all, if it is costly for publishers to maintain a staff to read slush, isn't it equally costly for agents to do the same thing?

As a matter of fact it is. Indeed, it could well be argued that it is more costly, because agents work on a much lower profit margin than publishers do. The average literary agency is staffed by two to five people including the boss. It is well nigh impossible for them to read manuscripts during the day when the phones are constantly ringing. That means taking reading home.

Reading at home is the cross that everyone in the publishing industry must bear. It often intrudes on our evening and weekend leisure time.

(Vacation time, too: my wife searches my luggage for manuscripts I try to smuggle to holiday resorts.) For agents, leisure time is too often occupied with reading manuscripts, contracts, and correspondence relating to our professional clients. It is difficult, and for some agents impossible, to devote quality time to the work of new authors.

Every agency that lists itself in the industry's directories receives a large quantity of unsolicited submissions from hopeful writers. I don't think my own agency is exceptional in this respect: on any given day, we receive between fifteen and twenty-five solicitations from unpublished or unestablished writers. The task of screening their queries, outlines, and partial and complete manuscripts takes my staff the better part of a morning. As you might expect, the material breaks down in the proportions of 5 percent interesting, 10 or 15 percent marginal, and the rest clearly unsuitable. (I hasten to add, unsuitable for us, but not necessarily unsuitable for other agencies.)

That means that I and/or my associates must find a way to seriously review ten submissions or more per week, excluding work by our regular clients. How much can I read without jeopardizing the interests of those clients? How much can I ask my employees to read beyond their normal burden of homework before they demand additional compensation? How can I ask outside freelancers to read manuscripts free of charge?

And that's just reading: What about replying? While much of the stuff we send back doesn't call for extensive analysis, many agents feel that it would be rude if not cruel to return it without a few lines of explanation, criticism, encouragement, or consolation. And if the material is above average, a thoughtful letter is certainly in order. Where is one to find the time, or the money to pay for that time?

I am not telling you all this because I want you to feel sorry for agents (*that* will be the day!), but because it's important for everyone connected with publishing and literature to realize that the economics of slush are as inexorable for agents as they are for publishers. We are faced with the dilemma of either cold-bloodedly returning this material unread and thus making it even harder for promising authors to get a hearing, or devoting serious attention to new authors at the expense of our clients' interests, to say nothing of our own.

For some agents, the solution is reading fees. These fees are designed to compensate agents, their employees, and their outside readers for the time they must invest in reviewing the work of new authors and cultivating the better ones. Of course, for anyone interested simply in getting a manuscript criticized, there are a great many reading services that do not, and do not claim to, perform agenting tasks. The quality of their services and the fees they charge vary widely. One can, though, often come away with a helpful analysis of one's manuscript and perhaps improve the quality of one's writing skills, as long as it's understood that the reading service cannot place the work with publishers.

It is when reading services are combined with agenting capabilities that some troubling moral issues arise. If a manuscript reading is offered with the implicit promise that the work will be offered to publishers, or if an agent accepts reading fees without offering anything by way of constructive criticism, authors will justifiably feel that they are being ripped off. Most agents can judge the quality of a manuscript within the first few pages, and critics of literary agency reading fee services feel that if the agent were honest, he or she would simply return the manuscript with the fee and a brief note stating that the work lacks merit or is unsalable.

It's hard to argue with these criticisms, but some agents who charge fees justify them on the grounds that they never mislead authors about the unpublishability of submissions; that the quality of their evaluations is high, and many authors genuinely benefit from them; and that from time to time, salable works and talented authors are discovered in agents' slush piles. I myself know of a number of books discovered in agents' slush piles that went on to get sold, initiating successful writing careers for their authors. And I can cite many authors who feel they profited immensely from literary criticism and marketing expertise for which they paid fees to agents. If handled properly, a fee system might provide one way of keeping stocked the literary breeding grounds that have been drying up on the shifting sands of modern publishing.

Unfortunately, some fee-charging agents have taken advantage of authors, and the taint of fraud hovers over the business of reading fees, making even the most ethically and responsibly run services suspect. As a result, the Association of Authors' Representatives has prohibited the practice among its members, for it's impossible to police it, and trade laws make it illegal for the organization to regulate the fees charged.

CHAPTER 34

Extraordinary Expenses

L ET'S TALK ABOUT the out-of-pocket expenses that agents charge to
their authors.

Among the commonest classes of such expenses are long-
distance telephone calls; faxes; photocopy of manuscripts and documents; messenger pickup and delivery of urgently awaited manuscripts,
contracts, and checks; special delivery and overnight mail charges;
purchases of extra copies of authors' books for exploitation of subsidiary
rights; international postal charges for submissions of books to foreign
agents and publishers; and loans to authors.

These are a perpetual source of friction between agents and authors,
and the policies on charged expenses differ from agent to agent. The
reactions to them differ from author to author, too. Some will resignedly
accept a deduction of hundreds of dollars, others will fight like trapped
beasts over a dollar that they feel has been improperly ascribed. But if
these charges are a source of irritation to authors, you should be aware
that they are not much fun for agents, either. The bookkeeping on them
is complex, energy intensive, time consuming, and thankless. It is also an
absolute necessity. Looking at it positively, "extraordinary" expenses help
us to make extraordinary deals, move properties and money faster, and
serve our clients more effectively. Extraordinary expenses would sap an
agent's profit if they weren't charged off to clients. While the debits may
not be huge for any individual author, in the aggregate they can be so high

that they could force an agency out of business if they were not paid out of author income.

Many an agent's session with his bookkeeper has been devoted to questions of what are appropriate deductions, how costs can be reduced, and how to get publishers to pick up some expenses that are currently laid on the shoulders of authors, and I assure you we take these matters very seriously. Never think that, since it's not our own money we're spending, we're unconcerned with holding costs down. Most agents lay the money out on behalf of their clients, and although they ultimately recover it from money flowing to those clients, they no sooner collect it from one client than they must lay it out for another. So we are always out of pocket in that respect, and it may therefore be fairly said that it is our money, and the less we can get away with spending, the less, you may be sure, we will spend.

Because the headaches surrounding this issue are intense, some agents have raised their basic commissions in exchange for the assumption of some or all extraordinary expenses. Authors selecting an agent will want to weigh the value of extraordinary expenses against the value of that additional commission—all other factors being equal in the choosing of an agent, of course.

The conflicts surrounding these expenses arise over the definition of what is a "normal cost of doing business" for an agent. It would be impossible for an agent to do normal business without making long-distance phone calls, making photocopies of manuscripts, or purchasing extra copies of books for servicing subsidiary rights. Yet the agent justifies charging some or all of such outlays to clients on the grounds that they are expenses the authors would have paid if they were operating on their own without an agent. A reasonable author, for example, faced with a choice of making a photocopy of his manuscript in response to an inquiry from a movie producer, or waiting until his book is published nine or twelve months later, wouldn't hesitate to opt for the former. But he could wait. His decision not to do so incurs an extraordinary expense for him. If he has an agent, his agent makes those decisions for him and advances the money to pay for the additional costs.

The line between ordinary and extraordinary expenses can get fuzzy, though. When I started my agency I charged clients for long-distance phone calls. It was easy to keep records of such calls when I had only a handful of clients; it was something to do while watching New York Giants football games. But as my firm grew larger the task of poring over multi-page phone bills became intensely agonizing, particularly because the years of my company's most rapid growth coincided with the period when the Giants were playing awful football, so that by the time I'd finished the task of charging calls to authors I was fit to devour carpets. Add to this the grousing of clients about being charged for what they contended was undeniably a normal cost of doing business and I was obliged to drop such charges. With phone bills running around $2,000 a month currently, I look back at my decision with pangs of wistfulness, but that's the way it goes.

Let's go over some other types of expense.

Faxes. With the tremendous advances in telephone technology, the necessity and cost of communication have declined sharply. But faxes are vital for furnishing written confirmation of deals when urgency is called for, and for expediting contracts. Faxes and long-distance phone calls are an absolute necessity in this age of high-powered international electronic negotiations, but even when they are cheap they are expensive. Yet, no author would want to risk blowing a deal by insisting that his agent convey decisions and information via old-fashioned airmail. As more and more agents and authors go online, we can expect even cheaper and more efficient means of transferring documents electronically, and perhaps at last agents will no longer need to charge their clients for this service.

Photocopies. The photocopy machine has been a prime factor in the transformation of the publishing industry into the high-powered business it is today, creating the immediate accessibility to material that makes for more dynamic book auctions and early sales of subsidiary rights. The process has also added to the burden of expense for author, publisher, and agent, and that burden upon even the smallest of agencies is tremendous. In New York City a price of ten cents a page is standard, with discounts offered for high-volume jobs. An agent must usually make at least one photocopy of any manuscript that he believes has subsidiary rights potential, so that he can make more copies from that one as the need arises. And the need arises all the time. If a book has any subsidiary rights potential at all he will probably need a dozen copies to service first serial submissions and to hit movie producers and foreign publishers eager for an early look. Figuring twelve copies of a three-hundred-page manuscript at eight cents a page, that's more than three hundred dollars for the job, including tax.

At any given time in the life of even a modest-sized agency, there may be between five and ten such literary properties in circulation, an outlay of two or three thousand dollars. I invite authors who think they can make their own copies cheaper to do so by all means, bearing in mind the cost of shipping those copies to their agents, the inconvenience of arranging for their own photocopying, and the time lost in getting sub-rights submissions in the works while the agent awaits the arrival of the copies shipped by his client.

By the way, an intermediate stage between manuscript and printed book is bound, uncorrected proofs, and agents frequently use these for subsidiary rights submissions. They cost about ten dollars a set on the average.

Messengers. Like most other businesses in New York City, the publishing industry runs at a breakneck pace, and while routine submissions, contracts, and checks are sent by ordinary mail or United Parcel Service, a day seldom passes in the life of a literary agency when some exigency or another doesn't require the use of a messenger, and sometimes the sheer importance of a project or deal demands use of a messenger to deliver a long-awaited manuscript or pick up a huge contract or check. The same exigencies demand the employment of special delivery or overnight express mail. Seldom do authors complain about these expenses as long as their agents use common sense in incurring them on their behalf.

In New York City, messenger services charge by the zone for routine errands, with one-zone deliveries and pickups starting at about $7. Parcels that are too weighty or bulky to go by bicycle (the standard messenger conveyance) must be picked up by van at extra charge. If you figure two or three calls daily for a messenger at a small to medium-sized agency (the largest agencies employ their own messengers rather than outside services), that comes to $400 or $500 a month. Overnight mail charges start at $10 or $12.

Next come *book purchases.* Although agents utilize manuscripts or proofs to exploit subsidiary rights to key books, much of the time we can wait until the book comes off the presses before offering those rights. Authors are entitled to a certain number of free copies, but anything beyond that must be bought, usually in hard cash, by the author or agent at a courtesy discount of 40 or 50 percent. If an agent is to do a thorough job of covering potential subsidiary rights markets—and sometimes the demand for a book extends over decades—he's going to need between twenty and fifty copies of a book. In the foreign market there are about a dozen key language territories, and in some cases the agent or his subagent partner in those territories will want to submit a book to more than one publisher at a time. Furthermore, after buying the rights to a book, a foreign publisher will usually request between two and five extra copies for translation, production, cover art, and other purposes.

If the book in question is a paperback original, the cost of buying extra copies is not excessive, but in the case of hardcovers the cost can be awesome. A $25 book discounted by 40 percent is $15, and thirty copies will set you back close to $500 including shipping costs. Publishers refuse to charge most such purchases to authors' royalties as they once did because so many books fail to earn out their advances and the publisher is thus left absorbing the cost of book purchases. So they demand cash on the barrelhead before processing book orders, and most agents cannot count on their clients to afford them or pay promptly. In any given month, therefore, an agency of any dimension will have to shell out $1,000 or more for book purchases. I try, when I negotiate contracts, to raise the number of free authors' copies to the maximum I can get away with.

Then there's the cost of marketing books overseas. Whenever possible—that is, in cases of routine submissions—agents use surface mail to submit books overseas. It may take months for books thus submitted to reach their destination, but when you hear how much it costs to airmail a book you may well decide the tradeoff between cost and time is an acceptable one. Airmailing a hardcover book costs four or five times more than shipping by boat; if the book is important or timely, if the author is eager to see results, or if there are guaranteed sales awaiting the delivery of a book, it is penny-wise and pound-foolish to send books via surface mail. But postage to service a book via airmail to all major territories can run $500 or more. If the book is hot, an agent may even airmail a copy of the manuscript. The cost is so obscene it will nauseate you. I try to remind authors that the cost of foreign submissions is easily wiped out by just one foreign sale, but they have a tendency to overlook this when they get a check with hundreds of dollars deducted for foreign postage.

Advances. You may not think that loans to authors should legitimately be classified as extraordinary expenses, but I suspect you would feel differently if you were sitting at my desk poring over that particular column in my ledgers. I can't speak for other agencies, but for mine, despite every effort to harden our hearts to pleas for advances, these "quick" loans to authors represent a larger debit than all the others that I have listed combined. An author who recently joined our agency told me he'd chosen me over two competitors because, "Another client of yours told me you were a sucker for a hard-luck story."

I suppose I am. At this writing, I have succumbed to the following hard-luck stories: (1) "My wife just left me and cleaned out our account" ($1,500); (2) "The hurricane damaged my roof and when the engineer inspected it he discovered extensive termite damage" ($2,500); (3) "I have to go into the hospital for diagnosis but they require prepayment" ($500); (4) "It's Christmas . . ." ($750); (5) "It's the end of the month . . ." ($650); (6) "The Internal Revenue Service . . ." ($1,250).

Most of these advances will be recovered within a month or two out of monies soon payable to my agency, but then, as surely as rent is due monthly and taxes quarterly, I will be besieged by a new wave of requests, so that the balance of unrecovered advances seldom drops below $10,000, which the clients are getting at a most attractive interest rate: 0 percent.

If robot-like efficiency were the goal I could slash many of these extraordinary costs to the bone. I could submit all manuscripts by fourth class mail; send checks and contracts to clients by routine mail; require clients to run off their own photocopies; submit books to foreign publishers via banana boat; and slam my teller's window to even the most abject appeals for loans. I would then take the savings and plunk them down on a hot sports car.

But then I start thinking, and at length I say to myself, How ridiculous it is to prefer the thrill of pushing a gorgeous piece of automotive engineering to the max on an open highway over the pleasure of hustling my tail off to cover a monthly out-of-pocket deficit of fifteen or twenty thousand dollars. But hell, a man's entitled to daydream, isn't he?

❧

CHAPTER 35

Bad News about Your Agent's Death

AS THE ACCUMULATION of publishing horror stories turns my hair grey, I have recently become reflective about the end of life, and that in turn prompts me to write about the problems writers face when their agents die. I have, of course, written about terminating your relationship with your agent, but that advice was predicated on his being alive. My omission is forgivable. Nobody likes to think about death, especially agents. Writers at least have an opportunity to immortalize themselves through their books. But what do agents have to be remembered by—their deals? Somehow the tribute, "He Negotiated the Sweetest Option Clause in the Industry," on an agent's tombstone doesn't have the lilt guaranteed to inspire pilgrimages to his grave.

In fact, his survivors and former clients might be inspired to shake their fists over his poor moldering body if he made inadequate provisions for the operation of his business in the event of his demise. Among the prizes of my horror story collection are those about authors whose money was tied up for years while their late agent's estate underwent probate.

These disturbing tales vividly point up the need for agents, while they are still vital and compos mentis (if anyone consciously electing to become an agent may be said to be compos mentis), to determine exactly how their estate administrators or business partners or employees will handle their business, especially cash flow in and out of their agency, until the formalities of probate are concluded. For, despite the remark by one publisher that the only good agent is a dead agent, the worst living agent in the world is better than the best dead one if the latter's passing creates a lot of aggravation for his clients. But much of it can be avoided by candid discussion of these matters between author and agent, and by some simple contractual measures in cases where the agent hasn't made appropriate provisions.

So, let's look death squarely in the eye and utter the unutterable: sooner or later your agent, like everybody else, has got to meet his maker. Despite the image of invulnerability and immortality agents try to project in order to intimidate publishers and reassure clients, actuarial statistics indicate that their track record in escaping the Grim Reaper is no better than anybody else's. And while autopsies do reveal some physiological characteristics unique to literary agents, such as overdeveloped spleens, ossified hearts, jaded palates, and a circulatory system of iced water, there are no indications of divine creation. This means that they are fallible just like you, and like you they don't pay as much concern as they should to the practical consequences of their death. But as the practical consequences of your agent's death may be to drive you close to bankruptcy, it's best for you to raise questions now while his body is still warm; if you choose to avoid the subject, you may be casting yourself to the treacherous winds of state probate law.

Let's talk about that law.

Although it differs from state to state, it is almost universally true that an individual's assets are frozen as soon as the authorities learn about his demise. This information is communicated to those authorities in a variety of ways: death certificates issued by doctors and hospitals, newspaper obituaries, cemetery and funeral home records, and voluntary reports by estate executors, next of kin, etc. As soon as the authorities have been informed, they are required to order the immediate freezing of all known bank accounts belonging to the deceased and the sealing of his personal safe deposit box. Except for insurance settlements and whatever liquid assets (cash, jewelry) may be converted for the use of the survivors, no funds are available to settle claims until the deceased's estate has been probated.

Entire court systems exist in every state for the probating of estates. The purpose of this procedure is to insure the proper settlement of claims on those estates. If the deceased made out a will, it must be reviewed to make certain it was properly executed; heirs must be located, signatures of the deceased and witnesses confirmed, and claims by heirs, legatees, and creditors examined. Even when the process proceeds without a hitch, it can take months and months. If the will is challenged, the delay may be even longer. We're talking about years, folks. And if the deceased left no will at all, requiring the appointment of a public administrator to sift through the deceased's affairs, well, you don't want to know about it.

This procedure applies equally to rich and poor, male and female, mighty and humble, to people of every race and creed, to industrial magnates, ditchdiggers, doctors, lawyers—and literary agents. Unless your agent is incorporated, it doesn't matter whether he has a thousand able people working for him, the best law firm in the country, and the most sympathetic survivors you could ever ask for: you will not immediately be able to get your hands on the money owed to you by your publisher.

Within days after your agent's death his agency checking account will be frozen, and whatever balance is in it will remain in it. Whatever funds are receivable by him, such as your advances and royalties, will go undisbursed while his estate is probated. Do you see a nightmare scenario shaping up? Wait, it gets worse.

You (or your lawyer, or the new agent you hired after three minutes of mourning for your last one) pay a visit to your publishers. You talk about your late agent. "Terrible thing," you say, clucking your tongue.

"Terrible," your publisher replies, but clucklessly.

Now you get down to business. "You know, royalty time is coming and you guys are going to owe me all this money. Those idiot lawyers for the estate are giving me a hard time about probate. So how about you paying the royalties directly to me, or to my new agent? If you want to go on paying the commission to the estate, fine, but the rest should go to me. Any problem with that?"

Your publisher's eyes are all sympathy, but his palms are turned up in a gesture of helplessness. "It's not that easy. We've referred the matter to Legal, and you know how they are."

"No," you reply through clenched teeth. "How are they?"

"Uh, very technical," says your editor.

What your editor means is that in the absence of clear-cut legal instructions, Legal can and will do nothing. And there's a lot about your agent's death that is not clear-cut. Did you have an agreement with him spelling out what commissions he was to take on your money? How can anyone be sure he didn't advance you money or incur some charges against your account (like that $435 in manuscript photocopy charges for that auction that flopped) that must be recovered? About the only things that are clear-cut are the contracts your agent negotiated with your publishers irrevocably requiring them to pay all your money to him! Legal cannot take the risk that the estate will sue your publishers for paying you money that rightfully belonged to your agent. The only thing Legal can do is point you in the direction of the bathroom so you don't whoops all over their carpet.

If your agent was incorporated you can breathe a big sigh of relief. Among the many reasons corporations exist is to furnish uninterrupted operation of the firm should the principal officer die. When a corporation is created, stock is issued. If it's issued to just the owner or a small number of people it's called a "closely held" corporation; or the stock can be issued or sold to a great many people. Either way, the principle is the same: the corporation is a business entity with a life of its own. Even if the corporation consists of just one person, the corporation survives his or her death. The corporate bylaws and minutes provide for the administration of the firm by other appointed officers or ones appointed by the heirs to the deceased's estate. The stock in the company is part of that estate, but no matter how horrendous the battle over the deceased's will may be, or even if he or she didn't make one out at all, the fiduciary function of the corporation cannot be interrupted. Of course, if it was a one-person operation there may be a lot of delay and confusion while your situation is being sorted out, whereas in a larger company there are usually other employees familiar with your account who can fill the breach left by your late agent and provide immediate continuity. But whether the corporation is great or tiny, its accounts cannot be frozen. Corporate law allows the firm to carry on while the late owner's estate is being settled.

Why then, you may ask, don't all agents incorporate? The reason is that it doesn't pay to do so if their revenues are modest. The start-up and administrative costs of a corporation are considerable, and the rule of thumb is that unless your firm is earning $100,000 annually or more (which, for an agent, means upward of $700,000 in sales depending on the size of his commission), it's not worth incorporating. I don't know exactly how many literary agents are currently incorporated, but a quick stroll through the pages of *Literary Market Place*, the directory of the publishing trade, suggests that at least half the listed agents are not incorporated.

If your agent is among these, what can you do to avoid the dreadful problems I've described? After consulting with a number of lawyers I would like to make a suggestion that will probably not endear either you or me to your agent but may rescue your money from the clutches of state probate law. And that is for you to ask your agent to sign a letter (with the signature notarized) directing your publishers, in the event of his death, to thereupon pay your net share of monies after commission directly to you and to pay only the agent's commission to the agency or its legal heirs or assigns. I don't know whether such a letter will stick with all your publishers, and it's impossible to predict whether it might be disputed by your late agent's estate, but it beats the scenario I described earlier. Speak to your lawyer about drafting such a letter, which might either be a "To Whom It May Concern" document or a notarized letter addressed to each specific publisher who publishes you.

You might also ask your agent what, if any, provisions he has made for the operation of his company in the event of his death, and whether his employees or heirs are sufficiently familiar with his business to administer it after he's gone. It may be that he has given the matter some thought and decided or even provided in his will to sell or assign his "agency of record" to some other agent with whom he feels his clients will be compatible should he die. It may even be possible for him to structure a sale or assignment to that other agent that is triggered by his death, as a means of avoiding tie-up of cash flow during probate. It's certainly worth exploring, given the alternative.

Even if your agent is incorporated, it's desirable to discuss candidly the measures he has taken against the possibility of his demise. Can his colleagues or employees take over the company? Can his spouse or other heirs? Does he contemplate liquidation of his firm or sale to another agency? Does he carry insurance naming the corporation as beneficiary to furnish it with operating cash during the transition period?

The questions we've raised here are important enough to be factors in choosing and remaining with an agent. For, while every literary agent hopes to live to a ripe age and die in bed, his flesh is heir to the same afflictions that strike so many others down before their time, to say nothing of muggers and crazed taxi drivers. Should your agent succumb to any of these, you will not want his tortured spirit to roam the earth forever howling over the colossal foul-ups and bad will he created by not planning ahead.

❧

MANNERS
AND MORALS

CHAPTER 36

Courtesy

EVERY SOCIETY CREATES rules to prevent anarchy, and the society of author-publisher-agent is no exception. Of course, the more civilized the society, the subtler its rules and the more sophisticated its sanctions for reinforcing them. The publishing business certainly fits the description of a civilized society, comprised as it is of well-educated, literate individuals operating in highly organized (sometimes, anyway) corporate entities and dealing in the extremely sophisticated activity of translating ideas into merchandise.

Actually, if you step far enough away from the sophistication of the publishing process you will see that it still boils down to a matter of seller, buyer, and broker struggling primitively with one another for dominance. Anyone who has lived in or studied the publishing anthill for any length of time can testify that there is as much plundering, treachery, rapine, and bopping on the head as may be found in the most aboriginal of civilizations. The only difference is that we prefer not to call these things by their names, as it sullies our self-image. I remember an editor describing the dapper, distinguished head of one of our most illustrious publishing companies: "Oh, he stabs you in the back like everyone else—it just takes you two weeks to realize you're dead."

In publishing, the rules governing behavior are codified into a system of protocol and etiquette called "courtesy." Courtesy is not always easy to define because editors, authors, and agents each have their own code and the three don't always harmonize. For instance, some agents feel there is nothing wrong with not telling an editor they are submitting the same manuscript to other publishers. From an editor's viewpoint, however, that is discourteous, for if an editor knows he is one of several considering a submission he will behave differently than he will if he thinks he is the exclusive recipient of the manuscript.

Editors may balk at discovering that an author has taken on a project for another publisher while under contract with them. Even though the author may not be breaching his contract (some contracts prohibit authors from working on any other book until the contracted book is completed), and even though the author completes the first book satisfactorily and on time, and even though the author took on the second project because the advance on the first was inadequate for him to live on while writing it, the editor may nevertheless feel that the author has discourteously affronted the monogamous spirit of the author-editor relationship.

Despite the quaintness of the word, a breach of courtesy can be a grave offense that leads to strained or even ruptured relations between an author and publisher or agent and publisher. I recall with a shiver how, as a tyro in the publishing business, I committed such a gaffe against the late and great Macmillan editor Peter Ritner, a blunt and bearish man who brooked no nonsense from callow upstarts. It happened in a swank restaurant at the height of the luncheon hour. I told him I had been speaking to another publisher about his author. "That," Ritner boomed at me in his awesome operatic baritone, "was most discourteous of you, sir." All that night I tossed in bed listening for the stomp on the stairs of Macmillan editorial assistants coming to frog-march me off for interrogation.

Space limitations prohibit me from enumerating all the points of protocol and etiquette that prevail in the editorial world, even if I knew what they were. Many of them are the same rules of the road that regulate other forms of social intercourse. Others are unique to our business. Until you feel completely comfortable in that world, until you know the players and are able to bend or break the rules with impunity, the following ten commandments ought to keep you out of the more serious forms of trouble.

1. *Keep your big mouth shut.* When speaking to agents and editors, refrain from criticizing other agents and editors. You must never assume that the person you are talking to cherishes the same poor opinion of

someone that you do. Many is the time I've listened to prospective clients complaining that this editor was a jerk and that publisher was a fool and this agent was a crowning idiot, and I've found myself thinking, "What's wrong with this guy?"

If you've had a bad experience, say as little as you can, and if you can't be charitable, perhaps it's best to say nothing at all. Lord knows, people in our business understand when you tell them you toured Chicago and Denver and there were no books in the stores, or your publisher originally promised you a 25,000-copy printing but ended up ordering only 7,500 copies. But for you to say, "My editor just sat there and did nothing, and my agent was too busy going to cocktail parties" may reflect worse on you than on those you so harshly judge, however deserving of criticism they may be.

2. *Don't be overly chummy with editors.* Whether or not you have an agent, be restrained in your dealings with editors. It is more important for them to respect your work than to like or love you. You must never forget that editors work for corporations dedicated to making a profit, and as often as not that profit is made at the expense of authors. However tight you and your editor may be, the time must inevitably come when you will want something he cannot give you, and he will want something you cannot give him. In the resulting negotiation, the closer your friendship, the harder it will be for you to hold out for the best terms. Your editor may care deeply about you, but his corporation cares deeply about its bottom line, and few editors will stake their job for the sake of an author.

From the viewpoint of an agent, the biggest discourtesy imaginable is for an editor to take advantage of an author's vulnerability. That's why many agents take strenuous measures to keep authors and editors apart and to funnel all communications through their agency. Many agents resist giving out their clients' phone numbers to editors or allowing any direct exposure of authors to publishing personnel. They are acting out of concern that editors may take advantage of authors if given the opportunity.

My own view is that a certain amount of contact is both necessary and desirable, and as long as authors are aware of the pitfalls of such contact, and keep their agents apprised of all developments, things cannot go too far wrong.

3. *Keep your big mouth shut.* Think before you speak. The things you tell an editor may not have the effect you intended and in fact may have the opposite one. The editor who granted you a nine-month delivery date

on your book may not be delighted to learn that you'll be finishing it four months ahead of schedule. He may in fact be appalled that a project as demanding as that one will take so little of your time, upset that you're not doing your research or that you're writing too fast or that the manuscript will come in too short. Better simply to say, "Don't worry, you'll get your book on time." If you do think you're going to finish it early and your editor thinks he would like to get it on an earlier list, you can say you'll try to turn it in sooner.

Volunteer as little information as possible, and try to think things through from an editor's viewpoint. *Should* you be telling your editor you don't want any more money this year? *Should* you be telling your editor you weren't terribly happy with the first draft but you're sure the final one will be okay? *Should* you be telling your editor you had to take on another writing project to make ends meet?

Authors volunteer all sorts of information because they feel the editor is their friend. But if you'll try to project yourself into the mind of your editor, or better yet of his boss, you might find yourself biting your tongue a little more often.

4. *Go through your agent for everything.* If you do have an agent, centralize all dealings through him or her. Contracts, submissions, delivered manuscripts should all be sent to your agent no matter how convenient it is for you simply to send the material directly to your editor. Aside from observing the procedural proprieties by doing things this way, you keep your publishers on notice that you prefer for them to deal with your agent rather than with you. Even your correspondence with your editor should be sent to your agent for review and forwarding. That way your agent may pick up on some things you probably shouldn't be telling. And if that sounds like censorship, it's better than committing a blunder that might injure your relations with your publisher.

5. *Keep your big mouth shut.* If you have an agent, he will brief you before you go into a meeting with an editor. Listen very carefully to what he has to say. A good agent will background you not merely on your immediate business with your editor but on such things as the state of your publisher ("They're hot right now," or "They're hungry, they haven't had a big book in three seasons"), the position of your editor ("He just joined the firm and he has to bring some good books in fast," or "He has no clout over there"), and other tidbits that will help you get a fix on conditions at your publishing house. Your agent will also tell you what to

say and, perhaps more important, what not to say. And if he tells you not to say something, then for crying out loud don't say it, or leave it for your agent to explain. Your agent undoubtedly has good reasons for with-holding certain information from your publisher, and those reasons may not always be clear to you. There may be undercurrents in his relationship with your editor that have nothing to do with you, or your agent may know something that you don't. He may be conducting negotiations with your editor for other authors besides you (there are other authors besides you, you know), and his dealings on your book may be part of a larger strategy. If your agent accompanies you to a meeting or luncheon, watch him so he can signal you with his eyes. Or sit beside him so he can signal you with a swift kick in the shins.

6. *Report everything to your agent.* In due time you may have direct contact with your editor and other staff members of your publisher concerning a variety of matters. Your editors might feel there's no point in bothering your agent about small stuff, so they will contact you directly. In most cases the business at hand will be routine, and requests will be innocent. But they can develop into problems if the author isn't alert or fails to discuss developments with his agent. Those routine queries about your manuscript by your copyeditor can develop into a request for a rewrite. The nice young lady who calls asking you to name some dates when you're free for promotional appearances may end up bullying you to accept a time that is inconvenient to you. I'm not saying it will happen every time, but it has happened in the past, and it can happen to you if you don't keep your agent au courant.

7. *Keep your big mouth shut.* When you're out with an editor, don't contradict your agent or question his handling of your work. And don't tolerate your editor's questioning of your agent's handling of your work. Publishers often have a vested interest in dividing authors and agents, and anything you inadvertently do to help them promote such divisions can only redound to your discredit and disadvantage.

8. *Don't play your agent and editor off against each other.* In your eagerness to please everybody, you may end up defeating yourself. On many occasions, for instance, an author and editor may have a friendship that long predates the relationship between author and literary agent. The introduction of the agent into that bond creates instabilities that may result in jealousy, tension, and even hostility, and the author sometimes fosters these emotions without realizing it, for it is, after all, highly

gratifying to have two people fighting over you. How often has a client said to me, "That dirty rat Joe down at Feemster House has been taking advantage of our friendship for years, so on that next contract I want you to wring every dollar out of him that you can." Then, a moment later, he'll add, "But go easy on the guy, okay? I mean, he and I are old friends."

Experienced agents are sensitive to the dynamics of friendships between authors and editors and don't barge into the middle of them like crazed water buffalos. If, however, your agent does feel he has to be firm or tough with your old buddy, don't interfere. That, after all, is what you hired him for.

9. *Keep your big mouth shut.* Don't spread rumors or gossip, however knowledgeable it makes you look. For, in the long run, it makes you look like, well, a gossip. Because this is a gossipy industry, discretion is a highly prized virtue, and one that far outlasts the pleasures of spreading the Hot Scoop about somebody. And because this is also a small industry, gossip has a way of turning on its disseminators. As in any small town, you never know who is a friend, ally, relative, or business associate of whom. Rumors are traced to their sources with far more ease than you would imagine. Don't be a source: You don't need enemies.

10. *And finally—Keep your big mouth shut.* When in doubt, err on the side of silence. Let your work and your agent speak for you. Whenever you feel that impulse to say something that you suspect may be out of line, consider that you really have only two choices: count to ten and call your agent, or count to twenty and call your agent.

Don't make your agent's job harder by putting him into the position of having to apologize for you or explain away some indiscreet things you may have said. "God!" an agent friend of mine once burst out. "My job would be so easy if it weren't for authors!"

Although we tend to lose sight of the fact, writing is still a profession. Behave professionally. As a wise person once said, the best way to save face is to keep the bottom half of it closed.

CHAPTER 37

Pet Peeves

I AM NOTHING if not fair and am perfectly willing to be convinced that the rotten things authors do are at least as rotten as the rotten things publishers do. But after half an hour of intense soul-searching (it is a waste of time to search an agent's soul longer than that), I have concluded that it just ain't so.

I have, however, compiled a list of pet peeves about authors accumulated over many years of association with them. I know that many of my publishing colleagues share my attitudes, so I trust that my complaints will not sound mean-spirited. And while I offer them to you with a light heart, some of them may be irritating enough to your agent or publisher to take the keen edge off your relationship with them. So, if you are a perpetrator of a few of the transgressions described below, I urge you to mend your wicked ways.

I must say right off the bat that among the things authors do that upset me, delivering manuscripts late is not one of them, at least most of the time. Lateness is the medium in which agents live. We breathe late manuscripts and eat late checks and drink late contracts. And lateness in a creative person is certainly more understandable and forgivable than it is in a business organization. I have never known an author to be deliberately late with a book, but I have known many a publisher to be deliberately late with a check.

What kills me is authors who don't *tell* me they're going to be late.

Publishers schedule books many months in advance, and in most cases are able to pull a book out of the schedule if given sufficient notice. In most cases, too, a publishers will grant the author a reasonable extension of the delivery date. If, however, out of embarrassment or some other reason (such as a moonlighting gig the agent doesn't know about), an author doesn't level with his agent, he will not only get himself into trouble, but his agent as well. An agent who knows the truth can go to bat for his client, make excuses, concoct a fib. But if an agent sincerely assures an editor that a book will be turned in in June because that's what his client told him, when the client knew all the time that there wasn't a chance in hell that he could make the deadline, the agent's credibility will be damaged.

I make very few inflexible rules for my clients, but this is one of them: no matter how embarrassing your reasons may be, I insist that you tell me the truth so that I can make proper excuses for you. (I, of course, have never lied on behalf of a client. What kind of agent would I be if I lied on behalf of a client?)

Lying to your agent is a mortal sin, but authors commit many venial ones as well, and oddly enough, it is the latter variety that drives me absolutely up the wall.

Take authors who misspell "Foreword," for instance. I strongly feel that anybody who turns in a manuscript containing a "Forward" deserves automatic shredding of his manuscript plus the first three fingers of his right hand. You would think I would not have to explain to professionals who make their livings with words that a foreword is a *fore-word*, a word that comes before the main text. But as the Forward-to-Foreword ratio on manuscripts submitted to my agency is about one out of three, I can see that the correct spelling cannot be stressed enough. (I hesitate, however, to criticize writers for not knowing the difference between a foreword, a preface, and an introduction, since I don't understand it either.)

The Forward-Foreword offense is part of a larger conspiracy to send me to an early grave. I am referring to authors who don't copyread their manuscripts before submitting them. An occasional, random typo is one thing, but when I realize that the author never bothered to reread his manuscript, have it reviewed by a good speller, or run it through the spell-checker on his word processor, a murderous rage comes over me and I am compelled to steal into the night to overturn garbage cans and scratch automobile fenders with my ring. Don't authors understand, I growl at alley cats as I kick them, that today's literary marketplace is so intensely competitive that a poorly spelled manuscript can lose somebody a sale?

A subspecies of the above-mentioned type misspells critical words and names, and misspells them consistently, focusing a glaring light on its own carelessness. I remember a Biblical novel in which the word "pharaoh" was spelled "pharoah" throughout, and in a book that long, that's a lot of pharoahs. I have often wondered why, if the word is pronounced *fayro*, lexicographers have chosen to place the *a* before the *o*. In fact, what is an *a* doing in the second syllable at all? Such speculations do not mitigate one's intense annoyance at having to correct such errors over and over again in saga-length manuscripts.

Speaking of repetitious errors, I'm reminded of those authors who print the title of their book at the top of every page of manuscript. I don't know where this quaint custom arose. I suppose it has its origins in the paranoiac fantasy that part of a manuscript will inadvertently be separated from the rest in a publisher's office.

Against this remote possibility must be weighed the not-so-remote one that the title you print on every page of your manuscript will be a lousy one. Like many publishing people I am a fanatical believer in the importance of titles: a good or bad one can significantly affect the fate of a book. All too often I'll get a good book with a bad title, and after kicking alternate titles around the author and I will agree on a new one. I'll then prepare a new title page only to discover that the discarded title appears on every page of the manuscript. Now what? I must now either go out with a badly titled book or have the entire manuscript reprinted just to knock the offending title off every page. Luckily, the advent of word processing makes it easier to run off modified manuscripts. Still, do us both a favor and leave the title off the top of every page.

On occasion an author will send me a book printed out in uncut, accordion form. I ask myself what terrible thing I did to this person that he should avenge himself on me so cruelly. Am I supposed to read his manuscript standing up, or to unfold it on my living room floor and creep down the room on my hands and knees? Am I expected to separate each page at the perforation after completing it? I think it's time that writers understood something about literary agents: their standard reading posture is supine, head elevated sufficiently to glance at a baseball game or sitcom on television. Now that I've revealed this tightly guarded secret, perhaps you'll be more considerate and instruct your printer to separate the pages of your manuscript.

One author used a poor font that made all lowercase *g*'s look like *s*'s and *s*'s look like *g*'s, so that words like "kissing" came out" kiggins" and "giggles" looked like "sissleg." I developed severe eyestrain after three pages and was certifiably brain-dead after fifteen.

These may sound like the querulous whinings of an excessively fastidious man, but most responsible agents feel it's better to catch problems in their offices than risk irritating editors, who, all other things being equal, might choose the clean manuscript over one requiring any editorial work.

No amount of work will rectify the manuscript that smells of tobacco smoke, however. Every once in a while I will open a manuscript box to be greeted with a gust of vile fetid air. "This manuscript stinks," I will comment to an assistant, "and I haven't even begun it." Heavy smokers don't realize that their habit imparts the same odor to typing paper that it does to clothing.

Occasionally I come across intriguing items nestled in the leaves of a manuscript, notably hair. Although the appearance of a long female hair may stimulate pleasant fantasies for me as I leaf through somebody's book, not all agents and editors respond quite so benignly, particularly if the hair is not human. So please, authors, fumigate and groom your manuscripts before posting them to your agents and editors.

And when you do post them, may I ask you not to have them bound or specially boxed or wrapped? Just a loose manuscript in a typing paper box wrapped and taped securely enough to get safely through the postal system. There seems to be a law of nature that the quality of a manuscript declines in inverse proportion to the elaborateness of its package. When I receive a manuscript bound by brass screws with a plastic embossed cover, lovingly wrapped in chamois cloth, set in a velvet-lined cedar box, shrink-wrapped, packed in turn in a fireproof strongbox secured with iron bands, I am prepared to stake my career on the likelihood that this book is one colossal dud.

There is a particularly lukewarm place in my heart for foreign authors who are obliged to use typing paper of different dimensions—approximately ½ inch too long and ¼ inch too narrow—from the standard American 8½ by 11 inches. I realize how chauvinistic it must sound to deplore the paper that was probably good enough for Thomas Mann, Jean-Paul Sartre, and Graham Greene, but because agents usually place manuscripts in submission boxes to protect them and present them attractively, it drives us crazy to get a misshapen manuscript from the Continent requiring Procrustean measures to package the submission.

Authors who submit their only copy of a manuscript are, to say the least, an intense source of curiosity to me. They brazenly challenge the immutable law causing such manuscripts to get lost in the mails. The advent of cheap photocopy services has stimulated a rise in lost manuscripts, for authors who used to type an original and carbon now type an original only and bring it to a photocopy shop, where another immutable law causes it to get mixed up with somebody's master's thesis. Again, the development of word processors will eventually make the question of lost manuscripts academic, but computers can crash and disks get lost. So keeping a hard copy is definitely a good idea.

Then there are the authors who administer tests to their agents. Some try a cute trick of turning one page in their manuscript upside down. If the agent returns the manuscript with that one page still upside down, it proves he didn't read the manuscript page for page. There are authors who quiz their agents about specific scenes and characters. A typical dialogue might sound like this:

AUTHOR: Did you like my book?

AGENT: Oh, yes, loved it, loved it.

AUTHOR: Great. What did you think of my character Pflonk?

AGENT: Pflonk? Terrific character. Nicely developed.

AUTHOR: Hah! Gotcha! There was no such character in my book!

I assure you that when it comes to an important book your agent reads your manuscript carefully. With so much riding on it, he has to. But most agents I know don't have time to read their clients' work page for page, nor do they need to in order to get a sense of its quality, organization, and pace. In fact, they don't even need to in order to sell it. With certain kinds of material, such as books in a series, a light once-over is enough to satisfy your agent that all is in order and the work follows the original outline.

Plainly, the evil that authors do may be categorized as Class B Misdemeanors, punishable by groans, rolling eyes, sighs of frustration, and indulgent smiles. I would like to think that you are as tolerant of your agent's foibles. Agents do have them. (I know this only from talking to authors). There is one extremely successful agent who likes to boast he's never read anything he's sold. And there's another who, every time he makes a big deal for a client, gloats, "That will pay for a new set of radials for my sports car," or, "Now I can put that new wing on my house."

I consider myself truly fortunate in not being possessed of any personality traits that irritate others. Well, maybe one or two. All right, maybe a few more than that. Okay, okay, so I'm riddled with them. But at least I know how to spell "Foreword."

CHAPTER 38

This Sporting Life

I F YOU'RE A sporting type you don't necessarily have to travel to Las Vegas or Atlantic City to find exciting action. It's right here on Publishers' Row. Behind the doors of every publisher and literary agency you'll find enough off-track gambling to satisfy the most reckless plunger. And while it's not, at first glance, as heady as chemin de fer or baccarat, the stakes are often just as high and the suspense as nerve-racking.

All business decisions are gambles to a degree. That is why one important Roman patron goddess of business was Fortuna, the same deity who presided over the fates of gamblers. Fortuna was depicted as blind, undoubtedly furnishing our language with the term "blind luck." However much the prudent businessperson attempts to minimize risk, however extensive the safeguards, warranties, disclaimers, escape clauses, and statistical precedents insuring the success of any business venture, there is always Blind Luck lurking just out of view, concocting some preposterous scenario, an unheard-of disaster, a combination of events that defies all odds, a random occurrence that mocks human intelligence and humbles the mightiest among us.

The risks essayed by publishing people may not be as glamorous or dramatic as those of, say, folks in the oil business, but the processes of evaluating information and acting on it are essentially similar. In fact, the analogy may be very apt, because in both fields you will find two distinct types. On the one hand, there is the wildcatter who risks everything on a hunch. On the other is the cautious investor who sinks wells over known and extensive oil pools that have been mapped and measured by geological experts. The wildcatter, risking all, walks away either a millionaire or a pauper; the conservative investor may spend nine dollars to make ten, but his return is as close to guaranteed as anything Dame Fortuna can deliver.

I have a tendency to romanticize the past and suspect I may be doing so when I say that it seems to me that publishers of an earlier era in our history took more risks. But from what I have read about our industry, and what I remember about the time when I entered it, publishers were disposed to gamble more than today's breed. This may be due to the fact that their companies were more independent than present ones are, and the founders of earlier publishing houses relied more heavily on their own taste and judgment rather than on the input of editorial committees, the pressures exerted by conglomerate managers and hierarchy, and the unsettling influence of bookstore chains. There are still some wildcatters in the publishing business if you know where to look, but I'll stand by my opinion that today's publishers conduct their business more conservatively than their forebears.

These publishers assess reading trends the way insurance companies assess actuarial data. They seek proven authors wherever possible, or make unproven authors prove themselves with extensive samples of their work. They do, of course, publish their share of first novels, midlist books, and works of serious literature, but their lists are amply weighted in the direction of books by or about stars, books that fit safe formulas or follow fads, and books developed with a view to making a sure profit. The phrase "downside risk" is frequently heard in the board meetings of today's publishing companies as the officers contemplate worst cases and invent catastrophic scenarios designed to chasten adventurous editors. They are reminded that only one book out of ten makes a solid profit for the company, and only five out of ten earn back costs and overhead. The resulting books are, predictably, seldom imaginative. The postwar trend toward publishing mergers and acquisitions and attempted mergers and acquisitions focused on companies with large backlists, like Harper-Collins, Doubleday, and Harcourt Brace. Backlist houses generate a great deal of guaranteed and easily harvested revenue to balance potential losses from gambles hazarded on best-sellers.

On any given day in the publishing industry, you can find countless numbers of people weighing odds and placing bets. The most common center of this activity is acquisition of books. The purchase of even a midlist novel is far more of a risky business than most authors think. Authors complain, "Why can't a rich company like Simon & Schuster or Random House take a chance on my novel for a lousy $7,500?" But that amount is just a fraction of the cost of publishing a book. The expense of manufacturing, distributing, advertising, and selling it, plus the publisher's overhead expenses covering rent, staff payroll, office maintenance, utilities, and the like, may bring the investment to ten times or more the advance that the firm paid the author for the rights to his book. Thus, as the fate of your manuscript is being weighed by a publisher, all those costs are being assessed against the projected revenue from book sales and subsidiary income.

If acquisition of a midlist book is as fraught with risk as this, what kind of gamble must a blockbuster be? Interestingly enough, in some respects it's probably less of one. A literary novel by an unknown writer is far more dependent on the vagaries of reviewers, word of mouth, and luck than is the latest novel by a best-selling author. Looking at the numbers on that author, a publisher can pretty much guarantee a minimum sale on the new book that justifies a huge offer, however good or bad that new book may be. When the bidding for the late James Clavell's *Whirlwind* came to rest at $5 million, with the hardcover-paperback price going to William Morrow and Avon, Tom McCormack, publisher of St. Martin's Press, wrote an article demonstrating how safe an investment $5 million actually was in light of Clavell's illustrious sales history.

Nevertheless, when the bidding for a big book or author gets frenzied, publishers can sometimes lose their heads in precisely the way that bidders at an art auction do. Then such unwonted and dangerous emotions as lust, greed, and vanity cloud the normal equability of a publisher's mind and you end up with one of those headline-making deals that elicits comments from people in the trade, at lunches for months afterward, that "they'll never earn that advance back in a million years." Sometimes publishers deliberately overpay to acquire a coveted author. That author's books may become a loss leader to make some kind of statement to the publishing industry, to authors and agents, and to the press. At other times, publishers overpay or seem to overpay because they genuinely believe they can earn their investment back. Some years ago, an agent conducted what is known as a blind auction on a very commercial first novel. Unlike the usual publishing auction where publishers are informed of each other's bids and allowed to raise theirs until top dollar is reached, in a blind auction each publisher must make one offer and one offer only, and that one must be his best. The auction was won for a price reported at $850,000; the next highest bidder came in for something like $250,000! Had the top bidder overpaid? In fact, the high price they paid stimulated a Herculean effort to recoup it, and I am reliably told that the investment was indeed recouped. So, one publisher's crazy gamble may prove to be another's shrewd investment.

Another form of legalized gambling conducted daily by publishers is known as "setting the printing." Here again, publishers do all they can to minimize the guesswork involved in determining the number of copies of any given book to be printed. The author's previous track record and the sales history of similar books on the publisher's list (as well as those on other publishers' lists) are among the key figures deliberated on by sales and production staffs.

Sales representatives solicit orders from buyers at bookstore and at bookstore-chain offices, and those orders furnish publishers with what is known as the "advance sale" numbers that enable them to fix a minimum print run. Worked into the calculations might be such pertinent information as movie, magazine, or foreign deals made on the book prior to publication, tie-ins of current events, the author's promotability, and other factors that promise to stimulate interest among potential consumers. Then some tricky number-crunching takes place. For instance, it is well known that the more copies printed in one print run, the cheaper is the cost per copy. Just as obviously, if a publisher prints too many copies, the losses from returns will usually outweigh the profits of a lower cost per copy. Usually, but not always. Publishers may sometimes "force" a large printing, gambling that the profit from a 150,000-copy printing that takes 50 percent returns will be higher than that from a 100,000 copy printing that takes only 40 percent returns.

Publishers gamble in quite a lot of other ways. They may try a daring cover concept or an unusual advertising campaign, offer an unusually high discount to lure stores to stock more copies of a book, or put an author on tour in the hope that the books sold on the strength of his or her charisma will make more money than what they would save if they did not put the author on tour at all.

The real hotbed of gambling activity is literary agencies, however. Perhaps because they are not heavily burdened by rigid organizational structures and procedures, and are responsible only to their clients, most agencies can maneuver faster than publishers and are more comfortable in an environment of risk.

On a typical day I am confronted with half a dozen situations that challenge my gambling acuity. Here are a few that I juggled the other day. What would you have done in my place?

1. I did a multiple submission of a nonfiction book and set the closing date for bids for a Friday. On Friday, three publishers called turning the book down without making an offer. A fourth made an offer of $25,000, barely acceptable but up to that point the only offer in town. Then the last house checked in. The editor adored the book and was totally confident that she could top $25,000, indeed top it substantially. But her boss was out of town and unreachable and she could not make an offer until the following Monday. Could I extend my closing date to next week? I asked the $25,000 bidder if he would do so. He said no, and he would withdraw his offer at the end of Friday. Should I turn him down and wait to see what, if anything, happens next week?

2. A publisher wanted to sign a fast-rising paperback author I represent to a long-term contract. The author's latest book had just been published and it figured to earn him about $10,000 in royalties above the $10,000 advance his publisher had paid him. The publisher's offer was a $60,000 advance, or $20,000 per book. The royalties on the three-book package were to be jointly accounted, meaning that even if any single book in the package earns more than $20,000, he will not be entitled to royalties until a total of $60,000 has been earned on the entire contract. The offer was attractive: The author is guaranteed twice the advance he currently receives. However, there is a strong possibility that if we contract for one book at a time, the value of the second or third book could be considerably higher than $20,000. Of course, it could also be considerably less. Should we go for the bird in the hand, or speculate on the two in the bush?

3. A best-selling paperback novelist has ambitions to be published in hardcover, and I have entered into discussions with two publishers. One is a hardcover house that does not own its own paperback firm, the other a hardcover-softcover combination. The former is a very prestigious company, but because it is not in a position to guarantee paperback publication it can offer no more than $250,000 for the author's next novel.

If the firm does well with it, however, a paperback auction might bring the author a headline-making $1 million paperback deal, and her 50 percent share of it would come to $500,000.

The hard-soft house is offering a $500,000 guarantee, and, as in all such deals, the author will receive a full paperback royalty instead of splitting it with her hardcover publisher, as she would have to do if she chooses the first option. The hard-soft house does not, however, possess the cachet of the hardcover-only house, nor does the deal have the publicity value of a paperback auction conducted by a hardcover-only house. But what if after we select the hardcover-only house that firm conducts a paperback auction that turns out to be a flop?

How I handled these situations isn't important in this context; what is, is the difficulty of calculating the odds, and being responsible for the consequences of a wrong guess. Most agents I know discuss these options with their clients, so that the decision is as well-informed as possible. Some agents make the decisions on their own, however, because they (and perhaps their clients as well) take the attitude that the agent knows best, otherwise why hire one? Early in my career I learned that that is not always the wisest course. I called a client who was making a good living writing paperbacks, and casually informed him I'd turned down a $2,500 offer for a quickie paperback. "You did what?" he snapped. It turns out he'd had some financial setbacks, had a couple of weeks of downtime, and would very much have appreciated the opportunity to make a few thousand relatively easy dollars, even though his going rate per book was closer to $20,000. Since then I've decided never to second-guess my client, even though I run the opposite risk of having a client say to me, "Why are you bothering me with these piddling offers?"

If I ever retire from publishing, I figure I will have received superb training for the career of bookmaker. But if I've learned anything, it's this: you can't possibly lose by betting that in the long run, publishers will make bigger profits on books than authors will.

I'm willing to lay ten to one on that.

CHAPTER 39

Back to Basics

A S THE STAKES continue to rise in the publishing business, writers are adopting a wide range of strategies to advance themselves out of the midlist and onto better-selling plateaus. I myself have recommended a number of such strategies in these pages. Recently, however, as I respond again and again to the question of what one can do to escape midlist oblivion, it's begun to dawn on me that many writers have been ignoring the most obvious answer: write better. The truth is that if all other things are equal, the author with better writing skills is the one who will move out of the pack.

Instead of reviewing what's selling these days and who is buying it, then, I thought it might be worth reminding you about some of the most common and flagrant writing transgressions to be found in a typical harvest of fiction works that fetches up on my desk. I hasten to point out that the perpetrators are by no means mere amateurs, but professional writers as well, so let those who are without sin skip this chapter.

I have to confess at the outset that as I was preparing my list, I realized that nobody has ever come up with a better formula for analyzing problem manuscripts than my late boss, Scott Meredith, and his "Plot Skeleton," which goes something like this: A sympathetic hero or heroine confronts an obstacle or antagonist, creating a conflict that must be credibly overcome through the protagonist's efforts. These efforts result in a triumphant resolution that is satisfying to the reader. Unsympathetic protagonists, inconsequential conflicts, and uninspired resolutions are the characteristics of most of the fiction that agents pop into stamped, self-addressed envelopes and return to senders. I have made notes, however, on some other fundamental failures that personally turn me off, and I've boiled these "sins" down to seven. I should add that the problems I am about to list are the type that jump out at me so quickly that I can usually make a determination about a book containing them after only a few minutes of reading.

1. *The Sin of Lousy Dialogue.* Many writers try to carry their books on narrative alone, leaving me hungry for some conversation. Often, when at last I do encounter dialogue, it's of a trivial "Hello, how are you?" "Fine, thank you" variety. By fanning a manuscript like a deck of cards, I can instantly perceive a paucity of quotation marks. Or, if you like your torture slow, you can read page by page waiting for somebody to talk to somebody else. Dialogue is an invaluable fictional device, yet many writers believe they can tell a story with a minimum of it. A playwright once said that a good line of dialogue reveals something about the speaker, the person spoken to, and the person spoken about. Without dialogue, a work of fiction becomes a tract.

A rapid scan of a manuscript often discloses the opposite problem, a book so replete with dialogue that it reads like a screenplay. In such books, the dialogue reveals little about anybody, because it's mostly talk, and you have to listen to endless conversations in the hope of seizing some nuggets of genuine story. It should be remembered that dialogue is not only a character-revealing device, it is also a form of action, but an excess of it is will have the opposite effect. Those guilty of this particular shortcoming should ask themselves in what way a dialogue scene moves the story forward. If too slowly, or not at all, you're doing something wrong.

Writers sometimes forget what dialogue sounds like when actually spoken, and they should therefore try speaking it aloud or performing it with another person. That way, they might avoid one of my all-time pet peeves, which might be described as, "What did you say your name was?

"John, we've been married for fifty years and you haven't given me flowers for the last thirty."

"Gosh, Mary, I hadn't realized it."

"It's true, John."

"Well, Mary, I'll just have to do something about that.

"I hope you will, John." etc.

2. *The Sin of Inaction.* I hate this one because it takes me so long to diagnose. I may have to read as much as half of a manuscript before I realize that nothing, in fact, is happening. This is also the most heart-breaking failure in terms of wasted time and talent, particularly when you realize that it is the most avoidable. Most of the time, it's the result of poor outlining or no outlining at all. By synopsizing your work before you begin, you will readily detect soft spots in your story.

A common offshoot of this problem is often found in mystery novels. I call it the "travel fallacy." After a crime is committed, our protagonist picks up a clue and visits a witness or suspect, where he picks up another clue and visits another person, and so forth. All that traveling from one place to another gives the illusion of action, but when you analyze it you realize that the only thing that has happened is the protagonist has gotten into a car or boarded a plane, boat, or bus and gone somewhere. But travel is not to be confused with action.

3. *The Sin of Skimpy Detail.* Many fiction writers believe that the best way to improve their craft is to study other fiction writers. Certainly one can benefit from reading the work of others. But if your spare time is limited you might benefit more by reading nonfiction. And not just history and biography but esoteric stuff like costumes of eighteenth-century France, Florentine church architecture, Samurai swords, and modern glassmaking. This will help to cure one of the surest signs of amateurism in fiction, the generalized description: "On the Czarina's desk lay a Fabergé egg." Don't you think a reader would rather read something like, "On the Czarina's inlaid walnut and ormolu escritoire a gorgeous gold Fabergé egg stood on a tripod of wrought gold. The egg was segmented with translucent green enamel trellising and inlaid with ceremonial scenes, miniature portraits of her children, and a particularly handsome portrait of Nicholas resplendent in blue uniform and gold epaulettes . . ." etc.

Though books about furniture-making or Russian enamels may not be as entertaining as the latest novel by your favorite writer, reading the former will ultimately pay bigger rewards in the rich texture of your writing.

4. *The Sin of Unimaginativeness.* Not only do writers fail to describe the real world in sufficient detail, often they portray imaginary worlds in inadequate detail as well. If that world is not thoroughly thought out, readers will know it and eventually lose attention. I find this to be particularly true of fantasy and science fiction, where it is all too easy to think readers will buy into a writer's world simply because it is alien. A planet warmed by binary suns may be a good premise, but if the writer does not describe in detail how these twin stars affect this world's ecology, culture or customs, the strangeness of the premise will soon wear off and the reader will be left in the equivalent of Akron, Ohio, in space. Worlds that never were possess as much detail as those that are or used to be, and the writer's task is to research those worlds as assiduously as a scholar might research ancient Thebes or Alexandria.

5. *The Sin of Weak Characterization.* A similar criticism applies to characterization: many writers simply do not "research" their characters in adequate depth. Making up character details as one goes along may work well for a rare few, but I get the impression that many writers have not "investigated" or "interviewed" their characters at length. The result is trite people.

The way to investigate your characters is to create dossiers on them that can later be reviewed as though one were a reporter going through diaries and scrapbooks. When and where was your character born and raised? Who were his parents, his grandparents? What events, friendships, circumstances affected his upbringing? What schools did he go to, jobs did he take, romances did he have? Whether or not you actually use all of the material you enter into your file or database, your intimacy with your characters will come through to your reader and they will feel you know more about the people in your book than you have revealed.

6. *The Sin of Clichéd Story.* The boredom factor is higher among agents and editors than it is among average readers, and a good thing it is, too. Writers don't always realize that stories that may seem unique to them are trite in the eyes of agents and editors. For every plot you write, we may see dozens of similar submissions. I freely confess to being easily bored, and I've stopped castigating myself for it, as I realize boredom is a critical symptom that the manuscript has gone wrong. I try to monitor the moment at which I started to lose my concentration and involvement, then to analyze precisely what it was that turned me off.

Much of the time, it's a story I've heard before. I am weary of Russian-

American nuclear confrontations, former-CIA vs. former-KGB cat-and-mouse games, Arab–Israeli terrorist machinations, female journalists turned detective, and Colombian drug lords doing just about anything. Not that these stories cannot be rendered fresh: indeed, that is precisely the point. I demand, I beg, that they be rendered fresh. But if I start to nod off, I know that the author has failed to approach a familiar story from an unfamiliar angle, and that's it for me.

7. *The Sin of Triviality.* In order for a book to feel big, it should deal with, or at least allude to, issues that go beyond the day-to-day concerns of its characters. Yet, many authors fail to give their story weight or dimension, and the result is often a book that feels trivial and inconsequential. Take a simple love story: boy meets girl and they fall in love. They have a jealous quarrel and break up, but they are eventually reconciled and end up getting married. Such a story is the stuff of a young adult romance, and that's probably where it will end up.

Now it is December 7, 1941. Boy and girl have met and fallen in love, but on that fateful day the Japanese attack Pearl Harbor and the world is plunged into war. Boy enlists and is shipped overseas to fight. In war-torn Europe he falls in love with a beautiful French girl, while at home girl has fallen in love with an older man in the munitions factory where she works. Boy and girl break up, marry their lovers. Years go by, both marriages go bad. Boy and girl look each other up, discover they still carry the torch for each other, and are reunited.

The difference between these two love stories is vast, but what is the essential difference? It's that in the second one, history, destiny, and war play a part in the story as if they themselves were characters. The war has taken a silly love story out of the realm of triviality and invested it with a dimension that approaches the tragic. It is not difficult for writers to add such dimension to their work but not all of them do so, and if it is missing, I quickly lose attention.

A team that is struggling is often told by its coach to go back to basics. That's not bad advice for struggling writers, either.

❧

CHAPTER 40

Lawyers (Groan!)

WHENEVER A CLIENT asks me if he should show a publishing contract to his attorney, I emit a noise not unlike that of a rutting moose whose girlfriend has just trotted into the woods with his rival. "Please," I beg, "anything but that. Take my firstborn. Take my co-op, even. But don't show your contract to a lawyer. He won't understand."

My attitude is by no means unique. Many publishing people consider lawyers to be humorless spoilsports placed on our planet to raise hypothetical questions about events that have only the remotest possibility of coming to pass. In response to our reassurances that "it will never happen" or "it doesn't work that way," they smugly cite *Gumbo v. Dittersdorf et al.* and send groaning agents back to the negotiating table to haggle over the nuances of such words as "book," "pay," and "publish." And whenever a breach of contract is imagined, these learned jurists are right there with their lawyer-letters, writs, petitions, and injunctions to hold the offending party to the explicit meaning of the contractual provision.

Most of the lawyers I know don't fit this caricature. They make serious efforts to understand the unique nature of publishing law; they are reasonable, thoughtful, realistic, and no more venal than anyone else; and they regard litigation as an extremely distasteful last resort. Nevertheless, by the very nature of their profession, lawyers tend to be extremely literal-minded about the language of contracts. And, sad to say, the literal language of publishing contracts is enough to induce cardiac infarction in even the most liberal of lawyers.

Lawyers ofttimes use legal precedents and forensic experiences that may be germane to coal mining, automobile manufacture, and real estate transactions, but are hardly applicable to publishing situations. Once an attorney is engaged, however, he has an obligation to show his client results for his fee. It is hard for me to believe that an attorney being paid $200 an hour or more will read a contract and hand it back to his client saying, "Looks okay to me," or, "I'd say your agent did everything that I would have done." It is far more likely that he will raise those hypothetical questions and will not be satisfied with an agent's breezy assurances that if This or That happens, it'll be taken care of. After all, most agents don't have law degrees, and while their experience must be respected, how can they predict with any certainty that This or That, or, even worse, The Other Thing, will not happen? Thus do agents frequently find themselves pushed by lawyers into composing contractual language applicable only to the red end of the spectrum of probability.

The involvement of lawyers in publishing contract negotiations often polarizes situations that might otherwise be settled through negotiation. Publishers hate lawsuits and with a few exceptions (described below) will do almost anything to avoid them. While litigation is certainly the ultimate weapon in a dispute, agents are adept at working out compromises that are scarcely different from settlements forged by lawyers after protracted litigation. The difference is that the agent performs gratis the same function for which a lawyer might charge thousands of dollars.

Most authors hold the legal profession in the same awe in which they hold the medical one. I would recommend a healthy dose of skepticism and common sense when it comes to dealing with the former, however. Practitioners of the law are of woman born like the rest of us. Their actions are often dictated by their emotions, their convictions guided by who pays them and how much, and they make as many mistakes and misjudgments as surgeons, engineers, stockbrokers—or literary agents.

You should regard contracts the same way. Contracts are solemn undertakings, yes, but they are not sacred covenants written in heavenly fire. Too many authors regard contracts as rigid structures of legal language constructed to thwart and constrain them. Actually they are flexible tools when used skillfully, and can liberate as well as restrict.

In the relations between publishers and authors or publishers and agents, a great many factors balance the literal language of contracts. Custom and tradition, market conditions, practicalities, and, above all, the power of the players affect the way any given contractual provision gets implemented, ignored, or defied. Let's look at some examples.

Not all contracts provide for a grace period in case an author delivers a manuscript late. Yet I have seldom heard of a publisher canceling a contract at the stroke of midnight on the day a manuscript is due. For practical purposes, a manuscript that is days, weeks, even a month or two late, can still be published on time without undue strain on the editorial or production staffs of a publisher. Now, an attorney may insist on specifying a grace period in a client's contract. Publishers don't like grace periods because they give authors another reason to be late, and authors have too many such reasons already. A zealous attorney might feel that that's a deal-breaker. In practice, if your publisher says, "Try to meet your deadline, but don't sweat it if you're a few weeks late," you can rely on that assurance ninety-nine times out of a hundred.

Friendships between agents and publishers mitigate the stringent language of publishing contracts. Despite a strict option clause requiring an author to deliver his next book to his publisher, on the strength of a tight friendship and an appeal to the goodness of an editor's heart an agent can often arrange for a one-time waiver of the option clause in order for the author to take on a project for another publisher—as long as that project doesn't compete with the work the author is doing for his regular publisher. "Thanks, I owe you one" is a common phrase heard in our business, and when the time comes for the publisher to lean on an agent for the return of favors, the agent may have to twist his client's arm a little to tidy up the debits and credits in the ledgers of obligation. Try to explain this system to a lawyer!

The most important factor by far in tempering the rigidity of publishing contracts is power. Don't let anyone tell you that might does not make right. While the language of any contractual provision may be plain as day, enforcing it is quite another matter if you don't have the money, status, influence, or leverage to do so. A first novelist has very little influence over a rich, powerful publisher, and no matter what his contract may say, it's going to be hard to compel his publisher to live up to every letter of his contract. If the author is a big name, however, the publisher's eager compliance may certainly be counted on. Indeed, a powerful author or agent can compel a publisher to do things that are not in the contract.

For instance, few contracts grant approval of cover art or jacket and advertising copy to authors, even big-name writers. Yet those stars are routinely consulted about such things, and if they don't like them they may well be able to get them changed or thrown out.

When contractual disputes arise, the interpretation that prevails usually belongs to the party with the most power. Nine times out of ten that's the publisher. An individual author of no particular clout may be able to enhance his legal leverage if he is represented by a strong agent, however. The agent who has a large and important clientele in, say, romance fiction may be able to gain advantages for an author who otherwise would have little standing against a publisher and who cannot afford to hire a lawyer.

One of the most important things that experienced agents know is precisely which issues publishers are prepared to litigate and which ones they will back down on. Authors who owe refunds of advances to publishers because of undelivered or rejected manuscripts are often harassed but seldom sued because it's too expensive for the publisher, as well as bad public relations. If there is a lot of money involved, however, a publisher may well go to the mat to recover its advance, or to resist having to pay the balance due on acceptance. The publisher's motive isn't entirely financial. As I pointed out previously, such disputes focus on an important issue: is an advance a loan recoverable by a publisher if the author fails to meet his obligation? Or is it instead a nonrecoverable investment?

Another issue that publishers are not afraid to go to court over is breaches of the author's contractual warranties, especially those for libel. With damages, settlements, legal and court costs, and insurance premiums reaching Olympian heights, most publishers are, I would say, prepared to sue authors they perceive to have dealt with them in bad faith.

Finally, publishers tend to get rather cranky about authors who play fast and loose with their option clauses, particularly big-money authors. The trend over the last decade or so has been for publishers to write more elaborate and tighter option clauses so that star authors cannot capriciously duck out of their obligations when another publisher waves a big check at them. I must say that option clauses are for agents what elaborate locks are for safecrackers. But even if you, your agent, or your lawyer discover a tiny loophole through which to escape from the necessity of submitting your next book to your publisher, there is nothing to guarantee that your publisher won't sue you anyway.

Other than breaching the acceptance, warranty, and option provisions of your contract, there aren't too many offenses you can commit that will land you in court, and even these may be worked out through negotiation most of the time. The same is true, perhaps even more so, for breaches or perceived breaches of contract by publishers. I can think of few so flagrant as to be worth an author's while to prosecute to the bitter end. The threat of a lawsuit, and its attendant bad publicity, may force a negotiated settlement that nets you as much as you would win in a full-blown lawsuit after you have paid legal costs. It you win, that is.

I say all this as a counterpoise to any boasts your lawyer may make that you have an open-and-shut case. Lawyers do their clients a disservice by encouraging them to think there is such a thing as an easy and inexpensive victory. Don't forget that it was an unagented writer, William Shakespeare, who wrote, "The first thing we do, let's kill all the lawyers."

❧

CHAPTER 41

"Let's Run It Past Legal"

HAVING ALIENATED THE legal profession in the previous chapter, I hope to return to grace with some high praise for one branch of the species.

It may be hyperbolic to refer to the legal counsels of publishing companies as "gray eminences," a term one usually assigns to the shadowy power brokers who manipulate the controls of vast corporate or political networks. But it would be no exaggeration to state that tremendous influence resides in the hands of the attorneys who counsel publishing executives on the legal aspects of their companies' operations. Few significant corporate decisions are made without clearance by a publisher's lawyers, and no book is published that has not somehow been affected by procedures originating in the firm's legal department. To the degree that the men and women of those departments are seldom colorful, their eminence may indeed be depicted as gray. But it must never be underestimated, because the power they wield over the fate of your book is both total and final. However headstrong the chief operating officer of a publishing company may be, he or she will almost never override a house counsel's advice.

Owing to the enormous number of legal affairs confronting every publisher, attorneys must be engaged to advise the firms' executives. Small houses with little money to spare for lawyers may hire a small firm or sole practitioner on an hourly or flat-fee basis to perform specific tasks such as drawing up incorporation papers, writing a lawyer-letter, or rendering an opinion about a specific situation. Larger publishers may engage an outside law firm for an annual retainer, which is adjusted if the time spent by the lawyers exceeds a prearranged ceiling. Fees and expenses of litigation are always a matter of separate arrangement, as they absorb extraordinary amounts of billable time.

The largest publishing companies maintain a salaried in-house legal counsel or staff to advise them on the countless matters arising out of the daily operation of the company. Or they may share the legal staff of the conglomerate of which the publisher is one component. In any event, some of the matters dealt with by the in-house counsel may be as minute as a single, but potentially actionable, provocative word in a manuscript; other matters may be as immense and complex as a corporate merger or a major litigation. The publisher's legal department is also in charge of contracts: not just publishing contracts, but those pertaining to everything from the office lease to a bank loan to a distribution deal to the acquisition of another publisher. If there is a notable increase in the time it takes for your book contract to be processed, as authors commonly assert these days, it may be attributable to the workload of the lawyer at the top.

Although routine contracts or deals for sums below a certain figure may never end up on their desks, most of them run very tight ships and insist on reviewing everything contractual that is generated in their bailiwicks. And there is scarcely a corner of the publishing company that does not in some fashion fall in a general counsel's bailiwick. Indeed, his office is sometimes a convenient dumping ground for many of those corporate problems that executives cannot pigeonhole and thus cannot deal with. "You should see some of the stuff I have to handle," one attorney told me. But he handles it decisively. "A general counsel is often a general troubleshooter for the corporation, and we solve lots of problems that are very far afield from our job description. You name it, they'll run it past Legal."

Here are some items that might appear on a typical day's agenda of the house counsel for a large publisher.

- The directors are concerned that the company is vulnerable to a hostile takeover. There is a great deal of stock on the market and its price is temptingly low. A raider might be interested in adding a publishing jewel to his conglomerate crown. A decision must be reached about buying back the stock and funding the maneuver.

- A news magazine has managed to get hold of a set of proofs of a major autobiography that the publisher is bringing out six months from now. Under the guise of a "news story" the magazine has summarized the juiciest passages of the book. The potential for selling first serial rights has been damaged if not ruined. The general counsel is contemplating litigation and is reviewing the legal precedents.
- This publisher is also at the other end of a possible lawsuit. An author has threatened litigation because, he claims, the publisher rejected his book in bad faith. He'd been hired by the publisher to write a biography of a glamorous starlet. But just as he turned in the manuscript it was learned that she'd been arrested for cocaine possession. The publisher rejected the book on the grounds that it was simply a poor job and wants back the large advance paid on signing the contract. The author not only doesn't want to repay the initial advance, but wants to compel the publisher to pay the money due on acceptance, too.
- A delegation of literary agents is scheduled for a meeting to discuss improvements in the publisher's royalty reporting system. The firm's management is loath to spend the large sum of money it will cost to revamp the computerized royalty statements for thousands of books. At the same time, management is anxious not to give offense to the agents and to the large number of authors they collectively represent. The house counsel must determine a negotiating position before going into that meeting.
- There are several high stacks of paper on his desk and coffee table requiring attention. One pile contains routine contracts and contract requisitions calling for his signature or initials. Another contains affidavits, depositions, briefs, and other court papers for him to review. Still another has corporate minutes and other company business for his comments, approval, or other action. And in yet another are some items demanding urgent attention: a subpoena to which a response must be made by Friday; a summary of the terms sought by an agent for a major book on which there is an auction closing at five this afternoon; and a memo from an editor containing the distressing news that a reader has pointed out a dozen passages in a book the company recently published that seem to have been lifted almost verbatim from a book published ten years ago.

- A staff attorney has completed a line-by-line reading of a recently delivered manuscript, a biography of the late great Senator Clemenceau Osterdonk. Osterdonk was allegedly a pederast, a sadomasochist, a drunk, a cokehead, an arsonist, an influence peddler, an ax murderer, and an embezzler with dandruff, halitosis, and athlete's foot—your typical politician, in other words. Although the laws of the land plainly state that one cannot libel a dead person, the senator's estate and its Rambo-type lawyer are ferociously protective of the hallowed reputation of their late lamented, and have threatened to nuke our publisher if he prints Word One of this scurrilous hatchet job. The book will, the lawyer contends, irreparably damage the family's business interests which are dependent on maintaining an image of the deceased as the closest thing to an angel that is to be found in this imperfect world.

The book was impeccably researched by a journalist of unassailable pedigree, then reviewed by his own attorney, who happens to be the world's authority on libel. Our publisher is not afraid to publish this insightful and entertaining book, but neither does it want to provoke a lawsuit it cannot successfully defend. So the publisher's counsel has a ton of questions, modifications, and requests for documentation to take up with the author, and on the corner of his desk rests this thousand page manuscript to which yellow Post-its are affixed. On each of these mini-memos a question has been raised, and there are so many sticking out of the manuscript it looks like a forsythia in bloom. The author must either alter the text to satisfy the attorney's requests, answer his questions in a point-by-point letter of response, or furnish sufficient documentation to demonstrate beyond reasonable doubt that the items in question rest upon a concrete foundation of fact. Even after the author has complied with all of the lawyer's requests, our house counsel will comb the manuscript again and pick a few dozen more nits before declaring it judgment-proof and fit for public consumption.

It's worthwhile for us to tarry over this function of our in-house lawyer. Every "flag" fluttering along the margins of that manuscript represents a fear fluttering in the heart of any responsible attorney. If the threatened lawsuit does materialize, it might take only one poor choice of phrase, one unsupported allegation, one overenthusiastic innuendo, one unattributable quotation to pave the way for a judgment against the publisher.

Old Rambo will be poised to pounce with claws and fangs bared, you may be certain. And not just Rambo, but the attorneys for anybody else mentioned in the book who may feel a victim of defamation, libel, or invasion of privacy.

The fact that the publisher holds a substantial insurance policy indemnifying it against adverse judgments in those areas is of no comfort to our attorney. In the first place, the policy calls for a sizable deductible, somewhere between $100,000 and $500,000, an unrecoverable expense that will make a painful dent in the publisher's profits. For another thing, if the insurance company believes that the publisher was negligent in its responsibility for purging the manuscript of assailable allegations, it may give the company a very hard time and may even cancel its insurance. "No publisher can afford to take that kind of hit," I was told by another attorney. Nor is it of great comfort that the publisher's contract with the author entitles it to recover some or all of its litigation costs and damages from authors' royalties. Rarely is there sufficient royalty revenue to balance the cost of an adverse judgment.

Our house counsel will therefore be forgiven if the queries he has raised in his review of the Osterdonk biography seem picayune. Let's look over his shoulder at a few of them:

Page 15. How do we know O. abused his half-sister when she was four months old? And what, precisely, do you mean by "abused"?

Page 26. Can you document that Uncle Floristan turned O. on to the kicks of Blue Nun administered intravenously?

Page 36. Can you support the innuendo that O.'s German shepherd was "a lot more than his best friend"?

Page 75. Were there any witnesses to O.'s "uncontrollable urge" to flagellate the family chauffeur?

Page 106. Re your statement that O. "bribed his way in one door of the Senate and bribed his way out the other door." Was anyone actually standing at the doors taking bribes? Names?

Page 140. Any documentation to verify that O. and Hermann Goering were "considerably more than nodding acquaintances"?

Page 141. Same question for Joseph Stalin.

Page 142. Same question for Al Capone.

Page 155. For my own enlightenment, can you explicitly describe the sexual contortion alluded to in the second paragraph?

Page 202. Did anyone actually observe O. picking his nose at the luncheon with President Eisenhower?

Page 261. Was O. actually divorced when he started his affair with Mister Ed?

Many such queries are exasperating for an author, particularly in cases where "everybody knows" that the subject of his biography slept with this or that person for years or beat his wife on a regular basis. If all you have to go by is a photo in a movie magazine of the subject escorting his alleged mistress to the Academy Awards ceremonies, however, or if not a single soul can be located who actually witnessed the subject striking his wife (or is willing to testify to that effect), you may be required by a prudent lawyer to fudge your language or throw the dubious passages out entirely.

Your publisher's general counsel does have a degree of discretion about some of the statements made in your book. If, for instance, reference to an affair has been made in half a dozen earlier biographies and the persons alluded to have never contested the references, the attorney may see fit to let your allegation pass, even though it does not rest on hard primary documentation. If he is a literary as well as a legal type, he may be reluctant to water a book down excessively because an overly "lawyered" book can be a ponderous bore. His recommendations may be challenged by publishing executives who feel he is being excessively cautious.

You the author have few options if your publisher insists on legal changes. Most publishing contracts permit a publisher to declare a manuscript unacceptable if the author fails to comply with requests to modify a manuscript to satisfy legal objections. In such cases the author must refund the advance paid on signing the contract, exactly as if he had turned in a book that was editorially unacceptable. The author may then seek a publisher that doesn't have quite so many compunctions.

I would think twice about doing that, though. For one thing, the same objections raised by the original publisher will undoubtedly be raised by others. And, more importantly, your publisher's attorney seeks to protect you as well as his company. You may find the legal vetting of your book upsetting at first, but after you cool down you will probably be grateful to have this eagle-eyed gray eminence on your side.

CHAPTER 42

Moral Rights

TODAY WAS ONE of the worst days of your writing career.

It began when the postman brought you an advance copy of your historical saga, an original paperback, and you started thumbing through it. To your dismay you discovered that over ten thousand words of text had been cut from your manuscript, and a number of sexy scenes modified if not downright bowdlerized. Your contract did give your publisher the right to make editorial changes, but you never dreamed they would go so far. You called your editor and were told the cuts were necessitated by pricing considerations, and the desexing had been performed to make the book more acceptable in certain markets.

No sooner had you recovered from that shock than you received a second in the form of galleys of a novel messengered to you by a packager you work for. The packager had engaged you as a writer-for-hire to write one of a series of novels it had created. Although the series is copyrighted in the packager's name, you'd insisted that your byline appear on your book. At the time you negotiated the contract, you thought that was a smart move. But when you started to review the galleys, you immediately realized that every sentence of your original text had been rewritten by the packager. Outraged, you phoned your packager, who informed you that as his company owns the copyright to your book, he could do anything he wanted to it.

As if these two horror stories weren't bad enough, you suffered the final insult when you attended a screening of the film that had been made from a spy thriller you'd written several years earlier. You were, of course, not so naive as to believe the adaptation would be absolutely faithful to your story, but you were scarcely prepared for the monstrous perversion portrayed on the big screen that evening. Except for the basic premise, the producer had thrown out every idea, every tasteful scene, every line of dialogue in your book. Surrounded by friends and family, you slunk out of the screening room humiliated to the very core of your being. In a black rage, you didn't even wait to return home but entered the nearest phone booth to call your lawyer. "Do you handle criminal cases?" you asked him.

"Some. Why?"

"Because I'm about to commit mass murder." It took three dollars in quarters just to tell him about the butchery that had been perpetrated on your work.

"Okay," he finally said when you let him get a word in edgewise, "here's what I suggest you do. Go straight home, do not attempt to murder anybody. Take out the contracts on your books and examine them carefully. Then call me again and I'll tell you what I'm looking for. You may have a case on a variety of grounds, but I'd be especially interested in any references to *droit moral*."

"Dwah wha'?"

"*Droit moral.* 'Moral right.' Bring your contracts to my office tomorrow. And don't forget your checkbook."

Tempting though it was to go on a killing spree, you took your attorney's advice and returned home, and after belting down a brandy straight you hauled out your contracts and pored over them, looking in particular for the phrase you had heard for the first time, *droit moral*. No luck in the contract for that historical, nor any in the one with your packager. But in the movie contract you struck pay dirt. Or so you thought at first. But as your finger traced the language your heart sank. You picked up the phone.

"No references to *droit moral* in my book contracts," you sighed to your attorney.

"I didn't expect any. And in the movie contract, you waived your moral right, yes?"

"Yes. So I guess that's the end of that."

"Not long ago I would have said yes," your attorney replies. "But there are signs that offer some encouragement. Whether or not the phrase appears in your contract, indeed even if you've waived your so-called moral rights, it may be that they are still recognized and enforced by the courts. I'll do a little research and have some thoughts for you when we meet tomorrow."

Your attorney is right, at least about the signs of change in the law, for an important event occurred on March 1, 1989, and it may presage some profound changes in the relationship between the buyers and sellers of literary and artistic works. On that date, the United States became a signatory of the Berne Convention, an international copyright treaty created to protect copyrighted works in the numerous countries that have signed it.

Included in the treaty is a provision giving artists the right to protect the integrity of their work even after it has been sold. That right is considered "perpetual, inalienable, and cannot be waived."

If your attorney didn't have time to research the Berne Convention and *droit moral* in great depth before you paid him a visit, he might have gotten an excellent summary out of *The Rights of Authors and Artists,* an American Civil Liberties Union handbook written by Kenneth P. Norwick and Jerry Simon Chasen, and published in paperback by Southern Illinois University Press. He might even, as I did, phone Ken Norwick for a briefing. Mr. Norwick is legal counsel to the Association of Authors' Representatives.

Mr. Norwick and his book point out that moral rights are distinguished from the property rights—that is, the rights that you have under the copyright law—that you convey when you license your written work to publishers and producers. *Droit moral* is described as "non-property attributes of an intellectual and moral character which exist between a literary or artistic work and its author's personality; it is intended to protect his personality as well as his work."

In other words, the distortion or mutilation of a work of art or literature could be considered a slur on the character of that work's creator. If you are wondering whether *Shootout at the Bensonhurst Riding Stables* or Book #16 in the Galactic Humungoid science fiction series may accurately be defined as literature, you will be comforted to know that the law offers lots of leeway on that score.

Droit moral embraces three major components: the right of integrity of the work, the right of paternity, and the right of divulgation. The right of integrity posits that a work is a direct expression of the creator's personality, and any harm done to that work reflects on the creator's identity itself. Unauthorized condensation of a literary work, expurgation of supposedly offensive passages, or rewriting of the text without permission are acts that might make it appear the author deliberatly designed the work that way, and subject him to unfounded criticism by his peers or condemnation by posterity. Even if critics feel the changes improve the work, those alterations misrepresent the author's original vision and are therefore a blot on his honor.

The right of paternity irrevocably associates the author's or artist's name with his work (or hers, though it's still called the right of paternity). Your byline cannot be taken off (or put on) without your express permission.

Finally, the right of divulgation gives artists and writers the right to decide at what point their work is finished and ready for exhibition or publication.

While principles of *droit moral* have been widely accepted beyond our shores, they have generally been rejected, or at least not recognized, by the U.S. courts. Thus, because these rights are not generally accepted by the legal system, if you want the protection that they offer you must negotiate for them in your contracts. If, for instance, you wanted to reserve the option to withdraw your byline from a book, you would have to state that explicitly in your book contract.

There have been some promising legal developments in this area of the law in the U.S. in recent years. In 1983, New York State passed an Artists' Authorship Rights Act that, among other things, prohibited exhibition or publication of a work of fine art "in an altered, defaced, mutilated form" without the artist's consent. The law also gave artists the right to claim or disclaim authorship of their works of fine art. The artist who believes his rights under this law have been violated can sue for damages. Similar moral rights legislation has been enacted in California, too.

The New York State act is limited to "works of fine art," and there's the rub. As Ellen M. Kozak, a lawyer and author of *Every Writer's Practical Guide to Copyright Law,* quipped in a piece on the Berne Convention in the *Science Fiction Writers of America Bulletin,* "Writers need not apply." But that may no longer be the case if the *droit moral* provisions of Berne are liberally interpreted in future court challenges.

You can imagine that not everybody greeted the ratification of Berne by the United States with banquets and fireworks. In fact, many publishers and movie and television producers lobbied passionately against it, even though some aspects of it protected their own rights. This was because they feared that the recognition of moral rights in the Berne Convention would threaten the traditional ways in which they have been producing and publishing their works. In response to those fears, Congress declared that Berne neither expands nor limits authors' or artists' rights to object to unauthorized modification of their work. The current thinking, then, is that you must seek remedies in other legal areas.

This bleak view, however, may not necessarily prevail in the days and years ahead. In the first place, many courts have recognized rights remarkably similar to "moral rights" under the guise of traditional trademark and copyright (and even in some cases libel) law. In what may be the most important example, a court found that a television network's substantial, unauthorized editing for television of a Monty Python movie violated the group's rights under American trademark law. Second, many people believe that America's entry into the Berne Convention should provide the impetus for greater recognition of moral rights in this country, and it has already encouraged a movement to lobby Congress to enact specific moral rights protection for authors and artists.

Somewhere out there are authors who will one day suffer the indignities hypothesized at the beginning of this article, and they will seek the protection of the courts using the *droit moral* principles recognized in the Berne Convention. I'll be sitting in the gallery when it happens.

❧

CHAPTER 43

Earn Big Bucks from Old Copyrights in Your Spare Time!

M AY YOU OUTLIVE your copyrights."

I'm not sure if that's a blessing or a curse. It is certainly an oversimplification of a highly complex process. Over the centuries, a body of laws has evolved to help authors enjoy the full benefits of their creativity, while at the same time enabling publishers and other legitimate licensees to exploit literary works exclusively.

For the most part, these laws are simple and clear, and they afford the protection for which they were designed. But some provisions may have precisely the opposite effect: denying benefits to an author or his/her heirs; others denying exclusivity or perpetuity to publishers, movie companies, and other licensees.

You may be among the majority of people who find the subject of copyright intensely boring. But some of its aspects directly affect your pocketbook or those of your heirs. So slap your face or pinch yourself and try to stay awake for some interesting revelations. I have drawn my information in large measure from *The Rights of Authors and Artists* by Kenneth P. Norwick and Jerry Simon Chasen; and from "A New Lease on Life for Old Books," an article by the late Carol E. Rinzler that appeared in the July 10, 1987 issue of *Publishers Weekly*. Rinzler's article in turn credits copyright attorney Frank R. Curtis for his article, "Caveat Emptor in Copyright," which appeared in the *Bulletin of the Copyright Society*, Volume 25, page 16. Mr. Curtis (no relation) augmented these sources with several telephone interviews, and I think I've got it right. But before you move on any of the following, consult a copyright attorney.

Let's start with a True or False quiz:

1. Your book was published in 1960 and you renewed the copyright in 1988 for a second term of twenty-eight years, as prescribed in the old Copyright Act that prevailed until 1978. In the year 2016, your book will go into the public domain and there is nothing that you or your heirs can do about it. True or false?

2. Your book was published in 1985. You may renew the copyright in twenty-eight years, then extend it for another twenty-eight. After a total of fifty-six years, your book will enter the public domain. True or false?

3. Your late husband wrote a classic novel in 1963. It sells ten thousand copies every year, and you and your publishers expect it will keep going at that clip for the foreseeable future. In 1991, the book's first copyright term expires, and you decide you want to recapture the rights at that time and auction the book off to the highest bidder. Your publisher screams, "You can't do that!" True or false?

4. Your book was published in 1989 and your publishers keep it in print. In 1999 you are bitten by a rabid oyster and die. Your publishers have exclusive control over your book until fifty years after your death—until the year 2049, that is—after which time it goes into the public domain. True or false?

5. You sold your book to the movies in 1989, and, as is the case in all movie contracts, you granted the producer the rights in perpetuity. There is no way you can ever recover those film rights, short of persuading the producer to sell them back to you. True or false?

If you answered "True" to any of these questions, you may well be depriving yourself or your heirs of valuable rights and revenue. Why don't you just throw them out on the streets right now, you miserable lowlife?

Before the overhauling of the federal Copyright Act took place in the mid-1970s and went into effect on January 1, 1978, terms of copyright were fairly straightforward. Copyright on a published work lasted twenty-eight years from publication date, and could be extended for another twenty-eight years by applying to the U.S. Copyright Office, the federal agency that implements copyright regulations. At the end of the total fifty-six year term, copyright expired and the book entered the public domain, entitling anybody to publish or otherwise exploit it without obligation or compensation to the original creator or licensees such as publishers.

Of course, most publishing contracts expire long before the full term of copyright has run its course. Owing to the brief (and getting briefer) shelf life of most books, authors may secure reversions of rights from publishers as soon as their books are out of print. But some books do become perennial sellers, remaining in print year in and year out. I am not referring merely to literary classics, but to works in such genres as science fiction, mysteries, and westerns.

Owing to widespread dissatisfaction with many aspects of the old Copyright Act on the part of authors, publishers, and other interested parties, Congress reviewed the rules and changed them, some significantly. One fundamental alteration was the term of copyright. Works published after January 1, 1978 are copyrighted throughout the author's lifetime plus fifty years. Simple enough, yes?

It should have been. But at the time the Copyright Act changes were being debated, some argued that the sudden change in term might prove unfair to certain authors whose works were published before the new law went into effect. In particular, attention focused on authors with valuable backlists that sell year in and year out, like Ernest Hemingway or Robert Frost. So Congress enacted a special grace period of nineteen years for any author whose work was published before 1978. Instead of fifty-six years for such authors, the term would extend to a total of seventy-five years after publication. If the author expired before his copyright, his direct heirs could take over copyright ownership for the duration of the term.

With the addition of that nineteen year grace period, our plot takes an interesting twist. For, when the fifty-six year copyright term on a pre-1978 book expires, the author or his direct heirs may terminate book contracts, recapture them, and exploit them for the duration of those extra nineteen years. And this is true *even though the work is still actively in print at the end of the fifty-sixth year.* In fact, it doesn't matter whether, in your original contract, you granted your publisher the rights to your book for the full term of copyright *and all renewals thereof.* Your right to recapture your property at the end of fifty-six years takes precedence!

To whom am I referring when I say that the author "or his direct heirs" can recapture the copyrights? Congress specified that "direct heirs" meant widow or widower, children, or grandchildren. Brothers and sisters, nieces, nephews, cousins, great-grandchildren, and live-in lovers need not apply. If you die before the end of that fifty-six year term, the recapture rights belong to your direct heirs, no matter what your will may say about copyrights to and revenue from your works. In fact, there is a little known and underutilized feature of the old law commonly referred to as the "Widows and Orphans Provision." It provides for certain beneficiaries to recapture rights to a pre-1978 book at the end of the first twenty-eight year period if the author died during that period.

As I said, for most authors of works published before 1978, these revelations will have little practical effect on their lives, for the process is dependent on books being kept in print for a very long time, and few works published then or now achieve that status. If you had a book published in 1970, and this year it has gone out of print, you may recapture the rights by demanding that your publisher either do a new printing or give you a reversion. If, however, that 1970 book becomes a classic, then you and/or your heirs may be able to recapture the rights at the times I've specified, even if the book is selling like hotcakes at the conclusion of the appropriate term. You or your heirs may then license the book to any publisher you or they choose (including your old publisher) for a new advance and royalties, and enjoy the protection of the law for an additional term as prescribed by that law.

Another little-known but fascinating fact is that you may be able to reclaim movie rights that you thought you'd sold "in perpetuity." That's because films are defined in the copyright laws as "derivative works"—adaptations that are substantially different from the original. And derivative works may be recovered during that period between the end of the fifty-six year term and the beginning of the nineteen-year extension. The law does not distinguish between movies that get made and those that do not.

If a film was actually made, it may continue to be exhibited at the end of the fifty-six year term, but technically you would have the right to sell a remake to another film company. As my sources point out, that isn't quite as exciting as it sounds at first. Because the Copyright Act is applicable only to United States copyrights, the copyrights on the original film taken out in foreign nations (as is customarily done in the movie business) would not be recoverable. Thus, even if you do recapture your rights from Paramount, for example, it would be hard for you to resell them to Universal because Universal would want to purchase worldwide rights, and you wouldn't be able to grant them.

For authors of books published pre-1978, the procedure for recapturing rights is rather complex and tricky. You have to serve notice to your publisher, film company, or other licensee (or to companies to which the original buyers assigned the rights) at least two years before the effective date of termination, and the termination date you pick must fall within five years after the end of that fifty-sixth year. If you fail to observe these rules, the publisher or other licensee gets to hold onto your property until it goes into the public domain, at which time it becomes fair game for anybody who wants to publish or adapt it.

The above facts are pertinent to those whose books were published before the revised Copyright Act went into effect. Is there anything that authors can do to reclaim rights to books published after January 1, 1978 if their publisher keeps them constantly in print? In fact, there is. For this class of books, the law provides for the termination of a contract thirty-five years after publication or forty years after signature date of the contract. If, therefore, you signed a contract in 1984 and your book was brought out in 1985, and assuming your publisher keeps it in print from that time forward, you or certain direct heirs of yours could terminate that contract in the year 2020 (thirty-five years after publication) or 2024 (forty years after the contract was signed).

Is any of this arcane information pertinent to your life? It was, for instance, in the case of Robert Heinlein's widow. She took advantage of the "Widows and Orphans Provision" and recaptured film rights to *Stranger in a Strange Land* after Heinlein died, according to Joel Gotler, the film agent who is currently endeavoring to license the rights elsewhere. She did it at the expiration of the twenty-eighth year after publication.

It is every writer's dream to write a classic, but as few of us know whether we've written one until we're old and gray (and, alas, some never live to know it at all), it is comforting to know that some protection exists for those whose work stands the test of time. In such cases, your biggest problem may be figuring out where to place a copy of this article so that you have a reminder in the year 2015, 2020, or beyond.

Publishers may have the advantage over you in such cases, as their calendars are set up to track copyright expiration dates. Unwary authors may, a short time in advance of those dates, receive letters from publishers offering to take care of the copyright renewal on the authors' behalf. By signing on the dotted line, those authors may lose the opportunity to recapture their rights or to renegotiate their contracts on improved terms.

If the information provided herein is a revelation to you, don't feel badly. I don't know of any authors who are aware of it. Most agents are not as versed in the mysteries of copyright as they would like to be. But for any agent interested in the longevity of his company, familiarity with these vital facts is a must. Those agencies that handle authors' estates may have a bit more experience in such matters, but as certain as death the issues I've described will arise for every literary agency and its clients. It's not too early to start thinking about and planning for them.

May you outlive your copyrights.

CHAPTER 44

Sacred Honor

L ET'S TEST YOUR ethics:

- An author under contract to write a book for a publisher delivers an awful, unpublishable, unrevisable manuscript, and his pub-lisher demands a refund of the advance paid upon signing of the contract, as is the publisher's right. The author agrees to refund all of the money except his agent's commission, but feels that his agent ought to refund the commission. The agent refuses to do so, since it's not his fault the author screwed up. Who's right?

- Two authors collaborate on a book under contract to a publisher. Both signed the contract and both are therefore equally liable for the warranties in that contract. One author is responsible for furnishing the research, the other for writing the manuscript. After the book is published, somebody sues the publisher and authors for libel. It turns out that the researcher provided his co-author with incorrect facts. Should the co-author be equally liable with his partner for the costs and damages of the lawsuit?

- Same situation, except that this time the researcher has done an unimpeachable job. The writer, however, turns in a perfectly lousy manuscript, and the publisher demands his down payment back. Should the researcher be required to repay his share?

- Agent A sold an author's first book to a publisher. The author becomes dissatisfied with his agent and leaves him for another, and

Agent B goes right back to the same publisher and sells the author's next book there. Agent A is very upset. After all, he established this author at the publishing company, and now Agent B is reaping profit from Agent A's labors. Is Agent A justified in feeling angry? And with whom should he be angry: the publisher, Agent B, or his former client?

- An agent sells a book to Publisher A, but before contracts have been signed, Publisher B hears about the deal. "If I'd known about this book, I'd have offered you twice as much money as Publisher A," says B. Should the agent try to get out of the deal? Should he tell Publisher A about Publisher B's remark and try to get Publisher A to match Publisher B's price? Was Publisher B out of line for saying something so provocative to the agent?

- A publisher signs a contract with an author to write a biography of the current, and currently popular, President of the United States. Before the book is finished, the President is embroiled in a scandal and his popularity plummets. The publisher then cancels the contract because it fears no one will buy the book under the new circumstances. But by that time the author has already delivered his manuscript. The publisher wants his down payment back. The author wants his acceptance check. Who's right?

The above are examples of disputes arising in the publishing business that can be said to fall as much into the category of ethics as they do of law. Although all of these cases could end up in court, they could all just as well be resolved by the application of business ethics. In fact, it may be said that they might not have arisen at all if the parties had considered their ethical positions when the problems began to develop.

The subject of business ethics makes front page headlines every day in one form or another. As I write this, the hot topic is the fortunes made by insiders trading on privileged information about corporate takeovers. But some other news stories of late, such as the trials of corrupt New York City officials, also raise acute questions about business ethics.

Ethics is a code of behavior bounded by morality on one side and the law on the other. It is based on a sense of right and wrong that is not necessarily dependent on what the law says one can or cannot get away with. The best definition of ethical behavior I've heard was furnished by *New York Times* columnist Russell Baker: it means, Baker said, that there are just some things that are not for sale at any price. Many people believe that ethical conviction has weakened in our time from what it once was, and fewer people ask themselves whether there is anything they hold so dear that they would not relinquish it no matter how high the price.

I can't speak for the world outside the little fishbowl that is publishing, but it does seem to me that people in our industry have held up better in the ethics department than corresponding workers in many other trades. I'm not talking about the ethical conduct of publishing corporations, but the behavior of the individuals who work for them. I would imagine this owes in some measure to the gentlemanly tradition of our industry and to the creative nature of the product we deal with. Still given the notably if not notoriously low pay scale for all but top publishing personnel, it's a wonder that one seldom hears of any instances of dishonesty in our trade. Years ago an acquaintance who worked in the ladies' garment business expressed amazement to me that the publishing industry operated so successfully without the payoffs and kickbacks that are prevalent in the garment business: "You can't drive a truck from Thirty-fifth to Thirty-sixth Street without shmearing somebody," he said, using the Yiddish slang for "bribe." Although there are opportunities or at least conditions for corruption, I know of no literary agents or editors who have ever done anything much more corrupt than using the company stamp machine to mail personal letters. Compared to our sister industry, the movie business, publishing is like a white-gloves tea party.

And, unlike so many other lines of business where a deal is not a deal until contracts have been signed and money changed hands, in publishing a handshake is usually firm enough to create a binding commitment from which one backs out only at the peril of losing the other party's trust forever. Whatever nightmarish problems may ensue once contracts have been signed, it can at least be taken for granted that the intent of the parties was and is honorable. And to me, that means a lot.

"Honor" is a word seldom heard in discussions of modern ethical values, though the time when men fought duels over it and women took their lives defending it existed less than a century ago. Honor in business dealings means, I suppose, taking responsibility for one's commitments, particularly when those commitments turn out unprofitably. If we look at it that way, it's easy to understand why honor in our business has become so difficult to maintain. The goal of the corporation—profit—is usually at odds with the sympathies of the editors. And the evolution of publishing into a highly complex corporate endeavor has meant the dispersal of responsibility to the point where, when one tries to assess blame for a mistake, one is left with a handful of mist.

It's easy to find people in charge at publishing companies, but not always easy to find people who will accept responsibility. The men and women who work in our trade are decent individuals, but the companies they work for seldom appreciate or reward employees for having moral scruples about corporate policies. Of course, agents are also responsible to a higher authority, namely their clients, so the challenge of doing the right thing is by no means restricted to publishing executives. But I wonder if we've forgotten that there may be an even higher authority. You know which one I mean.

Unfortunately, my qualifications for preaching about ethical conduct are less than impeccable. Although I happen to believe that I am morally above reproach, pure of mind and body, spiritually chaste, and extraordinarily humble, the only other person who thinks I'm a saint is my goldfish, and that's only because I feed him every morning.

Nevertheless, I do feel that honor in business dealings is an ideal worth striving for, if for no other reason than that it is good business. The agent who delivers on a promise will be trusted by a publisher the next time; the editor who stands by his or her word knows that an author or agent will accept that word the next time around. And although accepting responsibility can prove very costly—you can lose a job, a customer, a client, a lawsuit over it—I respect those who own up to commitments or mistakes far more than I do those who try to duck responsibility or pass the buck. And I prefer doing business with them, because I always know where they stand and know I can count on them to do the honorable thing in a crunch. When the mistake is mine and I own up to it, I feel better about myself, too. And maybe self-esteem is the only thing worth taking with you to the Great Beyond on Judgment Day.

When you examine in this light some of the hypothetical situations I offered at the beginning of this chapter, you can see that if the parties in any given dispute were to stand by their ethical responsibilities, the outcomes might be far less costly and bitter than if everyone looked to save his own skin. In fact, it might even create the kind of good will that binds people tighter than ever before. "It's my responsibility," says one party; "No, it's mine," says the other; and perhaps they have paved the way for splitting the difference or reaching some other kind of compromise that will generate mutual respect.

Honorable behavior calls for no small degree of courage, for it means making sacrifices and disdaining easy ways out. For an author to take responsibility for blowing an assignment, for a publisher to take responsibility for the failure of a book, for an agent to take responsibility for messing up a deal, a tremendous amount of honesty and fortitude are required.

And that's just honor. I haven't even gotten to sacred honor yet! But here I have to laugh. Show me the agent who, in the hypothetical case above, would not think long and hard when Publisher B says, "I'll pay twice the price if you can break your deal with Publisher A," and I'll show you a zombie.

そ

CHAPTER 45

Scruples

W E ALL KNOW that literary agents are supposed to determine whether books can be published. But should they decide as well whether some books ought to be published? Should publishers be passing moral as well as literary judgment on books being considered for publication? Do film and television producers have a responsibility to audiences to turn down projects that glorify criminals? I've been thinking about these questions a lot lately, and so, it seems, have many publishing people, even as they prepare their bids for the memoirs of this month's slasher, traitor, or Wall Street robber baron.

Virtually hours after Robert E. Chambers was charged with the sex-related murder of Jennifer Dawn Levin, Chambers's attorney was inundated by phone calls from authors, literary and film agents, movie producers, TV docudrama producers, book publishers and packagers, playwrights and screenwriters. More than one hundred bids were made, according to an article in the *New York Times* by columnist William E. Geist. One agent raved about how excited she was by what was quickly dubbed "The Preppie Murder" by the media. "It has money, sex, a defendant who is movie-star handsome, a lovely girl, and kids who seemingly had everything." Another agent said, "This is an upscale crime." And still another agent was quoted by Geist as saying, "To be completely venal about it, the people involved in this crime fit the demographics that TV is shooting for."

Not everyone could be completely venal about it, however. Another agent said, "It's like personal injury lawyers flocking to a car accident, but more ghoulish." And Robert Gottlieb, then editor-in-chief of Alfred A. Knopf, used a similar metaphor. "I find something deplorable about people pouncing on what are horrible human situations," he commented. "It's a little like ambulance chasing."

When a literary agent evaluates a manuscript for representation, he applies many criteria: Is it well written? Is it well organized? Is it dramatic? Is it entertaining? Is there an audience for it? Is it commercial?

Sometimes, however, a question arises of whether we feel the material ought to see the light of day at all, of whether it is "good" for the public to witness the reenactment of an unspeakably brutal murder, an anguishing kidnapping, or the machinations of a swindler who left countless trusting investors ruined. Almost every agent can recount how he or she has been approached by the perpetrator, or attorneys for the perpetrator, of some heinous crime or another. This alleged or convicted killer, gangster, traitor, spy, fraud, drug runner, madam, wants to write a book: would we be interested in handling it? Our commercial instincts immediately tell us the property could be a hot one. But is that all there is to it? Or are we obliged to consult our consciences as well as our mercantile sense when we formulate an opinion of a work's publishability?

Unfortunately, we can expect little help from publishers while we ruminate about the propriety of enriching felons with gains from the sale of their stories. With few exceptions, the first, second, and last impulse of most publishers is to stampede to sign up the recollections of a celebrated wrongdoer. One colleague tells me she had an opportunity to represent a convicted serial killer who wanted to tell his story. She called an editor to solicit interest in the book. "If they were entertaining murders we'd be interested," the editor replied, "but if they all sound the same, we'll pass." His only criterion, one which I can vouch is shared by many other editors, is, "Will these murders move books?"

It's easy for an agent to rationalize the handling of a criminal's story on the grounds that publishers are all but shoveling money at him to acquire it from him. "If I turn the book down," we reason, "one of my competitors will grab it and make those commissions. So it might as well be me."

Because the world in which criminals operate is often a dangerous and even violent one, I know of some agents who have declined to offer them representation out of fear that they, the agents, will come to harm. While I don't believe I've ever rejected a client for that reason, I would be less than candid if I claimed I hadn't spent some sleepless nights wondering whether one day a dark limousine would not pull up beside me as I strolled down the street, and several pairs of muscular arms would hustle me inside where a voice would direct the driver to proceed to the East River.

I overcame these paranoiac terrors by reasoning that nobody is very interested in harming agents, authors, or publishers to whom privileged information has been imparted by people with dark pasts. At least, I've never heard of anything more disturbing than a visit from an agent of the Internal Revenue Service (which can be horribly frightening, by the way).

So, while I can't blame an agent for turning down a client out of fear of reprisal, those grounds only beg the question of whether agents and publishers have a moral obligation to society to refuse to do business with malefactors.

The publishing industry is extremely sensitive to censorship of every kind, and what we are talking about here would seem to involve a form of censorship: self-policing. Ours is a liberal tradition stemming directly from the First Amendment of our Constitution; we abhor any attempt to suppress literature, however condoning or provocative of antisocial behavior that literature may be. The authors of our Bill of Rights did recognize, however, that the First Amendment could be taken advantage of by those who might see it as a license to publish whatever they wanted to without any regard for the good of the people. Over the centuries, numerous tests of the First Amendment have created a body of laws that curtail unrestricted use of the press.

But if the people themselves demand to read the first-person account of David Berkowitz, who randomly ambushed and killed six people during the mid-1970s, or Jean Harris, who murdered her lover, Dr. Herman Tarnower, or R. Foster Winans, who traded insider secrets on Wall Street, or Claus von Bulow, accused of attempting to murder his wealthy socialite wife, or Mayflower Madam Sydney Biddle Barrows or Preppie Murderer Robert Chambers or Bernhard Goetz or Jack Abbott or O. J. Simpson, isn't it a little sanctimonious for a literary agent to tell these potential clients to take their business somewhere else?

And there's something more. Suppose their books aren't exploitive, but in fact shed some important light on criminal behavior that might help someone curb those antisocial impulses and prevent recurrences of certain crimes? If a book helps us understand what makes David Berkowitz tick, what compelled Charles Manson to stage his Los Angeles bloodbath, or what caused convicted spy John A. Walker, Jr., to betray his country, doesn't that justify our involvement in it?

Fortunately, a number of state governments have relieved the publishing community of much of the burden of sorting these questions out. Spearheaded by the New York State legislature's revulsion at the prospect that David Berkowitz, who called himself Son of Sam, might sign a book deal and thus profit from his appalling crimes, New York and a number of other states passed laws requiring that the proceeds from such deals be diverted from the criminals to the victims of their crimes. These statutes have come, generically, to be known as Son of Sam Laws. There are variations on the basic principle. In some cases, the proceeds of book and film deals go to the victims and the next-of-kin of those victims; in others, the money goes into a general victims' fund that many municipal and state governments use at their discretion to pay victims of any crime committed in their precincts.

Some Son of Sam statutes narrowly define the types of crime applicable, others are broader and include or have argued to include such things as "victimless crime" (pimping, prostitution, illegal gambling, for instance), espionage (in which it may be said that the nation itself is the victim), and similarly ambiguous situations. Some interpretations embrace or attempt to embrace not just the author-criminal but the co-author, the publisher, and yes, the agent as well, meaning that their shares of revenue generated by the criminal's story are subject to forfeiture. How much easier it will be for us to be righteous, now that there's no longer any profit in agenting the memoirs of a miscreant!

As I have stated more than once, I'm no saint. I have handled my share of books by authors whose hands could scarcely be described as clean. I was the agent for several books by a man I knew only as "Joey," who declared himself to be a freelance hitman for the Mafia, claiming dozens of assassinations of Mob members who had broken the rigid code of that organization. In considering whether I should represent him, I weighed the fear factor, the profit motive, and my conscience, and managed to forge a delicate treaty with myself that enabled me to conduct my client's business in a state of relative guiltlessness. In the first place, I insisted that he never tell me his real name, address, or phone number, and indeed I never learned any of these until his death many years later. In the second place, I refused to let him tell me the real names of any victim, partner, or associate. In the third place, I refused to let him name names in his books.

As a result, as far as I knew, Joey could well have been a complete imposter and every word he wrote a total fabrication. (He was never convicted of any of the murders he supposedly committed, though the federal government finally nailed him for tax evasion.) If publishers believed his story and the public enjoyed his books and paid good money for them, that was fine, but I acquitted myself of any responsibility for the truth of Joey's identity or the terrible nature of his deeds. Even if everything he claimed was true, I was sufficiently distanced from his victims to feel no pang of guilt by association or any sense of being an accessory after the fact.

That (plus some nice commissions) was enough to get me through that test of conscience without excessive anguish. Joey himself was in his own way a charming, funny, Runyonesque character with a conscience of his own ("I never torture my victims, I never rob them, and I never kill them in front of their families," he boasted), a man who made the task of living with myself even easier. I was young and hungry for business, and it was all something of a lark.

I'm not sure whether the times have become more cynical since then, or I've become more thoughtful, but I don't know if I would, could, accept Joey as a client if he walked through my door again. I've stood before too many graves ever to think again of murder as a lark, even the murder of other murderers, which was Joey's stock in trade. And something happened to me that made it impossible for me ever again to see things the same way. Interestingly, it was a book.

Around ten o'clock on the evening of September 13, 1980, Eric Kaminsky, a promising twenty-two-year-old pianist, walked onto the downtown platform of the Eighth Avenue subway at 181st Street in New York City. He was attacked by two young assailants who robbed him, stole his wallet, stabbed him, and hurled his body onto the tracks. He was pulled back to the platform by witnesses, but by that time he had bled to death.

A few years later, his mother Alice contacted me. She had written a book about her son's murder and the subsequent trial of his assailants, and she wanted me to represent her. I read the manuscript the same night she sent it to me, and in a single sitting. My emotions were all but overwhelmed by the impact of her book. Unlike other books I had read written by the loved ones of victims, in which the authors eventually reconcile themselves to their loss, or forgive or even come to love the murderer himself, Alice Kaminsky's book was a volcanic outpouring of inconsolable grief and unmitigated anger untempered by the passage of time.

The following morning, still dazed by Mrs. Kaminsky's wrathful, righteous, Biblical fulmination, I phoned her to pledge my commitment to her and to her book, and to the memory of her son. She had called it *The Victim's Song*, a deliberately ironic twist on Norman Mailer's *The Executioner's Song*, a book recounting the life, deeds, and death of murderer Gary Gilmore, and indeed the penultimate chapter was called "Literature and Murder (Norman Mailer)." In that chapter she excoriated Mailer and other writers and indicted the publishing industry for glorifying murderers and romanticizing murder while ignoring or glossing over the tragedy of the victims and the enduring suffering of the victims' survivors. "Many writers are like scavengers who run like wild dogs to the garbage cans of sensational murders and who try to extract perfume from what is essentially foul," Mrs. Kaminsky charged. Until her son's death, she had been a member of the vast audience that finds murder, and books about murder, fascinating. "But murder takes on sinister significance when it occurs to 'me,' not to the 'other,' and then what might have seemed like a harmless pastime takes on the stench of what Geoffrey Gorer calls 'the pornography of death.'"

I ran off several copies of Mrs. Kaminsky's manuscript, and it was difficult to keep the emotion out of my voice as I pitched the book to the half-dozen editors I'd selected for the first round of submission. On the strength of my impassioned appeal, many of those editors read the book overnight and reported the next morning with voices similarly aquiver with powerful feeling. They were not only deeply affected by the book but also felt, as I did, that they could never quite look at things the same way again.

I was positive I would have a sale, possibly even an auction on the strength of those first reactions. But days and weeks passed, and at length the manuscripts began drifting back with the most abjectly apologetic notes I have ever received on a rejected book. What these notes said in effect was that although that particular editor has been tremendously moved by the book, the editorial board had raised some practical marketing considerations that made *The Victim's Song* a longshot. I was devastated, and launched a new round of submissions with practically religious zeal. The result was the same. Everybody was touched. Nobody bought the book.

It went to some twenty-five New York publishers. None of them made an offer for it. During that time, however, the publishing industry went into frenzies over a number of books by and about mad-dog killers, hoodlums, turncoats, flesh peddlers, and other culprits. Ultimately I had to report to Mrs. Kaminsky that I could not find a publisher for her book. On her own she took it to an out-of-town publisher who did bring it out. It received stunning reviews. One reviewer said the book is impossible to read without crying.

Not everyone will draw a moral from this story, but I did and I think you know what it is.

I have too much to atone for to preach that agents should be holier than anyone else. But agents are the primary interface between the real world and the world of literature, and we are therefore not without responsibility for what does and does not get published. Neither are you, the writer, nor you, the editor, nor you, the reader. As the publishing industry evolves from one peopled by individual men and women whose convictions informed the selection of books they published, to a collection of corporate entities dominated by the profit motive, questions of what is morally right and wrong to publish come up less and less often, or when they do the answer is usually a foregone conclusion. Whether the process can be reversed, I don't know. I would imagine that any editor who consistently votes down potentially profitable books on moral grounds will eventually find himself out on his righteous behind with instructions to take his scruples to a religious publisher where they belong. But a vote of conscience at an editorial board meeting is a vote nonetheless, and who knows how long and how far it will reverberate? For me, Mrs. Kaminsky's book still disturbs my complacency, and when those attorneys call to pitch to me the memoirs of their criminal clients, the memory of Eric Kaminsky's lifeless body sprawled across the subway tracks flashes into my mind and I grope for the courage to say, "Sorry, I'll pass."

❧

Index

"A List-B List Syndrome," 27
Abbott, Jack, 260
accounting, multibook deals
    and, 83
Ace, 68
advance sales, 223
advances
    acceptability provision and, 97,
        100–101
    audio deals and, 77
    book clubs and, 137–138
    escalators and, 92–93
    literary agents and, 33
    multibook contracts and, 83
    negotiating increases, 183–184
    payout schedules and, 86–91
    repayment of, 238, 254
advertisements, included in books,
    129–133
advertising, of books, 119, 127, 128.
    See also publicity

agent-packager, 153–155
"Agent's Corner," 11, 12
Alfred A. Knopf, 123, 259
American Booksellers Association,
    35
American Civil Liberties Union, 244
Annie, 68
Artists' Authorship Rights Act, 245
Association of Authors' Represen-
    tatives, 33, 193
audiotape deals, 76–79
audits, of publishers' books, 146–150
Avon Books, 142, 222

B. Dalton, 145
Baker, Russell, 254
Bantam, 244
Barnes & Noble, 145
Barrows, Sydney Biddle, 260
Barth, John, 169
Berkowitz, David, 260, 261

Berne Convention, 244, 245–246

best-sellers

    escalators and, 93–94

    length of, 170

    publicity and, 128

    risks in publishing, 222

Between Covers, 135

blind auction, 223

"blockbuster mentality," 172

boilerplate, 81

bonuses. *See* escalators

book clubs, 134–139

Book-of-the Month Club, 134–135, 137, 138

Bookman, The, 135

bookstore chains, 136

    buyers for, 141–145

    videocassettes and, 74, 76

bookstores

    buyers, 140–145

    versus book clubs, 135–136, 139

Bradbury, Ray, 171

Bradford, Barbara Taylor, 171

brand name sponsorship, of books, 131–133

breakout books, 168–172

Bulletin of the Copyright Society, 248

Cather, Willa, 138

"Caveat Emptor in Copyright," 248

Chambers, Robert E., 258, 260

Charles Scribner's Sons, 104

Chasen, Jerry Simon, 244, 248

China, piracy of intellectual property and, 69

Clarke, Arthur C., 171

Clavell, James, 222

"closely held" corporation, 203

collaboration, ethics and, 253

Color Purple, The, 169

computers

    determination of sales patterns by, 143–144

    editing and, 107–108

    speed and, 63–64

conceptualization, of books, 47

contracts

    acceptability provision, 97–101

    advertisements in books and, 130

    audio/video provisions, 75, 76

    cancellation of, 254

    department, 187

    disputes, 234–235

    drawing up, 61–62

    escalators and, 92–96

    grace period, 233

    lawyers and, 213–235

    multibook, 80–85

    option clause, 233

    payout schedules and, 86–97

    provision to audit books, 146, 147, 149–150

    renewal of, 163

    Writers Guild of America Basic Agreement, 65

copy editing, 106–107

copyright

    duration of, 247–252

    history of, 69

    reversion, 249, 250, 251

    Widows and Orphans Provision, 250

    work for hire and, 69–73

Covenant, The, 137

Curtis, Frank R., 248

Dell, 100
Dickens, Charles, 64
distribution, audits and, 148
Doubleday, 75, 144

editorial boards, 20, 21, 49, 98–99,
    221, 264
editors
    as literary agents, 23
    as writers, 63
    courtesy and, 209, 210, 212–213
    criticism and, 175
    responsibilities of, 104–109
    "satisfactory progress" payments
        and, 88
    sales conferences and, 111–112,
        113–114, 140–141
    submissions to, 176, 186, 189,
        190
    written inquiries to, 181
encyclopedias, work for hire and,
    70
escalators, 92–96
*Every Writer's Practical Guide to
    Copyright Law*, 245
Executioner's Song, The, 263
expense projections, authors', 165–
    166

Fehrenbach's Law, 39–40
film adaptations of novels, 67
    agents and, 151–155
    copyright and, 250–251
    decline of, 156, 157–158
    escalators and, 93, 94–95
    for television, 159–161

selling, 183
    theatrical release options and,
        156–158
film industry, changes in, 152–153,
    157
First Amendment, 260
flat fees, tie-ins and, 66, 68. *See also*
    copyright, work for hire
Fleischer, Leonore, 68
Francis, Dick, 172

Gale, Spencer, 144, 145
Geist, William E., 258–259
genre writing
    length, 170
    multibook contracts and, 80–81,
        82–83
    See also series, fictional.
ghostwriting, work for hire and, 70–
    71
Gilmore, Gary, 263
Godfather, The, 172
Goetz, Bernhard, 260
Gorer, Geoffrey, 263
Gottlieb, Robert, 123, 259
Guest, Judith, 190

hard-soft deals, 58, 90
hardcover
    distribution, 121–122
    publicity, 127
    returns, 148
hardcover and paperback publi-
    cation, distinctions between,
    54–59
HarperCollins, 172
Harris, Jean, 260
Heinlein, Robert, 171

Heyer, Georgette, 170–171
high concept, 47
How to Be Your Own Literary Agent,
    11, 12
Hughes, Langston, 40
Hunter, Evan, 36

ideas, 45–47
income projections, 120, 163–164,
    165
inflation, effect on advances, 86–87
inspiration, writers and, 45–46, 63
Ironweed, 169
Irving, John, 169

Jakes, John, 171
James, Henry, 49, 64
Jedi Story book, The, 68

Kaminsky, Alice, 263, 264
Kaminsky, Eric, 262, 264
Kennedy, William, 169
King, Stephen, 138, 139, 170
Kozak, Ellen M., 245
Krantz, Judith, 171

lawsuits, acceptability provision
    and, 98, 99–100
lawyers
    as literary agents, 23
    publishers' counsel, 236–241
    publishing contracts and, 231–
    235, 237, 243
Levin, Jennifer Dawn, 258
libel, publishers' counsel and, 239–
    241
literary agencies, comparison of
    organizational structures

of, 23–28
literary agents
    advantages of having, 21
    as editors, 33
    author-editor relationship and,
    106
    book clubs and, 138
    building authors' careers, 29–30,
    38–41
    business expenses, 194–199
    changing, 30
    collaborations and, 31
    commissions and, 91
    courtesy and, 209, 211, 212–213
    death of, 200–205
    diplomacy of, 174–178
    effective timing and, 179–184
    ethics and, 254, 256
    film adaptation agreements and,
    151–155
    idea development and, 46–47
    incorporation and, 203–204
    influence over publishers, 18–22
    moral judgment and, 258, 259,
    260, 260–264
    patience of, 185–188
    pricing and, 22
    profit-and-loss projections and,
    118
    reading fees and, 189–193
    relationships between, 29–31
    responsibilities of, 32–37
    risk-taking by, 224–225
    sales conferences and, 110
    work for hire and, 73
Literary Guild, 135, 137
Literary Market Place, 204
L'Amour, Louis, 170, 171

MacDonald, John D., 169

Macmillan, 209

magazines, electronic rights and, 73

Magic Mountain, The, 65

Mailer, Norman, 263

Manson, Charles, 261

manuscripts
  late, 214–215
  legal changes to, 240–241
  proofreading, 215–216
  proper form for submission, 216–219
  reading fees for unsolicited, 189–193

market projections, 49

mass market publishing, publication dates and, 123

McBain, Ed, 36

McCormack, Tom, 222

Meredith, Scott, 36, 226

Michener, James, 137, 171

midlist books, 127, 138, 169, 170, 222

Monty Python, 246

moral rights, 242–246

morals, 258–264

movie agencies, 152–153, 154–155. *See also* film adaptations

multibook contracts
  accounting and, 83–85
  advantages of, 81–82
  disadvantages of, 84
  genre writing and, 80–81, 82–83
  publicity and, 82
  work for hire and, 73

"negative option," 134–135

"New Lease on Life for Old Books, A," 248

New York Times, 69, 83, 93, 123, 169, 254, 258

Nixon, Richard, 99

nonfiction, publicity and, 128

Norwick, Kenneth P., 244, 248

novelizations, of films, 65–68

One Minute Relationship, The, 34

option clauses, 81

options, adaptations of novels and, 157–161

Ordinary People, 190

outlines, as sales tools, 48–50
  fiction and, 52–53
  nonfiction, 50–52

packagers, work for hire and, 72, 73

paperback revolution, the, 129

paperbacks
  advantages of, 58
  advertisements in, 129, 136
  changes in, 55, 56
  distribution, 122
  proofreading of, 107
  publicity and, 126–127
  returns, 148

payments, overdue, 177, 187

payout schedules, 87–90

Perkins, Maxwell, 104, 109

Pinnacle, 34

"PITA" factor, 188

"Plot Skeleton," 226

Portrait of a Lady, 65

printers, audits and, 148

printings, sales conferences and, 112

probate law, 201–202
profit-and-loss statements, 22, 49,
    116–120
proofreading, 106–107
public domain, 248, 249
publication date, 121–124
publicity
    book clubs and, 135
    bookstore buyers and, 143
    multibook deals and, 82
    publishers and, 119, 125–128
publishers
    audio and video rights and, 74,
        75
    contracts and accounting
        departments, 60–61, 62, 187
    costs, 118–119, 126–127
    entertainment companies,
        alliances with, 75–76
    moral judgment of, 259
    reading of manuscripts and, 20
    switching, 181, 184
    tie-ins and, 66–67
    work for hire and, 72–73
Publishers Weekly, 93, 123, 180
publishing
    courtesy, 208–213
    ethics, 253–257
    risks in, 220–225
publishing industry, changes in, 11,
    12, 13, 21, 47
    bookstore chains and, 141–142
    editorial/business schism, 49
    editorial responsibilities, 104–
        106
    manuscript submissions, 189–
        190, 191
    paperback publication, 55–56

profit-and-loss projections, 117–
    118
publication dates, 122–123
risk-taking, 221
use of outlines, 48–49
Putnam, 172

Random House, 68
Reader's Digest Book Club, 137, 138
reprint deals, escalators and, 93, 94
reprint market, collapse of, 118
reserve against returns, 148–150
Return of the Jedi, The, 68
returns, audits and, 148
review coverage, 57
revisions, payout schedules and, 89
rights
    audio/video, licensing, 75–76,
        77–78
    novelization, 66
    subsidiary, 196, 197
    See also copyright.
Rights of Authors and Artists, The,
    244, 248
Rinzler, Carol E., 248
Ritner, Peter, 209
Robbins, Harold, 171
royalties, 238
    accounting of, 77
    audio, 75, 76–77
    audits and, 147, 148, 150
    book clubs and, 138, 139
    profit-and-loss projections and,
        119
    tie-ins and, 66

Safire, William, 99
sale conferences, 110–115

bookstore buyers and, 140
  scheduling of, 121–122
sales projections, 118
Scherman, Harry, 134–135
Science Fiction Writers of America
  Bulletin, 245
screen plays, 65–67, 158
"sell-through," 118
series, fictional, work for hire and,
  71, 72–73. *See also* genre
  books
"setting the printing," 223
Shadows on the Rock, 138
Sheldon, Sidney, 171
Shylock, 35
Simpson, O. J., 260
"slush pile," 189, 190
Society of Authors' Represen-
  tatives, 33–34
Softweed Factor, The, 169
Son of Sam Laws, 261
Squirm, 68
St. Martin's Press, 222
Steele, Danielle, 171
subsidiary revenue, profit-and-loss
  projections and, 118
Susskind, David, 183
synopses, for film adaptations, 160

Tarnower, Dr. Herman, 260
taxes
  payout schedules and, 91
  self-employment and, 164, 165,
    166
Tebbel, John, 135
television adaptations of novels,
  66, 95–96, 159. *See also* film
  adaptations of novels

termination clause, 81
tie-ins, 65–68
Travis McGee, 169

Victim's Song, The, 263, 264
videotape, material appropriate
  for, 79
Viking Press, 190
Vinge, Joan, 68
von Bulow, Claus, 260

Waldenbooks, 144
Walker, Alice, 169
Walker, Jr., John A., 261
warranties, 81
Whedon, Julia, 100
Whirlwind, 222
William Morrow, 99, 222
World According to Garp, The, 169
Writers Guild of America Basic
  Agreement, 65
writing
  as a full-time career, 162–167
  common problems, 227–230
  speed versus quality, 62–64, 67

Allworth Books

Allworth Press publishes quality books to help individuals and small businesses. Titles include:

Writing Scripts Hollywood Will Love by Katherine Atwell Herbert
(softcover, 6 × 9, 160 pages, $12.95)

The Writer's Internet Handbook by Timothy K. Maloy
(softcover, 6 × 9, 208 pages, $18.95)

The Writer's Legal Guide, Revised Edition
by Tad Crawford and Tony Lyons (softcover, 6 × 9, 304 pages, $19.95)

Business and Legal Forms for Authors and Self-Publishers,
Revised Edition by Tad Crawford (softcover, 8½ × 11, 192 pages, $19.95)

The Copyright Guide by Lee Wilson
(softcover, 6 × 9, 192 pages, $18.95)

The Internet Research Guide by Timothy K. Maloy
(softcover, 6 × 9, 208 pages, $18.95)

The Internet Publicity Guide by V. A. Shiva
(softcover, 6 × 9, 208 pages, $18.95)

Electronic Design and Publishing: Business Practices, Second Edition
by Liane Sebastian. (softcover, 6¾ × 10, 200 pages, $19.95)

Artists Communities by the Alliance of Artists' Communities
(softcover, 6¾ × 10, 192 pages, $16.95)

Travel Photography: A Complete Guide to How to Shoot and Sell
by Susan McCartney (softcover, 6¾4 × 10, 384 pages, $22.95)

How to Shoot Stock Photos That Sell by Michal Heron
(softcover, 8 × 10, 208 pages, $19.95)

Please write to request our free catalog. If you wish to order a book, send your check or money order to Allworth Press, 10 East 23rd Street, Suite 400, New York, NY 10010. Include $5 for shipping and handling for the first book ordered and $1 for each additional book. Ten dollars plus $1 for each additional book if ordering from Canada. New York State residents must add sales tax.

If you wish to see our catalog on the World Wide Web, you can find us at Millennium Production's Art and Technology Web site:
http://www.arts-online.com/allworth/home.html
or at **http://www.interport.net/~allworth**

Visit Richard Curtis Associates, authors' representatives, at:
http:www.curtisagency.com